MOUND SITES OF THE ANCIENT SOUTH

MOUND SITES OF THE ANCIENT SOUTH

A GUIDE TO THE MISSISSIPPIAN CHIEFDOMS

ERIC E. BOWNE

THE UNIVERSITY OF GEORGIA PRESS

ATHENS AND LONDON

Friends Fund
a
publication

PHOTO, PAGES ii–iii:
Sunset at Aztalan.
(Photography by Daniel
Seurer, Seurerphoto
.squarespace.com)

PHOTO, FACING PAGE:
Stan South using a
camera and photo tower
to record subsurface
archaeological features
in an excavation unit at
Town Creek. (Courtesy
of the Research Labora-
tories of Archaeology,
The University of North
Carolina at Chapel Hill)

Publication of this work was made possible, in part, by
a generous gift from the University of Georgia Press
Friends Fund.

© 2013 by the University of Georgia Press
Athens, Georgia 30602
www.ugapress.org

Designed by April Leidig
Set in Arno Pro by Copperline Book Services, Inc.
Maps by XNR Productions

The paper in this book meets the guidelines for permanence
and durability of the Committee on Production Guidelines
for Book Longevity of the Council on Library Resources.

Manufactured in Singapore for Imago USA
17 16 15 14 13 P 5 4 3 2 1

Library of Congress Cataloging-in-Publication Data
Bowne, Eric E. (Eric Everett), 1970–
Mounds sites of the ancient South : a guide to the
Mississippian chiefdoms / Eric E. Bowne.
    p. cm.
Includes bibliographical references and index.
ISBN 978-0-8203-4498-0 (pbk. : alk. paper)
ISBN 0-8203-4498-2 (paperpack : alk. paper)
1. Mississippian culture — Southern States.
2. Chiefdoms — Southern States. 3. Mounds —
Southern States. 4. Southern States — Antiquities.
I. Title.
E99.M6815B68   2013
975'.01 — dc23   2012034309

British Library Cataloging-in-Publication Data available

CONTENTS

FOREWORD

ERIC BOWNE HAS WRITTEN a guide to what remains of the ancient world that existed in the American South from about AD 1000 to the 1600s. Many people have conceptions of ancient worlds that existed in their homelands before them. This is true of Europeans who learn in school about the world of ancient Greeks and Romans. Mexicans learn in school about the ancient Aztec world that once held sway in their homeland. And the same is true of Peruvians, who are quite aware of the world of the ancient Incas. Many other examples from around the world could be cited.

All these ancient worlds have been discovered and reconstructed as much through archaeological research as through documentary research. It is therefore striking that contemporary Americans have no such notions of the ancient worlds that existed in their homeland. This is especially notable in the American South, where an ancient world most assuredly did exist before the arrival of our European and African ancestors.

As described by Bowne in chapter 1, this was a world of Mississippian Indians who occupied in the Ancient South an area closely paralleling that of the Old South. Both the lifeway of the horticultural Mississippians and the lifeway of the agriculturalists of the Old South were shaped by the mild, moist climate and rich soils of the South. In both lifeways, for example, diets depended on corn, beans, and squash, and houses were built to shield residents from the mild winters while allowing them to enjoy the utility and pleasure of porches, verandas, piazzas, and ramadas to gain respite from the hot summer sun.

Like other worlds that have existed on our globe, the Mississippian world of the Ancient South included within its borders a number of polities, which dealt with one another through peace, diplomacy, athletic contests, economic exchanges, and war (especially, it seems, war). These Mississippian polities were not states with populations numbering in the millions, but chiefdoms with populations numbering in the thousands or tens of thousands.

All were governed by chiefs who led by means of various kinds and degrees of power or influence: persuasion, jawboning, religious authority, threats, military violence, and so on. A chief had to deal with day-to-day problems within his polity as well as with those involving neighboring chiefdoms. Archaeologists have doggedly reconstructed the ups and downs of many of these chiefdoms, and the Europeans who explored the South in the 1500s and 1600s observed them in action and left written descriptions of what they experienced. Much is now understood about the Ancient South, but as readers of this book will see, much remains to be reconstructed and explained. When one explores the past, every answer begets a dozen questions.

This guide is primarily intended for people who want to visit archaeological sites and museums where they can see the physical remains, scholarly interpretations, and artistic representations of Mississippian chiefdoms. In clear language and using well-chosen drawings, photographs, and artists' representations, Bowne gives summary descriptions of the more important Mississippian sites, with histories of the research that has been done on them, and with brief narrative accounts of our present understanding of the historical experience of the chiefdoms to which they belonged.

For laymen, this book will be a treasured introduction and guidebook to the Ancient South. For undergraduates, it will be a handy introduction to what is by now a vast archaeological and historical literature. And for adventurous high school students, it will open doors of understanding to an unsuspected world.

Charles Hudson
FRANKFORT, KENTUCKY

PREFACE

THIS BOOK IS INTENDED to appeal to a wide range of people with varying degrees of interest in southeastern Indian societies and archaeology. First and foremost it is designed to serve as a guidebook for people interested in visiting late prehistoric Native American archaeological sites and museums in the South. The book covers more than twenty such sites, thirteen of which are featured. For these featured sites, the discussion takes in the environmental setting, a current site description, archaeological research, and site history. Each location is discussed in enough detail to enhance a visit without requiring additional reading. Visitors interested in learning more about the climate and environment of the Ancient South or the lives of the people who inhabited it should read chapters 1 and 2 as well as the box features found throughout the text. I have tried to stay away from unnecessary jargon, and a glossary of frequently used terms is included.

I believe that this text can be of use to the beginning student of southern prehistory. In addition to providing a basic historical framework for the Mississippian archaeological period and descriptions of a number of important sites, the book includes a fairly extensive bibliography containing popular and academic books, edited volumes, and articles from national and regional academic journals. A sample of chiefdom theory is included as well.

This guidebook is intended also to highlight the importance of preserving and visiting these and other archaeological sites. The archaeological record is finite, and protecting it for ourselves and posterity should be considered a civic duty. Archaeological remains are useful to archaeologists only if they are recovered in context, that is, without having been disturbed by pothunters or looters. Removing artifacts from archaeological sites is against the law. Please take only photos on your visit.

Above all, I hope this book will serve as a vehicle for transporting the reader in some small way to the Mississippian world of the Ancient South. Enjoy.

ACKNOWLEDGMENTS

I WAS FIRST INTRODUCED to the Ancient South in 1993 when I took Dr. Charles Hudson's course "The Rise and Fall of Southeastern Chiefdoms" as an undergraduate at the University of Georgia. He painted such a clear and vivid picture of those societies in his lectures that I was captivated, and as a result I have been studying the region and its Native peoples ever since. In many ways, this guidebook is a tribute to the superlative teaching career of Dr. Hudson. Thank you, Charlie.

Of course the production of this guidebook was possible only with the help of a great number of individuals, all of whom deserve recognition and credit.

Thanks to XNR Productions for the beautiful original maps.

The staff at the University of Georgia Press exhibited great patience in shepherding the project to fruition. The Press provided me with a grant during the summer of 2004 to gather the data for this book. Since then, I have accepted two visiting professorships and a tenure-track position, moved five times, been helped by three editors, gotten married, became a grandfather, and started a degree program. In the interim, this project came to feel like a houseguest that overstayed its welcome. I can only imagine how the staff at the Press felt. Special thanks should be given to Regan Huff and Sydney Dupre, who are responsible for finally bringing this albatross home to roost. Thank you all.

In compiling the information for this guide, I received an immeasurable amount of help from the dedicated employees of the archaeological parks, state historical sites, national monuments, and museums included in the book. Special thanks should be given to Mary Bade, Jim Barnett, Tim Bauman, Robert Birmingham, Bill Bomar, Jefferson Chapman, Robert Connelly, Lonnie Davis, Steve Davis, Kim Dunnigan, David Dye, Chris Goodwin, Carla Hildebrand, Liz Horton, Mark Howell, Bill Iseminger, Adam King, Liz Leigh, Mike Linderman, Jeff Mitchem, Dennis Peterson, Jennifer Price, Tess Pruett, Martha Ann Rolingson, Daniel Stephens, Ben Swadley, Cheryl Taylor, and Michael Wiant.

FACING PAGE:
View from the stairs ascending Great Temple Mound, Ocmulgee National Monument.

xi

This work benefitted greatly from the editorial comments of Greg Waselkov and an anonymous reader, as well as those of Charlie Hudson.

In the summer of 2005, while working as an adjunct professor at Appalachian State University, I taught a summer course that traveled to many of the mound sites and museums featured in this book. It remains one of my most satisfactory teaching experiences, in part because I learned so much from my students during our time together that June. They were Allison Clark, Matt Cook, Daniel Covey, Charlie Edens, Lisa Hummel, Andrea Juliani, Bob Kollm, Marc Lewis, Kyle Mears, Josh Neale, Dylan Philyaw, Justin Scarborough, Logan Seamon, Carly White, and Laura Yoder. The logistics and supervisory responsibilities for the journey were shared with my very good friends from graduate school Dr. Brian Campbell and Dr. Josh Lockyer. Here's to many more journeys together, boys.

I have had the pleasure to study under and work with some of the best archaeologists in the business, and I would be remiss if I did not acknowledge their influences, direct and indirect, on this work. At the University of Georgia, I was honored to have David Hally, Steve Kowalewski, and Mark Williams serve on my doctoral committee. At Appalachian State University, my colleagues included Cheryl Claassen, Larry Kimball, and Tom Whyte, all of whom helped me establish myself as a professor. At the University of Mississippi, I had the pleasure of working with Jay Johnson. My archaeological colleagues at Wake Forest included Paul Thacker and Steve Wittington.

Colleagues of the nonarchaeological sort also contributed to this work in subtle but important ways. Thanks to Robbie Ethridge, Dan Martin, Greg Reck, and Jeanne Simonelli.

I met my wife about the time I started this project, and she has been a constant source of encouragement, ideas, and help ever since. I could not have done this without her support.

Any mistakes within are my own.

MISSISSIPPIAN SITES AND MUSEUMS

The following Mississippian sites and related museums are described in detail in this book.

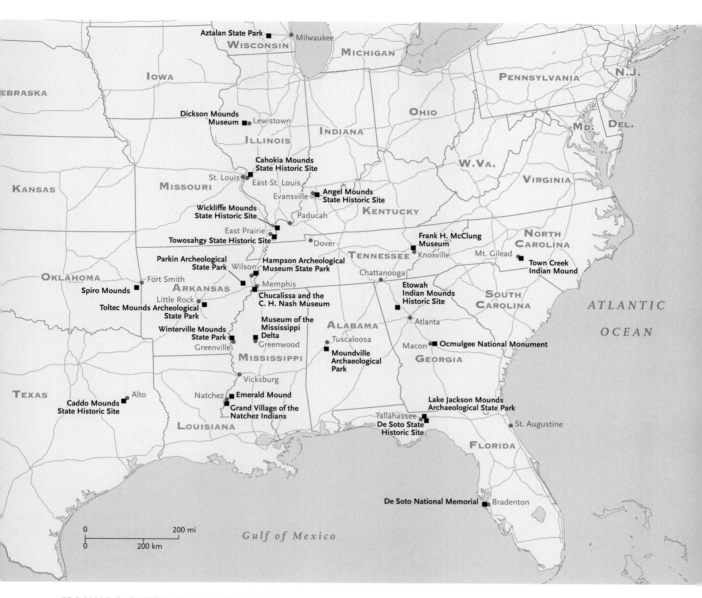

Aztalan State Park ■   ● Milwaukee
WISCONSIN   MICHIGAN

IOWA

Dickson Mounds
Museum ■ Lewistown
ILLINOIS

PENNSYLVANIA   N.J.

OHIO   MD.   DEL.

Cahokia Mounds
State Historic Site
St. Louis ● ■
MISSOURI East St. Louis
Evansville ●   Angel Mounds
State Historic Site

KANSAS

Wickliffe Mounds
State Historic Site ■
East Prairie ●
Towosahgy State Historic Site ■
Paducah ●
KENTUCKY

VIRGINIA

W.VA.

NORTH
CAROLINA

Frank H. McClung
Museum ■
Dover ●   Knoxville ●   Mt. Gilead ●   ■ Town Creek
Indian Mound
TENNESSEE

Parkin Archeological
State Park ■
Wilson ●
Hampson Archeological
Museum State Park ■
Chattanooga ●
Memphis ●
OKLAHOMA   Fort Smith ●
Spiro Mounds ■
Little Rock ●
ARKANSAS
Toltec Mounds Archeological
State Park ■
Chucalissa and the
C. H. Nash Museum
Etowah
Indian Mounds
Historic Site ■
Atlanta ●
SOUTH
CAROLINA

ATLANTIC

OCEAN

Winterville Mounds
State Park ■
Greenville ●
Museum of the
Mississippi
Delta ■
Greenwood
MISSISSIPPI
ALABAMA
Tuscaloosa ●
Moundville
Archaeological
Park ■
Macon ● ■ Ocmulgee National Monument
GEORGIA

TEXAS
Caddo Mounds
State Historic Site ■
Alto ●
Natchez ● ■ Emerald Mound
Grand Village of the
Natchez Indians ■
Vicksburg ●
LOUISIANA
Lake Jackson Mounds
Archaeological State Park ■
Tallahassee ●
De Soto State
Historic Site ■
St. Augustine ●
FLORIDA

De Soto National Memorial ■ ● Bradenton

0 ———— 200 mi
0 ———— 200 km
Gulf of Mexico

MOUNDS SITES AND MUSEUMS

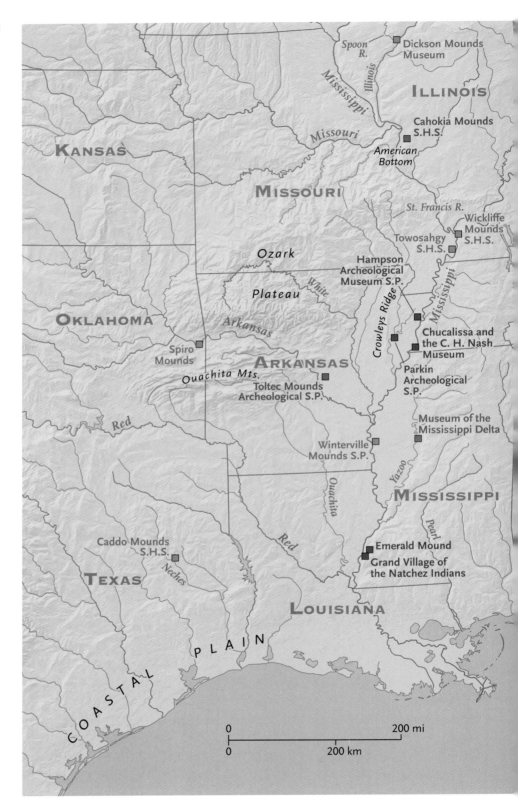

Spoon R.

Dickson Mounds
Museum

ILLINOIS

Mississippi

Illinois

Cahokia Mounds
S.H.S.

Missouri

American
Bottom

MISSOURI

KANSAS

St. Francis R.

Wickliffe
Mounds
S.H.S.

Towosahgy
S.H.S.

Ozark

Hampson
Archeological
Museum S.P.

White

Plateau

Crowleys Ridge

Mississippi

OKLAHOMA

Arkansas

Chucalissa and
the C. H. Nash
Museum

Spiro
Mounds

ARKANSAS

Parkin
Archeological
S.P.

Ouachita Mts.

Toltec Mounds
Archeological S.P.

Red

Museum of the
Mississippi Delta

Winterville
Mounds S.P.

Yazoo

MISSISSIPPI

Ouachita

Pearl

Red

Caddo Mounds
S.H.S.

Emerald Mound

Grand Village of
the Natchez Indians

TEXAS

Neches

LOUISIANA

C O A S T A L   P L A I N

0   200 mi

0   200 km

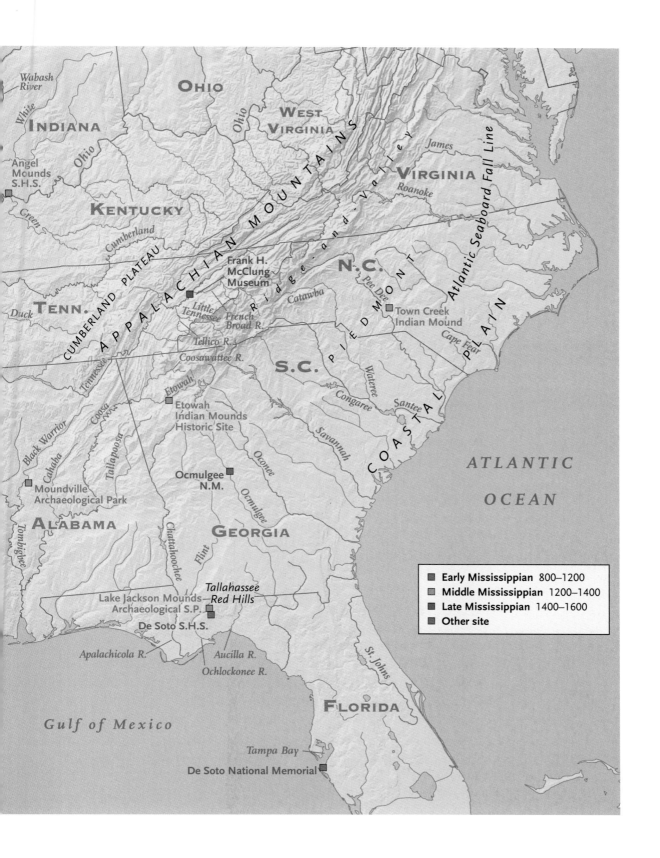

Wabash
River

OHIO

White

INDIANA

WEST
VIRGINIA

Ohio

VIRGINIA

James

Atlantic Seaboard Fall Line

Angel
Mounds
S.H.S.

Ohio

Roanoke

Green

KENTUCKY

Cumberland

Frank H.
McClung
Museum

APPALACHIAN MOUNTAINS

Ridge-and-Valley

N.C.

Pee Dee

Town Creek
Indian Mound

CUMBERLAND PLATEAU

Duck

TENN.

Little
Tennessee

French
Broad R.

Catawba

Cape Fear

Tellico R.

P
I
E
D
M
O
N
T

Coosawattee R.

Tennessee

S.C.

Watere

C
O
A
S
T
A
L

Black Warrior

Coosa

Etowah

Etowah
Indian Mounds
Historic Site

Congaree

Santee

Cahaba

Tallapoosa

Oconee

Savannah

ATLANTIC

P
L
A
I
N

Moundville
Archaeological Park

Ocmulgee
N.M.

OCEAN

Tombigbee

ALABAMA

Chattahoochee

Ocmulgee

GEORGIA

Flint

■ Early Mississippian 800–1200

Lake Jackson Mounds
Archaeological S.P.

Tallahassee
Red Hills

■ Middle Mississippian 1200–1400
■ Late Mississippian 1400–1600

De Soto S.H.S.

■ Other site

Apalachicola R.

Aucilla R.

Ochlockonee R.

St. Johns

Gulf of Mexico

FLORIDA

Tampa Bay

De Soto National Memorial

MOUND SITES OF THE ANCIENT SOUTH

CHAPTER ONE
THE ANCIENT SOUTH

WHAT FOLLOWS IS a guide to the late prehistoric native peoples of the American South, particularly a group of societies known collectively to scholars as Mississippian chiefdoms. The concept "chiefdom" refers specifically and exclusively to societies characterized by the hereditary transfer of leadership positions and by a social system that included both elites and commoners but that had not reached the size or complexity of a state. The chiefdoms of the Ancient South were dubbed "Mississippian" because their way of life first developed in the wide Mississippi River Valley, where the largest Mississippian site was built at a place called Cahokia. These Mississippian chiefdoms did not conform to popular ideas about Native American life.

Mississippian societies were ruled by powerful leaders with the ability to raise armies of warriors from among their followers. They often lived in fortified towns, and they buried their chiefs and other important citizens in earthen mounds surrounded by riches acquired through pillage and long-distance trade. The Mississippians were quite interested in and knowledgeable about the movements of the stars and planets, and they built monuments that were also tools of astronomical observation. Using archaeological information and the accounts of sixteenth-century Spanish explorers, scholars have begun to understand something of the lives of these remarkable peoples.

Although most Americans have heard of Indian groups such as the Cherokee, Choctaw, and Creek, the societies depicted in this book have received almost no attention in the popular media, though to be fair, only in the last few decades have scholars come to understand something of this extinct social order. When the media do depict these societies, they tend to lump them unceremoniously with even earlier societies and refer to them all as "Mound Builders." Many groups built earthen mounds throughout eastern

North America during the last few thousand years; however, they can in no way be considered part of one mound-building culture. Piling up earth into symbolically potent creations was merely a widely shared trait.

The moundbuilders that we are interested in, the Mississippians, built their mounds for burial and as platforms for elite residences and temples. Their societies were found only in the South and only during the Mississippian Period, between approximately 900 and 1600. This time and place characterize what is referred to as the "Ancient South." Charles Hudson developed the concept of the Ancient South as a complement to the "Old South," a much more familiar idea referring to the era of slavery and cotton growing before the Civil War. In the minds of most Americans, including most southerners, this is the "ancient" history of the South. This guide shows, however, that the true beginning of the South as we understand it today began with the rise of the Mississippian chiefdoms.

The Mississippians were farmers, just like the Euro-Americans who eventually replaced them across much of the landscape. The same places in the region that were attractive to Mississippians were later attractive to the immigrating Europeans, and for the same reasons. As subsistence farmers, both groups sought the rich soil of the bottomlands in spots that received copious amounts of rain and little frost. Both groups dealt with many of the same problems of cultivation and came to interact with the land in similar ways. Like Mississippian peoples, the newcomers constructed their houses and outbuildings on the highest ground near the fields, sometimes on long-abandoned Mississippian mounds, and founded many of their most important towns at old Indian sites.

Daily activities depicted in a reconstruction of life in an elite neighborhood adjacent to Monks Mound and the Grand Plaza at Cahokia. (Cahokia Mounds State Historic Site)

The similarities extended to the kitchen as well. Mississippians and Euro-Americans grew many of the same foods and prepared them in much the same way. Women in Mississippian societies stewed vegetables until they were soft and limp and cooked nearly everything in animal fat, though they used bear fat instead of lard. By 1540, when southern Indians and members of the Hernando de Soto expedition sat down to eat the first recorded barbecue in the South, the technique had already been a tradition for many hundreds of years. And it is still in use today, of course, though in most cases beef, chicken, and pork have replaced deer, bear, and turkey.

In other words, the heritage of the Ancient South is in many ways the heritage of all southerners. Therefore, the responsibility rests on all of us to understand something of it and to enjoy and protect the remains of those once-great southern societies to which we owe so many of the region's long traditions. An exploration of the Ancient South naturally begins with an examination of the origins of Mississippian societies.

The Mississippian Transformation

During the ninth and tenth centuries, the majority of peoples in what would eventually become known as the American South adopted a new way of life. This way differed from the old in many respects, but two were particularly important: the adoption of corn as the staple of the diet, and the development of politically and militarily formidable chiefdoms. Scholars once believed the new way of life spread from the Mississippi Valley as a result of an expanding and conquering population, but it has since been shown that in most cases the transformation was due to more indirect forces. Mississippian practices were adopted because they were perceived to be a successful way of organizing society and because it took a chiefdom to compete with another chiefdom. That is to say, chiefdom organization spread not only because it represented successful technologies and political principles but also because nonchiefdoms were vulnerable to the military might of their newly organized Mississippian neighbors and had to adapt or else lose their independence.

Southerners had grown corn in small amounts since about 200. It entered the region from one of three places: eastern Mexico, South America's Caribbean coast, or the American Southwest — probably the last. Dozens of generations passed before a variety that did well in the climate of the South was bred, but that development may have triggered the rapid and widespread intensification of corn horticulture after 900. Corn was more productive and easier to store than the native plants on which southerners had previously relied. But corn also made more demands on its cultivators than the native plants, demands that altered their lifestyles. In a sense, with the adoption of corn as the major crop, southerners went from being gardeners to being farmers. In addition, nascent chiefs used the ability to store corn for long periods to their political advantage.

Before the Mississippian transformation, societies in the region were relatively small, and leaders arose haphazardly whenever an individual could accumulate enough influence, wealth, and charisma to command the loyalty of followers. But one's position disappeared at death; it was not passed on to offspring. Mississippian chiefdoms, by contrast, were the first societies in southern history to include an elite segment characterized by the hereditary transfer of power. Although precisely how this elite segment of society developed is impossible to discover, it can be traced in part to the chief's ability to reduce risk. Once corn began to provide the lion's share of a population's caloric intake, that population became more vulnerable to the effects of crop failure, which the chief mitigated by collecting part of every harvest to hold in public trust. In addition, chiefs seem to have legitimized the permanent hierarchy of the new political order by expanding their ritual actions and connecting them with the perpetuation of the sacred order of the universe. People began to see the chief as a representative of their principal deity, symbolized by the sun. Thus Mississippian societies merged the functions of religion and government.

Another important difference between chiefdoms and earlier southern societies had to do with warfare. Because of their relatively large populations and the presence of storable food, Mississippian societies could sustain substantial military forces. Nonchiefdom societies lacked not only numbers and sufficient stored food but also leaders with the power to command the military allegiance of their people. Chiefdoms were thus much more capable and efficient in military operations than the societies that preceded them. Although armed conflict was a regular part of Mississippian life, chiefs seem to have risen to power in part because they were able to narrow the scope of violent conflict. That is, chiefdoms were larger societies spatially and numerically than those that had preceded them, and because chiefs demanded cooperation within the chiefdom and unity against outside enemies, they were able to create wider areas of peace than those that had characterized pre-Mississippian life.

In exchange for participation in these chiefdoms, the common people received several benefits. By giving part of their harvest to the chief, they "bought" insurance against future crop failures. In exchange for occasional military service and communal labor, commoners were assured of peace with their neighbors and help against foreign enemies. Finally, by giving fealty to a representative of their god, they received spiritual gains in this world and the next. That said, costs and benefits were not shared equally between the chiefly elite and the commoners. Before the workings of chiefdoms can be explored in detail, however, we must examine the region in which these societies developed.

The Climate and Environment of the Ancient South

The landscape of the Ancient South differed in many important ways from that of the current South. Much of the Ancient South was covered in vast forests, and a significant percentage of those forests were old growth. Old-growth trees were huge, with lots of space between them, and because their limbs and leaves formed a canopy that kept out much of the sunlight, there was little undergrowth, making travel much easier than is possible in today's dense, second-growth southern forests. The rivers of the Ancient South were not dammed and ran much cleaner and clearer than they do today. The flora and fauna have changed greatly as well. Many plant species we associate with the South had not yet been brought to the region, including peaches, kudzu, bluegrass, and peanuts, and the same can be said for animal species such as cows, pigs, horses, and chickens. On the other hand, several animals common in the Ancient South are now extinct or nearly so, such as passenger pigeons, Carolina parakeets, ivory-billed woodpeckers, and red wolves. Some plant species have also been lost, including the American chestnut, once the most common tree in the southern Appalachians. In other cases, native plants have had their ranges much reduced through competition with foreign species; for instance, English privet has taken over many of the areas where river cane once thrived.

In addition, the physical boundaries of the Ancient South differed from those of the modern South. Because of climatic differences, the South was larger than it is today. Specifically, between about 900 and 1300 the world experienced what has come to be known as the Medieval Warm Period, a stretch of particularly good weather during which the population of Europe grew, the Norse began to colonize the extreme north, and many of the great European cathedrals were built. In the Ancient South, the climatic episode coincided with the development and maximum growth of Mississippian societies. During that four-hundred-year period, the region extended as far west as eastern Oklahoma and as far north as the American Bottom around modern St. Louis. There were even short-term Mississippian settlements in northern Illinois and southern Wisconsin during the eleventh and twelfth centuries.

The Medieval Warm Period was followed by a climatic episode known as the Little Ice Age, which lasted from approximately 1300 to 1850. The Little Ice Age consisted of a series of unpredictable stretches of cold years interspersed

ABOVE

The Parrot of Carolina, by Mark Catesby. Flocks of raucous and vividly colored Carolina parakeets were common in the Ancient South. (Mark Catesby, *The Natural History of Carolina, Florida, and the Bahama Islands*, 1731–43)

RIGHT

The Largest White-bill Woodpecker and the Willow Oak, by Mark Catesby. Because of its club-like bill, the ivory-billed woodpecker was a potent symbol of war in the Ancient South. (Mark Catesby, *The Natural History of Carolina, Florida, and the Bahama Islands*, 1731–43)

with more moderate weather. In Europe during this time, the Norse colonies were abandoned, there was much famine brought on by crop failure, and several episodes of bubonic plague. In the Ancient South, the boundaries of the Mississippian world contracted until they closely resembled those of the South today. Many of the largest Mississippian centers were deserted, and although some were later reoccupied, others were abandoned forever, including the sites in the American Bottom and those farther north. Although climate alone was not responsible for this, the effect of climate on chiefdom societies was considerable. Mississippian farmers needed at least two hundred days without frost and at least forty-eight inches of rain each year in order to grow the crops necessary to sustain their societies.

Not all places within the Ancient South were valued equally by the Natives of the time. The Mississippi Valley is where the Mississippian way of life developed, though it first emerged in what we would today consider the Midwest, around St. Louis. It is difficult to overstate the size of a river that drains approximately 1.25 million square miles and counts among its tributaries such major rivers as the Ohio, Missouri, Arkansas, and Red. The Mississippians viewed the river as a great serpent undulating across the land. For an idea of what the Mississippi River was like in its natural form, before the modern levee system was installed, we have to turn to such authors as Mark Twain in *Life on the Mississippi* (1883) and Thomas Nuttall in *A Journal of Travels into the Arkansas Territory* (1821).

The vast floodplain of the Mississippi was covered with old-growth southern floodplain forest dominated by bald cypress, tupelo, sweet gum, and several varieties of submergible oaks. Mississippian peoples lived on the highest land available, the natural levees, but regular flooding would have been a fact of life. The Mississippi system is essentially a tremendous meander belt (a snaking, twisting watercourse) through a shallow valley marked by soft soils. As the river passes along its S-shaped path through the floodplain, water flows fastest along the outside edge of the bends, which results in soil being removed from those banks. The slower water on the inside of the bends cannot keep the soil particles suspended, so they are deposited on the inside bends. The S-shaped curve eventually becomes so pronounced that it takes on the appearance of a horseshoe. At that point, even a small flood can result in the horseshoe curve being cut off from the main channel if the river "jumps" over the small neck of land between the ends of the horseshoe, shortening the river and turning the S-shaped curve into a lake known as an oxbow.

The shores of oxbow lakes were among the best places to live for Mississippian farmers. The levee soils between oxbows and the main river channel were the richest soils for corn horticulture in the entire Ancient South. The

Formation of an oxbow lake. The adjacent levee soils and abundant resources made these lakes attractive places for Mississippians to settle. (Mississippi River Commission)

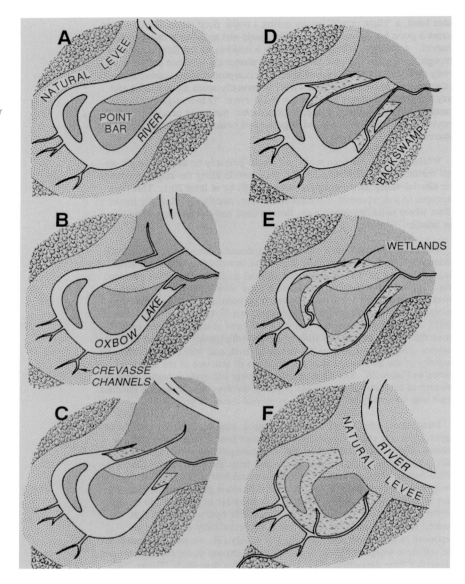

lakes were full of turtles and many slow-water fish species, such as buffalo fish, gar, and catfish, that commonly weighed as much as eighty to one hundred pounds. Fast-water species, including freshwater eels, lived in the many tributaries. Countless migratory birds used the Mississippi Valley as a flyway, so during certain seasons the oxbow lakes teemed with several species of geese and ducks. A number of valuable plant species grew throughout the valley, perhaps none more important than river cane, which was abundant along the Mississippi and other waterways throughout the Ancient South. River cane was used for scores of purposes by Native peoples. (See the box feature River Cane, page 9.)

River cane (*Arundinaria gigantea*) is a species of bamboo that is native to the south-eastern United States. Cane grows very rapidly and favors disturbed soils like those associated with hoe horticulture, so it could always be found growing near Mississippian fields. It thrived in the same water and temperature conditions as corn, and, in fact, Euro-American colonists judged a land's fertility by the height of the cane they found growing on it. River cane often grew in brakes, that is, large areas where it choked out almost all other plants. It was difficult to move quickly through the dense canebrakes, and it was impossible to move quietly through a canebrake because of the rustling of dry leaves and stalks. For these reasons, they were excellent places of refuge for both men and beasts. In addition cane was a good source of browse (shoots, twigs, and leaves used by animals for food), and because it was evergreen, it continually attracted animals desired by Mississippian hunters.

River cane was used as raw material for such a huge variety of items that its pervasiveness was analogous to that of plastic today. Cane has several characteristics that recommend such extensive use: it is hard yet quite flexible, easy to split or hollow out, and water-resistant. River cane was often split into withes of varying thickness and then used in the construction of baskets. Fancier baskets featured designs woven from dyed withes. Split cane was used to weave mats, which covered the inside walls and floors of houses and served as a base layer of bedding. Tightly woven split-cane mats could be used to shingle the roofs of houses, and long cane withes were one of the materials used in the construction of house walls. (See the box feature Mississippian Homes, pages 30–31.)

Tools made from river cane included fishing spears, blowguns, arrow shafts, and scalping knives. There is some evidence of the use of cane shields during the Mississippian period, but this practice was discontinued after the introduction of firearms. Fish traps, known as weirs, were often constructed of cane. Mississippian peoples sometimes made rafts out of river cane, though their preferred watercraft was the dugout canoe. (See the box feature Dugout Canoes, pages 22–23.) Small stalks of cane were often fashioned into pipe stems that could be attached to clay or stone pipe bowls. Flutes were generally made from cane as well. Light-duty fences, such as those placed around gardens, were constructed of whole stalks of river cane placed vertically into the ground and lashed together. Finally, cane could be used to make torches, and was burned like firewood as a source of fuel because it was fairly smokeless when thoroughly dry.

The Mississippi Valley was far from the only place conducive to the Mississippian way of life. The Atlantic Seaboard Fall Line was particularly attractive to Mississippian farmers. Not technically a physiographic province, the fall line is actually the boundary area between the Piedmont and the Coastal Plain. In prehistoric and early historical times, the line, which begins in New England and traces a J-shaped course down the coast and across the mid-South, where it turns slightly to the north again in west-central Alabama, was the major east-west corridor for travel and communication along its southern end, not least because of the good river crossings along its entire length. The fall line was also where swift-running rivers emerged from the relatively narrow, rocky riverbeds of the higher country and dumped the soil and nutrients they were carrying into the slow-moving, languid rivers of the low country. In the Coastal Plain, rivers mimicked the meandering of the Mississippi, but on a reduced scale. The fall line featured wonderful bottom-land soils and plant and animal species, and its inhabitants could easily access the resources of both the Piedmont and the Coastal Plain.

On both the eastern and western sides of the southern mountains lay elevated plateaus; the Piedmont is the eastern one. The Piedmont begins in the Northeast as a narrow strip of land between the mountains and the coast, but widens considerably in the South. A southern mixed-hardwood forest dominated by oak, hickory, and pine covered most of the gently rolling Piedmont hills, which reach five hundred to a thousand feet high. The Piedmont forests were much different from the ones we see today, as evidenced by the description left us by the colonial botanist William Bartram in his *Travels* (1791):

> We rise gradually a sloping bank of twenty or thirty feet elevation, and immediately entered this sublime forest; the ground is perfectly a level green plain, thinly planted by nature with the most stately forest trees, such as the gigantic Black Oak ... whose mighty trunks, seemingly of equal height, appeared like superb columns. To keep within the bounds of truth and reality, in describing the magnitude and grandeur of these trees, would, I fear, fail of credibility; yet, I think I can assert, that many of the black oaks measured eight, nine, ten, and eleven feet diameter five feet above the ground, as we measured several that were above thirty feet girth, and from hence they ascend perfectly strait, with a gradual taper, forty or fifty feet to the limbs.

The rivers of the Piedmont tend to alternate between moderately developed floodplains and narrow shoals. Shoals were excellent places to catch fish and mussels, and they were used also as fording places. Piedmont forests were home to many of the most important plants and animals available to Mississippians, including deer, turkeys, persimmons, pecans, and hickory nuts.

Mineral resources in the Piedmont included hematite and limonite (also known as red ochre and yellow ochre), which could be ground into a colored powder, mixed with other ingredients, and used as pigments.

Much of the Ancient South was composed of the Coastal Plain, often referred to as the low country. The Coastal Plain was covered by a forest type known as "pine barrens," which began near the coast and ran inland for 75–150 miles. At least three-fourths of the forests were composed of longleaf pines, which require fire in order to release their seeds. Thus while the frequent hot fires of the region tended to kill deciduous trees, they fostered the proliferation of longleaf pines. The result was a fire climax forest of which nothing remains today. Pine barrens were essentially deserts because they offered little for game animals to eat — and so were generally shunned by Mississippians as uninhabitable. The exception was within the floodplain valleys of the rivers, where tree species such as sweet gum, beech, magnolia, and live oak thrived and where the plants and animals needed by people could be found, though not as abundantly as elsewhere in the Ancient South. Yaupon holly (*Ilex vomitoria*), a plant used to make an important beverage, was native to the area also. (See the box feature Black Drink, page 18.)

The Coastal Plain boasted other important resources, such as marine shells and chert, a flint-like stone particularly suited for the production of tools. Shells from the Atlantic and Gulf Coasts were widely traded inland and fashioned into both useful and decorative items, from hoe blades to jewelry. Also widely traded was Coastal Plain chert, a tan-colored stone that changes to a reddish pink when heated before being made into tools. The estuaries behind the barrier islands and coastal peninsulas were exploited for a variety of fish, shellfish, and birds. Despite such resources, much of the Coastal Plain was unsuited to the Mississippian way of life. Mississippians found beaches to be unsuitable for habitation; besides being subject to violent weather, they supported few game animals, the soil was too poor for growing corn, and fish traps could not be set along the beaches.

The southern mountains were not a particularly coveted location for the Mississippians, either. In general, Indians lived in the mountains only where rivers cut through, and even there the river valleys tend to be narrow because of the hard underlying rock, with poorly developed floodplains. Farmers had to deal with early and late frosts that were difficult to predict. As a result, the Mississippian way of life came late to the mountains, and the mountaineers of the Ancient South developed smaller chiefdoms than those in other parts of the Mississippian world. The predominant species in the mountain forests was the American chestnut, a tree that grew to enormous dimensions. Unfortunately, the American chestnut is now subject to a blight that was introduced through the imported Chinese chestnut, which invariably kills

An Appalachian family in front of a chestnut tree in the early twentieth century. Such trees provided Mississippians with an abundant harvest of nuts each fall. (Smoky Mountains National Park)

the American species long before the trees reach maturity. Humans, bears, and deer alike loved the sweet chestnuts and would travel great distances to gather the fall harvest. The mountains also contained both copper and mica, which were passed along trade routes throughout the Ancient South.

Mississippian peoples found the Ridge and Valley Province much more suitable than either the coasts or the mountains. Along the western edge of the mountains lay a series of northeast-trending parallel ridges with narrow but fertile valleys between them. The ridges vary between one thousand and three thousand feet in elevation, and from the air they look like a strip of corduroy lying along the foot of the mountains. The province was blanketed by forests dominated by oak, hickory, and pine, from which Mississippians hunted and gathered an astonishing array of animals and plants, including deer, black bear, turkey, wild grapes, pawpaws, hickory nuts, and a variety of berries. The Ridge and Valley was a good source for grey-black chert, which, like the chert of the Coastal Plain, was widely traded throughout the Ancient South. The Mississippians who populated the region tended to build their capitals near the edge of the province, near its juncture with the Piedmont. The places where rivers entered the Ridge and Valley from the Piedmont contained the most fertile soils in the province and offered residents a location from which to efficiently exploit the resources of both regions.

CHAPTER TWO

THE MISSISSIPPIAN WORLD

D URING THE HEIGHT of the Mississippian period, in the thirteenth century, there were at least fifty large Mississippian chiefdoms and many small ones scattered throughout the Ancient South, and the total population of the region was at least several hundred thousand. Despite the tremendous linguistic and cultural diversity among these societies, there were enough similarities to allow them to have more than a basic understanding of one another. A number of general Mississippian traits constitute a setting that can rightly be referred to as the Mississippian world. This chapter explores important aspects of this nearly lost world, including subsistence practices, settlement patterns, social and political organization, kinship, belief systems, and warfare.

Horticulture

It is important to try to understand how the Mississippians experienced their landscape. How did the constraints of the environment shape the Mississippian way of life? Conversely, how did Mississippian farmers alter and shape the environment to suit their needs and desires, and what were the results, intended or not, of their actions? Mississippians practiced what is known as a mixed economy, meaning that in addition to growing foods in their fields and gardens, they gathered wild plants, hunted, and fished.

By far the most constraining activity of the Mississippian world was the cultivation of corn. Initially, a prospective field had to be cleared of old-growth trees, which were so large they could not be felled with stone axes. Instead, the trees were "ringed," that is, a continuous strip of bark was removed near their bases the year before the field was to be planted. In this way, farmers killed the trees, which stopped producing leaves; sunlight could then reach the forest floor. The crops were planted among the standing skeletons of the dead trees, which over the ensuing years would gradually lose their limbs and finally their trunks, leaving stumps that would eventually rot completely away.

Preparing the fields was the first of many arduous tasks. Corn must be protected throughout its growing cycle from the birds and animals that like it as much as humans. Weeds must be continually combated. Finally, once harvested, corn must be kept completely dry — not an easy task in the warm and humid South. Corn is very hard on the soil, quickly depleting its nitrogen content, and so the cultivation of corn required the very best soil available. This was especially the case for Mississippian farmers, since they did not use fertilizer. The loose floodplain soils coveted and exploited by Mississippians were easily tilled and thus compatible with the available farming equipment — mainly the hoe, since Mississippians lacked both plows and domesticated draft animals.

When planting, Mississippian farmers sometimes used a ridge-and-furrow technique that resulted in neat rows of crops, but more often they practiced a haphazard-looking intercropping technique. Small hillocks of earth just a few inches high were piled up randomly throughout a field, and two or three corn kernels were planted in the top of each one. The hillocks not only absorbed the heat of the sun more quickly than the surrounding soil, but also helped protect the young seedlings from drowning. Around the base of the hillocks, farmers planted beans, which used the cornstalks for support as they grew. As nitrogen fixers, beans help reduce the damage corn does to the soil. Squash was planted between the hillocks to help hold moisture in the soil beneath its wide-spreading leaves and to prevent weeds from taking hold in the fields.

Early corn was planted near houses, and late corn in the fields, but only after wild foods had ripened, giving crows and other corn thieves something besides corn to eat. Crows are particularly persistent raiders of fields right after corn sprouts, as are deer and raccoons. Once corn is dry on the stalk, a number of bird species become interested in it as well. Mississippians had several methods of protecting their crops from birds and animals. Small raised and shaded platforms were often built in the fields, and both the elderly and the young often had to take turns as human scarecrows. Gourd birdhouses were hung for purple martins, and wrens and swifts were encouraged to nest near crops, where they could feast on bugs. Occasionally, fires were built at night along the perimeter of the fields to discourage nocturnal feeders.

The lack of fertilizer and corn's voracious appetite for nitrogen meant fields periodically had to be left fallow for several seasons in order to regain their fertility. These so-called old fields were soon overgrown with a tangle of underbrush that included several edible species attractive to humans and game animals. Thus, old fields were useful even when they lay fallow. A field deemed ready for use again was burned off to prepare it for planting. Mississippian towns had a patchwork of fields and old fields on their perimeters. If a town had been recently founded or its population was growing rapidly, then some of the fields would be new enough to contain standing dead trees in various stages of decay as well as fields that more closely resembled our own conception of farmland.

Mississippian farmers planted kitchen gardens where they grew pumpkins, sunflowers, and a variety of greens. Tobacco, bottle gourds, and yaupon holly were grown in the gardens, too. (See the box feature Black Drink, page 18.)

Gathering

Both men and women gathered a wide variety of raw materials from the forests, fields, and rivers, including cane, mussel shells, tool stone, and a variety of plant fibers. Some medicinal plants were cultivated, but most were gathered and then dried in the rafters of houses or corncribs. In addition to medicinals, Mississippians gathered an amazing variety of wild foods, which formed a vital part of their diets. Mississippians possessed an intricate botanical knowledge, covering food and nonfood plants, accumulated over hundreds of generations.

Fruits were particularly important because they provided a number of essential vitamins — that is, vitamins that the human body cannot make on its own. Persimmons, a rich source of vitamins C and B_2, were perhaps the most important fruit, but dozens of others were eaten as well, including wild grapes (such as muscadines and scuppernongs), wild cherries, wild plums, maypops, crabapples, pawpaws, and pods of the honey locust. Berries gathered seasonally included small wild strawberries, blackberries, raspberries, huckleberries, gooseberries, mulberries, serviceberries, and others. Nuts were vital to the Mississippian diet, particularly hickory nuts, which were prized for their oil. The oil, which was obtained by boiling the nutmeat and skimming off the substance that rose to the surface, was known as "hickory milk" and was used much like olive oil. The nutmeat was also eaten, either fresh or after being pressed into cakes and dried. Other important nuts included chestnuts, pecans, walnuts, and acorns. Mississippian peoples ate wild seeds, greens, and roots and tubers, including wild onions, leeks, and Jerusalem artichokes. Mushrooms, however, were not much used.

BLACK DRINK

Mississippian societies made a drink from the leaves and twigs of the yaupon holly, a plant still used today throughout the South as an ornamental shrub. The plant contains caffeine and is, in fact, the only herbal source of caffeine not currently exploited on the world market. The beverage produced from yaupon holly was much like coffee, tea, or mate and was known by a variety of names during the early historical period. The English often referred to it as "cassina" or "yaupon," and the French as "*apalachine*," after the Apalachee Indians, who first introduced the drink to the Spanish. The beverage was sometimes referred to simply as "black drink" because of its color, but the southeastern Indians called it "white drink" because they associated it with purity and used it ceremonially. The scientific name of yaupon holly (*Ilex vomitoria*) comes from the European association of this beverage with a common southeastern Indian practice: on certain occasions, men in important political positions would drink copious amounts of this concoction and then vomit in order to attain a state of ritual purity. Although the vomiting was often violent (achieved by pushing on the abdomen), it was due not to toxins in the plant, but to drinking a large volume of liquid in a short period of time. But Euro-Americans mistakenly credited the plant with having emetic properties, and so its scientific name reflects that misconception.

Yaupon holly was best when picked in early to midsummer, although it was harvested and used at other times of the year as well. Black drink was made by roasting the leaves of the yaupon holly and steeping them in boiling water. It was deemed ready to drink as soon as the liquid would no longer scald the skin. After the beverage was brewed, it was given to men to drink in a prescribed order that reflected their individual places within the hierarchy of the chiefdom. Black drink was seen as a symbol of peace and was thus commonly prepared for visitors. At least in later times, black drink was consumed daily by the men of the town while they talked in the public square, and though this was seemingly a casual consumption of the beverage, the making and serving of it still followed a ritual prescription.

Black drink was often consumed out of large shell cups, sometimes described as dippers. These cups, which averaged eleven to twelve inches in length but have been found as long as sixteen inches, were made of three types of shells: lightning whelk (often mistaken for *Busycon perversum*, a smaller species), emperor helmet, and horse conch. Cups were made by removing the columella (central column or axis) of the shell (which was often turned into a pendant), grinding and polishing the edges, and sometimes engraving the outside.

The ceremonial consumption of black drink, depicted in an engraving by Theodor de Bry. Vomiting in this context was considered to be an act of ritual purification. (Beinecke Rare Book and Manuscript Library, Yale University)

Fishing

Mississippians were industrial fishermen who sought large catches. They ate catfish, buffalo fish, trout, bass, sturgeon, eel, paddlefish, gar, and many other varieties. In addition, they frequently ate turtles and many types of fresh-water mussels. Fish were taken in a number of ways. Fish weirs, basketry traps that allowed fish to swim in but not out, were commonly used. Dip nets were used from dugout canoes and from shore, as were larger, weighted nets requiring the coordinated action of a group of people. Spearfishing was done at shoals and from dugout canoes. (See the box feature Dugout Canoes, pages 22–23.) Both nets and spears were sometimes used at night from dugouts that contained fired-clay basins in which a small fire could be lit to attract fish. Trotlines with many baited hooks were strung across stream channels and periodically checked for fish and turtles. In late summer, when many of the backwater ponds were quite shallow, Mississippians even poisoned fish with concoctions made of buckeye and devil's shoestring. When placed in the water, these plant poisons killed the fish, which then floated to the top, where they could be scooped out. Because the poison did not affect the flesh, the fish were safely edible.

Life at the Etowah site: fish being gathered from basketry traps known as weirs, water being collected in jars, and children frolicking in the river. (H. Tom Hall, National Geographic Stock)

Native fishing techniques, including spear and net fishing, depicted in an engraving by Theodor de Bry. The fire built on a clay base in the dugout canoe was meant to lure fish at night. (Beinecke Rare Book and Manuscript Library, Yale University)

Hunting

By far the most important game animal was the white-tailed deer, which was sought after not only for venison but also for hides, bones, antlers, and sinews. Turkeys, also important, were quite abundant. Bears were hunted mainly for the oil that was rendered from their fat and then used for both cooking and cosmetic purposes, but their fur, meat, and sinews were used also. A number of small mammals were eaten regularly, including squirrels, raccoons, possums, rabbits, and even beaver. Passenger pigeons were taken in large numbers from their roosts at night, and thick oil was rendered from their fat and used like butter. Other birds commonly eaten by Mississippians included quail and wood ducks. Migrating waterfowl such as teal, Canada geese, mallards, pintails, cormorants, mergansers, and shovelers were taken in season. Some animals were hunted but not eaten, such as the cougar and the wolf, which were killed for their pelts. Many birds were destroyed to obtain their feathers, including hawks, eagles, buzzards, owls, woodpeckers, and dozens of brightly colored songbirds, such as the now-extinct Carolina parakeet.

Successful hunting often included magic, and always included prayers of forgiveness for the taking of life. Boys spent much of their youth practicing the finer arts of tracking and stalking as well as marksmanship, and adult men spent countless hours at the hunt during their lives. The main hunting weapon was the bow and arrow, and men usually hunted alone or in small

groups — attempting through stealth to get so close to an animal that they could not miss. They sometimes hunted from blinds. Hunters used calls to attract a variety of animals, including deer and turkey. The most sophisticated deception, however, came in the form of elaborate deer-head decoys that masked the humanness of the hunters and allowed them the opportunity to move close to a grazing herd. Communal hunting methods included fire surrounds and the use of dogs. Dogs were particularly effective against bears and cougars, which they could often drive into trees from where they were easily killed. Small mammals could be trapped or snared, and many were killed by boys using river-cane blowguns and darts of locust wood with thistledown fletching. Poison was not used, however, so the darts were effective only against small birds and mammals.

Native hunters using deer-head decoys to approach their prey at close range. Engraving by Theodor de Bry. (Beinecke Rare Book and Manuscript Library, Yale University)

The Yearly Round

Mississippians, like their historical descendents, divided the year into lunar months. Each month was associated with (and possibly named for) a ripening food or particular weather condition, and the months were grouped into two seasons: the warm season and the cold season. The beginning of the cold season marked the start of fall hunting. Most adult males spent part of the season hunting in small groups that included wives, sisters, brothers, sons,

DUGOUT CANOES

The peoples of the Ancient South used dugout canoes carved out of the trunks of individual trees to transport themselves along the many creeks and rivers of the region. These canoes were unlike the watercraft generally associated with Native Americans, the birch-bark canoe. Birch-bark canoes were common in the Northeast but were not used on southern rivers, for a number of reasons. The material needed to make or patch these canoes (certain types of bark and resin) was not readily available in the South. In addition, southern rivers contained many "sawyers," trees that were snagged underwater and bobbed continuously up and down, sometimes readily apparent and other times quite hidden. Sawyers were more than capable of tearing out the bottom of a bark canoe, but had little effect on southern dugouts. Mississippian peoples did occasionally make a type of bark canoe out of elm or cypress, which could be constructed quickly and used for a single river crossing if a ford was unavailable or unadvisable.

Dugouts were long, narrow boats with a very shallow draft. Consequently, they could tip over easily, but under the direction of skilled boatmen, dugouts were quite maneuverable and very fast. They were generally paddled but could be poled on sufficiently placid water. Dugouts varied greatly in size—the largest could accommodate as many as sixty or seventy people in three rows, while the smallest held only three or four. Unlike lightweight bark canoes, it was difficult or impossible to portage dugout canoes, that is, to carry them from one water source to another, so dugouts often had to be left unguarded along the shores of rivers. As a result, the peoples of the Ancient South devised a number of ways to hide them. The simplest way was to drag a dugout under the cover of nearby vegetation, but some Mississippians left the bark on the outside of the canoe so it could be turned over and made to look like just another downed tree. Since dugouts were made of rot-resistant wood, they could be sunk with large stones and retrieved later.

Pine and cypress were the most common trees used in the construction of dugouts, but others were used as well, including poplar. Trees downed in storms were used if possible, but often they had to be felled, not an easy task given the size of tree needed and the tools available. Since trees of the right size could not be chopped down with stone axes, they had to be brought down with the tandem use of fire and axes. After splintering the wood around the base of the tree, Mississippians would start a fire to help bring down the tree, protecting the section to be used for the dugout by plastering it with a thick layer of wet mud. Once the tree fell, the process had to be repeated at the far end of the section of log to be used. Once the log was reduced to the desired length, it was plastered completely with wet mud, with the exception of the top side of the log, where the hollowing-out process began. After splintering the wood along the top, Mississippians would start a fire there. From time to time the fire would be put out and the inside of the log scraped clean. Then the inside walls would be plastered with mud and a new fire built, with the process repeated until the log had been appropriately hollowed out.

Since dugout canoes took an enormous amount of time and energy to create, they were considered quite valuable. They were very sturdy, could carry a large amount of cargo, and could last for generations with little repair. Mississippian villages generally had one good canoe landing, and larger towns often had several.

Stages in the construction of dugout canoes, depicted in an engraving by Theodor de Bry. (Beinecke Rare Book and Manuscript Library, Yale University)

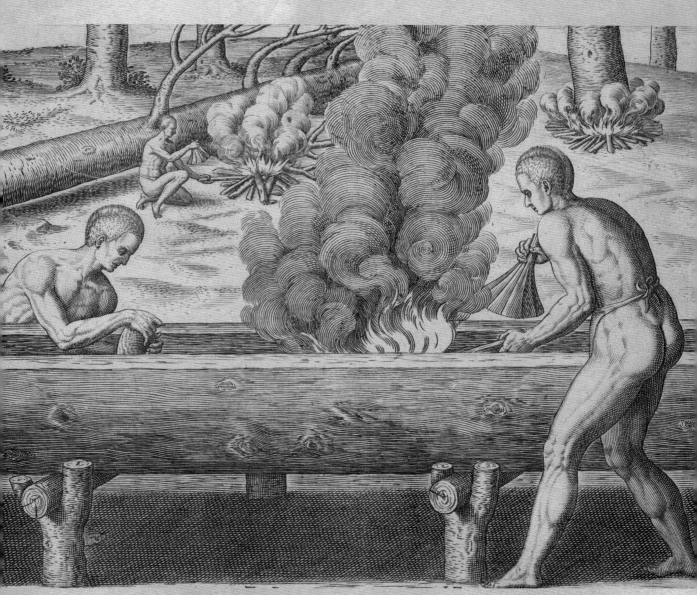

and nephews. For a few weeks, they camped in the territory of the chiefdom and its buffer zones, killing animals, preserving meat, processing hides, collecting feathers, and rendering fat for oil. If they did not encounter any of their enemies in the wilderness, they returned home with large supplies of meat, skins, and other animal products.

When the weather began to warm, people traveled in family groups to their favorite fishing camps to harvest and dry large stores of fish. Anyone might go on these trips, because they were closer to the village and of shorter duration than the fall and winter hunts. But the onset of the warm season, in April or May, primarily signaled the time to plant. While the early corn was being put in near the houses, the men cleared the fields surrounding the village. About a month after the early corn was sown, the late corn was planted in the fields. Many wild foods, especially fruits, became ripe during the warm months, when they had to be gathered and stored away for the winter. As the warm season ebbed, people enjoyed a period of leisure.

Many chores had to be kept up throughout the year. Men maintained buildings, made and repaired tools, and ruminated over the affairs of the chiefdom. They generally spent several weeks each year engaged in war as well. Women cooked and cared for children in addition to weeding, gardening, collecting fuel, processing hides, and making clothing and pottery. (See the box feature Pottery, page 25.) The affairs of men were concentrated beyond the village — hunting, fishing, and war. Even when they were home, they talked incessantly about matters beyond the boundaries of the chiefdom. The affairs of women related to the village, the fields, and the patches of woods close to town. It was there that the influence of women was most keenly felt, and women were a powerful and respected force in the Mississippian world.

Cooking

Mississippians were particularly fond of soups and stews, and when their meat wasn't boiled with vegetables, they grilled it over an open flame. Corn, beans, and squash were the staple ingredients of most dishes. They made several varieties of bread as well, including fritters cooked in bear grease, bread baked in a Dutch oven made of two pots, boiled dumplings, and cornbread, which was wrapped in cornhusks and then boiled. Seeds were often added to bread batter before it was cooked, and bread was sometimes smeared with a butter-like substance made from the oil of hickory nuts, rendered passenger pigeons, or bear fat, as well as from live oak acorns, which produce an oil similar to almond oil. Uncooked vegetables were almost never eaten, so the idea of a salad would have been unappetizing to Mississippian peoples.

The history of pottery in the South began more than two thousand years before the Mississippian way of life developed. The work of Mississippian potters, who primarily were women, was more advanced than older forms; it is on display at virtually every site discussed in this guidebook. Pottery vessels were created from a paste made of clay and additional ingredients, known as temper, that kept the pot from breaking during firing. Before the Mississippian period, temper could be plant fibers, pebbles, or sand. Mississippian potters began using shell, which was first burnt and then crushed into fine particles. This material, which was far superior to other tempers, allowed potters to create a wide variety of vessel shapes with thinner yet stronger walls that conducted heat more evenly, resulting in increased cooking efficiency. The use of shell-tempered pottery was widespread, though not universal, in the Mississippian world.

Once the shell was added to the clay, the clay was rolled out into long, snakelike pieces. On a flat wooden board that rested on the potter's lap, the pieces were coiled into a variety of vessel shapes. The most common vessels were cooking pots (some with a capacity of several gallons), jars, bottles, bowls, and shallow pans or dishes on which food was served. Once the walls of a vessel were built up, they had to be smoothed by hand with a river rock or a pottery trowel—a common item in Mississippian museum displays. When several pots were ready, a wood fire was built and the pots were set around it to be heated and further dried. Once the bed of coals was ready, the pots were placed on top of it, covered with more fuel, and fired for an hour or so. Mississippian potters did not use kilns.

Vessels were not glazed, so water could seep very slowly through the walls of the pot. As the moisture evaporated, both the contents of the vessel and the vessel itself were cooled. The color of vessels varied according to the clay and the firing techniques used, but was usually buff, gray, brown, or black. Sometimes Mississippian pots were painted—often red—before firing. Although utilitarian pottery was decorated only occasionally, Mississippian potters created an array of ornamental vessels as well. Surface designs were added after the initial drying period. Designs were often stamped or pressed into the vessel by carved wooden paddles or paddles wrapped with fabric or cord. Sometimes corncobs were used to make impressions as well. In addition, pottery vessels were sometimes incised with designs carved into the clay before firing. Images found on pottery are found also on shell artifacts such as gorgets (ornamental collars) and cups. Mississippian potters created a wide variety of human and animal effigy pottery as well, and these vessels are featured prominently in museum displays.

A number of common Mississippian vessel types. These exquisite reproductions were produced by the accomplished potter Tammy Beane.

TOP: Fish being broiled over an open flame. Engraving by Theodor de Bry. (Beinecke Rare Book and Manuscript Library, Yale University)

BOTTOM: A couple tending a pot of fish and corn. Soups and stews were common fare among the people of the Ancient South. Engraving by Theodor de Bry. (Beinecke Rare Book and Manuscript Library, Yale University)

Plates and bowls were used mainly to serve food; there were no individual place settings. People dipped into serving bowls with their own spoons and ate from common plates, often with their hands. Each house normally had a pot of sofkee ready to eat at any time. Sofkee was a sort of gruel similar to grits, made of cracked hominy treated with wood-ash lye. Corn could be parched and ground into meal using long wooden pestles and mortars made from a section of log. When reconstituted in water, this parched cornmeal was used as the main source of sustenance while traveling. Meats, fish, fruits, and vegetables were preserved mainly by drying. Meats and fish were not salted because Mississippians did not generally have excess salt. Salt was not available everywhere, and like farmers in all times and places, Mississippians had to acquire it via trade for use in their diets. Salt was traded from the coast and from areas near salt springs and salines, which produced water from which salt could be rendered and were common in parts of Alabama, Arkansas, Kentucky, Louisiana, Missouri, and Tennessee.

Elite Involvement with Subsistence

The economy of Mississippian chiefdoms was based on what anthropologists refer to as a domestic mode of production. That is to say, each household pursued the same domestic activities — farming, hunting, fishing, and gathering — and each household could produce all the food required by its members. Farming, however, could be a risky endeavor, and since Mississippian peoples received most of their calories from their horticultural produce, crop failure could be devastating. The likelihood of this happening allowed for the emergence of leaders who promised to ameliorate the threat.

In addition to collecting a portion of each family's harvest, chiefs probably first encouraged the practice of double-cropping. Mississippians planted two successive crops of corn each year near their houses, and although the huge bottomland fields were planted only once each year, double-cropping added a substantial amount to the annual harvest. In fact, it may be this practice on which the whole Mississippian finance system was based. Chiefs kept their corn in cribs like everyone else, but chiefs had corncribs not only in their towns of residence, but in all their subject towns as well, where it was collected and stored until needed.

To accommodate that arrangement, each family put more land under cultivation, placing additional demands on local resources. Further, although exact figures are not known, it is clear that the population of the region increased during the Mississippian period, and denser populations would have been more adversely effected by crop failure. A chief could easily deal with small problems such as those caused by localized flooding or mammalian or avian pests. The chief would simply dip into his supply of corn and take care of the few families involved. For more widespread problems, such as a severe drought or a killing frost, a chief might have been more hard-pressed to provide relief.

Although a chief may have had enough food to take care of his people in most circumstances, whether minor or severe, he was certainly loath to give it up, and the food collected from subjects was generally not returned in full. Instead, the chief used much of the collected food to finance a lifestyle befitting a chief. In fact, chiefs redistributed food primarily as a system of elite finance and only secondarily as insurance against famine for commoners. On the other hand, no matter how much or how little power a Mississippian chief had, convention forced him to be extremely generous. Anytime a person was allowed an audience with a chief, food was served, and generally it was an ostentatious meal. A chief was expected to hold huge feasts for all the important ceremonial events of the year as well as for important social and political occurrences, such as an elite marriage or a declaration of peace or war. The food for such events came, of course, from that collected from a chief's constituents.

A chief felt the bite of famine when disasters forced him to dip so far into his corncribs that it was difficult or impossible to properly play the part of leader and host. The elite did not go hungry, however, no matter the condition of the commoners. At many of the Mississippian sites for which bioarchaeological evidence exists and has been tested, it is clear that the elite were in much better health than the commoners. When evidence of nutritional stress is found among commoners, the same signs are often absent from elites living at the site. In some cases the elites were taller than commoners by an average of one or two inches — a clear indication of long-term, not just emergency, differences in nutrition.

Chiefs received fresh food too from commoners. Evidence collected from throughout the Ancient South suggests that the choicest parts of deer were brought to the chief, who rarely dined on any other parts if the supply of venison was abundant. In more densely populated areas, especially those hemmed in by war, elites were often the only people who ate deer regularly. Gifts were made to the chief of the choicest of all food — newly ripened fruits and nuts, freshly caught fish, and treats that were harder to come by, such as honey. Chiefs received the choicest tobacco, yaupon holly, and other garden produce. In short, the chief was entitled to the finest of all things produced within his chiefdom.

With this bounty of food, chiefs fed their own extended families. Besides his kinfolk, a chief supported people roughly comparable to priests — keepers of esoteric and arcane knowledge. Chiefs helped finance artists and craftspeople — for instance, the best potters, those with considerable ability at cutting and incising shells, or those who could produce stone tools with particular skill. Additionally, a chief might finance the families of military specialists, who continually trained for war and acted as a sort of chiefly guard as well as a constant physical reminder of the chief's power.

Chiefs' power, however, varied with the size of their chiefdoms. The more wealthy and productive a chief's society and the more demands made of it, the more a chief was able to set himself apart from the commoners through the system of elite finance. Powerful chiefs of the Mississippian period could feed many families and support a large number of artists and craftspeople as well as what amounted to a small private army. On the other hand, the chief of a small society could afford to feed only his extended family well, to be generous to commoners only at the right times, and to support a handful of other families, perhaps a few priests, a dozen or more artisans, and at least a score of military men.

The Settlement System

Regardless of size, chiefdoms were spatially organized in similar ways. To begin with, they occupied areas that were environmentally well suited to the Mississippian way of life. Each chiefdom had a primary mound center, which served as a capital and the home of the chief. In addition, most chiefdoms had at least one secondary mound center, which served as home to a subchief. Both primary and secondary mound centers had resident populations, but in some places those populations were mostly elite, with the commoners spread throughout the territory of the chiefdom in homesteads, a pattern referred to as "dispersed settlement." Other Mississippians conformed to a "nucleated settlement" pattern, in which mound centers were densely packed "urban" towns with hundreds and even thousands of commoners living in proximity to the elite. Each chiefdom, regardless of arrangement, was separated from neighboring chiefdoms by buffer zones — places devoid of permanent human settlement.

Settlement Location

Mississippian farmers usually located their settlements near their fields, that is, along the levee ridges of remnant or active river channels, often near the confluence of two physiographic provinces. Those who lived in homesteads rather than towns did not need a dense concentration of appropriate soil, so homesteads were found in more diverse settings. In all cases, people tried to locate their houses (see the box feature Mississippian Homes, pages 30–31)

MISSISSIPPIAN HOMES

WINTER HOUSE. The typical residential structure used by Mississippians was similar to later structures sometimes referred to as "winter houses" because of their insulating properties. The size and shape of winter houses varied somewhat throughout the Ancient South, as did some building techniques, particularly roofing, but most winter houses conformed to a basic pattern. They were dark (no windows) and smoky (poor ventilation). Winter houses were square or rectangular one-room buildings ten to thirty feet long on each side. The walls were built of small round posts set vertically into the ground, evenly spaced with a few inches between each. Long split-cane withes were then woven between the posts, and both sides were plastered over with mud mixed with plant fibers. This construction technique is known as wattle and daub, with the wattle referring to the cane withes and the daub to the mud plaster. The plastered walls were sometimes covered with cane mats and sometimes painted with images. Roofs were very steep and included eaves to facilitate the runoff of rainwater away from the walls of the building. Thatch was probably the most common roofing material, but the plants used to produce it varied considerably across the region. Shingles, often made of cypress bark, were regularly used in some areas, and split-cane mats were sometimes used as an inner roofing layer that was then covered by thatch or shingles. Floors were often dug down to a depth of one or two feet, and the excavated earth was banked around the bottom of the outside walls for insulation. Entrances were occasionally placed in the middle of a wall but were more often located in corners. Entrances were quite small, often requiring a person to stoop to enter. The opening was covered with a blanket or woven mat, and a windscreen in front of the entrance helped cut down on the inevitable draft. In the center of each house was a hearth, which was used primarily for heat, as most cooking was done outside. Fire was a constant hazard as the updraft lifted sparks toward the smoke hole at the apex of the roof. To prevent fires from starting this way, the inside of the roof around the smoke hole was daubed. Raised beds were built along the walls. These sleeping platforms were built of cane, covered with split-cane mats and animal-skin blankets, and often separated by partitions that could afford a modicum of privacy. Storage space was available under the beds and in the rafters, and some Mississippian groups also dug storage pits in the floors of their houses.

RAMADA. Ramadas were freestanding porches, square or rectangular structures more lightly built than winter houses. The roof, the most substantial part of a ramada, was designed to keep out the summer rains and, more importantly, the summer sun. Ramadas had no walls, though they sometimes had a raised floor to protect against flooding and to facilitate air circulation under the house as well as through it. A large ramada could be used by the occupants of multiple winter houses.

CORNCRIB. Corncribs were small storage sheds built on legs several feet high. They had steep roofs and small doors that were sealed with mud when not in use. The walls and roof were plastered to keep out bugs and moisture. Burrowing rodents were unable to dig their way into these structures, and climbing mammals such as squirrels and raccoons were discouraged by village dogs and children with blowguns. All manner of foodstuffs were stored in them, mainly corn and beans. The space below the corncrib was used as an outdoor kitchen. The overlying structure protected cook fires from the elements, and the smoke from the fires helped keep bugs away from the corncrib.

An example of Mississippian construction techniques. Note the wattle-and-daub earth-embanked walls and interior partitions and benches. (Thomas Whyte, Frank H. McClung Museum)

above the level of seasonal floods, which were a regular part of Mississippian life. Nonetheless, settlements sometimes had to be abandoned temporarily because of high water. The location of Mississippian settlements was not determined completely by environmental factors; the history of certain locations seems to have made them particularly appealing as well.

One of the best-studied regions of the Mississippian world is northwest Georgia. Of the forty-eight mounds discovered on twenty-seven sites in the area, thirty-one have been professionally excavated. In twenty-nine instances, the construction and use of the mound lasted between seventy-five and one hundred years, with new construction episodes occurring every fifteen to twenty-five years on average. Seventeen of the sites with mounds were originally founded between 1000 and 1150, while only ten more were founded during the long stretch between 1150 and 1600. About half of these twenty-seven sites had more than one period of occupation separated by periods of abandonment. In other words, a particular site was often the home of a chiefdom that would last about a hundred years, after which the site was abandoned for a few decades before being occupied by another chiefdom.

It thus seems Mississippians were attracted to previously occupied sites. This pattern was probably related partly to choosing an ideal environmental location, but the Mississippian world was never full — there were other choices available. So this practice of reoccupation might have been related to the oral history of the site itself.

Capital Towns and Mound Centers

No matter its physical location, a chief's capital town was the metaphorical center of the chiefdom, and the center of every capital town was its mound and plaza complex. Capitals included at least one mound and an adjacent plaza but often included several mounds, some or all of which helped define the public space of the rectangular plaza. The Mississippians built the majority of their mounds in the form of a truncated pyramid, that is, they were shaped like pyramids with their tops cut off, leaving a platform on the summit. Mound summits held the houses of the chief and often those of other elites, as well as temples and special buildings where the dead were prepared for burial. Many of the mounds also contained burials, but some Mississippian burial mounds were conical instead of flat topped.

Mounds varied greatly in size, from only a few feet to one hundred feet tall. Individual mounds were not built all at once; instead, they were added to a little at a time, sometimes over a span of many decades. The buildings on the summits were burned down or dismantled as a prerequisite for erecting

a new structure on the same spot. Before the Mississippians put up the new buildings, however, they covered the mound over with an additional mantle of earth, thereby increasing not only its height but its overall size as well. The number of times a mound was added to, and when those additions occurred, varied both within and between chiefdoms, but available evidence suggests that additional mantles were added at least every fifteen to twenty-five years. Some have argued that the interval was related to the practical maintenance of buildings, while others envision it as the span of a particular chief's reign. It was likely a combination of those and other factors, many of which we could not possibly know.

Generally adjacent to the mound was the plaza, which, though less dramatic than the earthworks that surrounded it, was truly the heart of Mississippian towns. The plaza was essentially a public square, and even non-mound towns had one. Plazas were flat, rectangular, open places generally

An overhead view of Cahokia, the largest Mississippian settlement, located near present-day East St. Louis, Illinois. (Dennis Simon, National Geographic Stock)

capacious enough to accommodate a large number of people. The size of plazas varied with the size of towns, but many of them had room for several hundred people, and the largest ones could easily hold a few thousand. Plazas were regularly swept clean, and because of the constant attention, they were often outlined by a small berm of earth about the size of a speed bump, though sometimes larger. In some cases the sweepings from the plaza were added to mound fill or placed around the base of the pole that each plaza generally contained. The large-circumference posts were often quite tall and would not have been easy to erect, requiring some engineering skill and a relatively large crew. The posts were potent symbols, but of exactly what we cannot be certain.

Although the exact layout of each mound site was unique in its details, they were all variations of the same plan. The chief's house usually stood on the summit of the largest mound on the edge of the plaza. At times the summit of the mound might be edged with a stockade wall for purposes of defense. A very tall, steep mound would have been accessible only by stairs. Alternatively, walls erected on mound summits were sometimes of lighter construction and were used as privacy fences, perhaps especially in the case of low mounds. A large ramada (a roofed, open-sided structure) under whose shade a chief could receive visitors was often built directly in front of the chief's house on the summit. Taller mounds offered nice breezes as well. Around the chief's mound but not directly intruding on the plaza were corncribs where the chief stored the food gathered as gifts from his people.

If the chief's mound was large enough, it might also include a temple or a mortuary house for the preparation of the dead. If not on the same mound as the chief's house, the temple was often built on a separate platform mound adjacent to the plaza. In some cases the chief's mound and the temple mound faced each other across the length of the plaza.

Within each temple could be found the sacred fire, which symbolized the fire of the sun and was kept burning continually. The sacred fire was tended by priests and guarded so that no one would profane either the fire or the temple. The smoke of the sacred fire carried the prayers and benedictions of the chief and the priests to the heavens. It was believed that a terrible calamity would befall society if the sacred fire were allowed to go out and the celestial connection severed. Another common feature of Mississippian temples was a pair of statues, human figures, one male and one female, which represented the first chief and the mother of the chiefly heir. The bones of past chiefs and other elites were also kept in the temple, each skeleton bundled up and stored in a cane basket, wooden box, or pottery vessel. (See the box feature Burial Methods, pages 36–37.) Often the treasures of the chiefdom were stored in the temple as well — exotic goods acquired through trade or

Paired male and female statues recovered from Mound C at Etowah. The figures may represent, in accordance with the principles of matrilineal kinship, the original chief of Etowah and his sister. (Photo courtesy of David H. Dye)

warfare. The roofs of temples were often adorned with wood sculptures of animals, generally birds. Finally, outside the temple near the door or along the path to the door were often displayed the severed heads of enemy warriors mounted on spears.

In the larger capitals the plazas were literally surrounded by mounds of various sizes that served as platforms for the houses of other elite persons. Sometimes a capital had more than one mound-plaza complex, but such instances were rare and restricted to some of the largest and most important Mississippian places, such as Cahokia, Etowah, and Winterville. Even when the elite did not build their houses on mounds, they still located their dwellings near the plaza in what amounted to an elite neighborhood. The houses of commoners were located beyond those of the elite, farther from the plaza district and extending to the wall if the town was fortified. This was similar to the medieval pattern of nobles living in the castle district in relative opulence while the rest of the town lived in their shadow with much less, and the poorest located closest to the outer walls of the settlement.

Buffer Zones

Chiefdoms were separated from one another by uninhabited wilderness areas known to archaeologists as "buffer zones." Buffer zones were more than political boundaries. Members of a chiefdom could hunt, fish, and gather wild foods in the forests, swamps, and rivers of buffer zones, and firewood and other nonfood resources abounded there as well. But buffer zones were

BURIAL METHODS

Mississippian peoples underwent both primary and secondary burials—primary burials refer to the interment of the body shortly after death, and secondary burials refer to those in which the body was "processed" in some way before the final burial. Evidence of cremation is rare, though scholars currently have a poor understanding of its place within Mississippian society. The most common type of processing was the defleshing of bones, which required bodies to decompose until such time as their flesh could be easily and completely removed. Once the flesh was removed, the bones were bundled together and kept in baskets or buried. Bodies not defleshed or burned were buried in either an extended or a fetal position, and often all the burials of a particular society would face in the same direction. Sometimes people were buried individually, and sometimes multiple interments took place. In all cases, the handling of the dead was considered a polluting act, so people who performed the act had to be ritually cleansed afterward. Among commoners, the kin took care of this chore, but there may have been special people who handled the bodies of the elite.

In most Mississippian societies, in fact, there was a marked contrast between the treatment of elites and the treatment of commoners upon the occasion of their deaths. Commoners were often buried in the floors of their houses, presumably under the bed in which they slept, after which the house was generally burned down and then rebuilt. Some societies used cemeteries instead of floor burials; some used a combination of the two. Although some people were buried with nothing more than their clothes, others were interred with one or more mundane or utilitarian items. Women were buried with pots and men with tools, though generally only the stone ones have been preserved. At times, common burials included nonutilitarian items—most often freshwater-shell beads—that were interred with both sexes in the form of necklaces and bracelets. Occasionally, a person would be buried with a dog, presumably a hunting dog. It is also likely that perishable items were included in most burials, such as food for the journey to the afterlife.

Mississippian elites were often buried in mounds or special cemetery plots, with both primary and secondary interments. The most elaborate graves were stone- or log-lined tombs within the mounds themselves; presumably, these contained 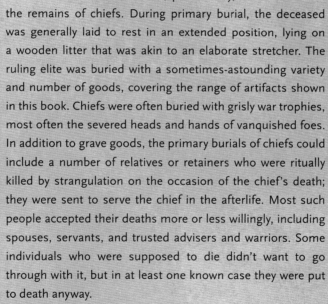 the remains of chiefs. During primary burial, the deceased was generally laid to rest in an extended position, lying on a wooden litter that was akin to an elaborate stretcher. The ruling elite was buried with a sometimes-astounding variety and number of goods, covering the range of artifacts shown in this book. Chiefs were often buried with grisly war trophies, most often the severed heads and hands of vanquished foes. In addition to grave goods, the primary burials of chiefs could include a number of relatives or retainers who were ritually killed by strangulation on the occasion of the chief's death; they were sent to serve the chief in the afterlife. Most such people accepted their deaths more or less willingly, including spouses, servants, and trusted advisers and warriors. Some individuals who were supposed to die didn't want to go through with it, but in at least one known case they were put to death anyway.

The burial of a group of important persons in a chamber below the base level of a relatively small mound. Later burials were often added to the mound itself. (Artwork created and provided by the Interpretive Services Branch, Texas Parks and Wildlife Department; permission to use provided by the Texas Historical Commission)

contested areas that lacked clear boundaries; chiefdoms "shared" them, though each one claimed more than its neighbors were willing to concede. Consequently, buffer zones could be dangerous places where it was possible to run into enemies.

Men tended to travel farther afield while hunting than women did while gathering, so the most frequent encounters were between enemy warriors out on hunting expeditions. During an active war between chiefdoms sharing a buffer zone, war parties would lurk in the wilderness in the hopes of ambushing people out doing chores. The size of the buffer zone affected the level of danger. Some were so small it took less than a day to cross them, and others were so large it took more than a week. No matter their size, buffer zones were actively defended because their maintenance was important for the continued well-being of the chiefdom.

Settlement Pattern and Size

As mentioned earlier, Mississippian chiefdoms conformed to one of two general settlement patterns, nucleated or dispersed. Densely settled towns were fortified, which suggests that violence was the main reason for people living in such close quarters. When that threat could be reduced, people generally chose to live in homesteads with some space between one another. Settlement patterns alternated between nucleated and dispersed, depending on political conditions. During periods of intense warfare, the members of a chiefdom were forced to live behind walls for safety and in order to launch their own raids without fearing for the safety of their families at home. Periods of peace, on the other hand, were characterized by people living in small hamlets and individual homesteads that lacked defensive walls and were scattered throughout the territory of the chiefdom, therefore putting less strain on local resources. Capitals, however, were often fortified even when the majority of the population lived in homesteads. People thus had a place to retreat to if threatened as well as a place to safely store their extra corn when away from their homesteads on the long fall hunts.

Some Mississippian chiefdoms were quite small, controlling perhaps ten to twelve miles square, plus additional space in the surrounding buffer zone. Such chiefdoms often included no more than two or three secondary mound centers in addition to the capital, and might contain as few as five hundred people, which would have given the chief an effective fighting force of up to one hundred warriors. An area of ten or twelve miles square could also be densely populated with a few thousand people, including several hundred warriors. Some Mississippian chiefdoms were even larger, with impressive multimound capitals and half a dozen or more secondary mound centers, as well as many nonmound towns or homesteads spread throughout a region of more than twenty miles square. Such a chief would have counted at least a thousand warriors among his several thousand constituents. This seems to have been about the spatial limit of a chief's ability to command real coercive power over people, though chiefdoms could and did get much larger than that. Under such circumstances, however, a chief's hold on the farthest reaches of his territory — out beyond twenty-five or thirty miles — was much more tenuous than that which he enjoyed closer to home.

Political Organization

The size of Mississippian chiefdoms was limited by certain aspects of their political systems, particularly the lack of specialization in administrative duties. Chiefs ruled their chiefdoms directly. There was little delegation of authority, so a chief's presence was regularly required throughout the chiefdom — and a chief had to be timely in dealing with matters as they arose. Thus it seems from archaeological and historical evidence that a chief could exert real control only over an area roughly equivalent to a circle whose radius was the distance he could travel in a day. That distance depended on environmental particulars. For instance, travel by water allowed for greater distances to be traveled than was possible on land. But many other factors were important. How was the capital located in relation to the chief's subject towns? Was the chiefdom spread over more than one river system? Was its settlement pattern nucleated or dispersed?

For a chiefdom only ten or twelve miles square, a chief could easily travel to all the towns or homesteads within his domain in less than a day's travel. But what about chiefdoms twenty or twenty-five miles square, with a half-dozen secondary mound centers? In such a case it would be difficult for a chief to travel to the remoter regions of his domain in a single day. Instead, a chief had to be able to travel easily to all his minor mound centers, where he could speak with the subchiefs, who, in turn, could travel to the towns and homesteads in their districts and relay the wishes of their lord. Subchiefs, because they were possible usurpers of the chief, had to be kept under regular scrutiny, and a half-dozen subchiefs were all that a single chief could effectively manage. It is easy to see why very large chiefdoms were unstable.

Leadership

Since chiefdoms lacked bureaucracies, chiefs had a wide range of duties. They collected surplus food, which they stored, used, and redistributed as they saw fit, taking on roles like those of a modern banker or insurance agent for the chiefdom's people. The chief served as mediator — one with the final word — for problems that threatened the equilibrium of the chiefdom, though minor disputes were probably solved through other channels. The chief oversaw the design and construction of mounds, stockade walls and bastions, weirs, and other large-scale projects, and he could periodically draft the chiefdom's people to work on such projects.

In addition to his civic duties, the chief conducted relations with other chiefdoms. Chiefs were in charge of all military actions and could demand war service from able-bodied men of the society. Chiefs were responsible also for long-distance trade and other peaceful interactions with neighboring chiefdoms. Finally, chiefs also functioned as religious leaders, though each had a number of ritual specialists, or "priests," who acted as advisers.

Despite chiefs' wide range of responsibilities, their coercive power was limited. That is to say, chiefs ruled with the consent of the people, backed by the weight of tradition.

Every secondary mound center was presided over by a subchief chosen by the chief, often from the chief's lineage or that of one of his wives. Within their jurisdictions, subchiefs had many of the same powers and responsibilities as the chief. They collected the gifts for the chief, settled disputes, and organized building projects, just as the chief did at the capital. On the other hand, the food they collected wasn't theirs alone to dispose of as they wished — a significant percentage of it was sent on to the granaries of the chief at the capital. Nor did subchiefs have the authority to send warriors against an enemy chiefdom without the permission of their lord. If something happened to a chief, however, a subchief had a legitimate claim to the office.

Evidence suggests that every chiefdom had one or more translators. Chiefs often had to deal with foreign languages in their trading endeavors, and some chiefdoms incorporated peoples of more than one language. Translators were used for more than just diplomatic occasions. For example, they were probably chosen for their oratorical skills as much as for being multilingual. Translators may have regularly delivered speeches on behalf of the chief and may have kept track of and periodically recited the chiefdom's oral history. It is also possible that they were commonly used as diplomatic messengers, with a recognized right to safe passage between chiefdoms.

Every chief and subchief also had a personal cadre of warriors whom they helped support. These men were chosen from among the best warriors in the chiefdom, and many were probably taken from among the commoners. After all, a ruler would want to be protected by people who had absolutely no chance to gain the chieftainship if anything happened to him. The prospects of the cadre thus rose and fell with the fortunes of its chief, since there was no guarantee its members would retain their social position when a new chief took office. These military specialists led a chief's army in battle, and in some cases carried the chief around on a litter. The head warrior likely acted as the chief's general and probably had real coercive power over his warriors during times of war.

In addition to the subchiefs who resided at secondary mound centers, chiefs invested some authority in village headmen, one of whom was appointed for each nonmound town or district of homesteads. Unlike subchiefs, headmen were commoners, though they were probably chosen from among the most influential and respected commoner families in a particular town. Village headmen were responsible for many of the same things as subchiefs, but their authority was restricted to a single village, and they did not receive the same benefits that accrued to subchiefs. A headman maintained the plaza and council house of his village, but his primary duty was to make sure the village gave sufficient gifts of food, labor, and military service to the chief.

The chief chose his own subchiefs, translators, and headmen. But the office of chief itself was inherited, which was one of the most distinctive characteristics of Mississippian societies. Around 900 in the Mississippi Valley, societies began to embrace a political system featuring a permanent office of chieftainship that was filled from an emerging elite stratum of society. Social position and political position became intimately connected. The leaders of pre-Mississippian societies, by contrast, ruled by the consensus of their followers, not by the authority that came from occupying a position previously held by a relative. Pre-Mississippian leaders came to their positions because of personal ability — a blend of charisma, generosity, wisdom, warrior might, and oratorical skill — but also because of their past successes. They could lead only as long as others were willing to follow them, and there was no guarantee that their offspring would have the characteristics or abilities of a leader, much less be followed as one.

Social Organization

Although hereditary chieftainship is in many ways analogous to the monarchies of our own past, we have little frame of reference for understanding the social world of the Mississippians. Most Mississippian societies, as well as the historical southern Indians who followed, were organized according to matrilineal kinship principles, not the bilateral kinship principles of American society today. In matrilineal kinship systems, a person's blood relatives were restricted to the males and females on the mother's side. Thus, not only was no one on a person's father's side of the family considered blood relatives, none of the children of males on a person's mother's side were considered blood relatives either. So, for example, an uncle on a person's mother's side was a relative, but his children (the person's cousins, in modern terms), were not. Although it may at first seem confusing, the matrilineal kinship system of Mississippian societies was based on just a few principles.

One of the most important relationships in the Mississippian world was that between a boy and his maternal uncle, who served all the functions Americans normally associate with fathers. A maternal uncle was responsible for educating and disciplining his sister's children, particularly the boys. That is not to say that a man's own children were not important to him — they were — but he was primarily responsible for the upbringing of his sister's children. Men tended to treat their own children as a favorite uncle might — they spoiled them and enjoyed them, perhaps in part because they weren't ultimately responsible for them. Another important relationship in the Mississippian world was that between brother and sister, who were closer in many ways than husband and wife and raised children together with no chance of divorce. Despite such closeness, they lived in separate residences, often in different parts of the village or in different villages altogether.

Mississippian societies were not only matrilineal but also matrilocal, that is, men moved in with their wives when they got married. Extended families were composed of mothers and their children, maternal aunts and their children, and maternal grandmothers. The only males considered related by blood who lived in an extended family home were a woman's unmarried sons. All the adult males living within the matrilineage were simply husbands, whose only ties to one another were through the women they married. The females of each matrilineage owned the houses they lived in (despite the fact that their husbands built them), the gardens and fields they worked and the produce from them, and the children they bore — children always stayed with their mother's people.

Although women controlled most of the property and all the progeny of a chiefdom, most of the effective political power resided with the men. But women could and did have quite an influence over the men of their lineages, and female chiefs were not unheard of, though rare. Whereas women were able to put all their concerns and resources into their own lineages, men were obligated to both their own lineage and that of their wife. Their principal allegiance, however, was to the lineage of their mother. Marriage, in fact, was a fairly brittle relationship and could be easily dissolved. This does not mean it was taken lightly. Marriage was more than just a relationship between individuals — it was a relationship between lineages, and bad blood between lineages could turn deadly.

Lineages were grouped together into a number of clans. A person was born into his or her mother's clan, and clan affiliation never changed, nor could a person belong to more than one clan. People who belonged to a particular clan believed themselves to be related to all the other people and lineages that belonged to it, but they could not always trace the relationship. Each clan was associated with a particular animal, or sometimes a plant or natural phenomenon like wind, and each clan had members in several towns in the chiefdom. A person could depend on the hospitality of clan members, even strangers, when traveling through the realm. Unlike lineages, however, clans were not economic units. They didn't work as groups or keep their fields and houses in the same area the way lineages did, and they didn't function as political groups.

Lineages and clans were exogamous, meaning a person could not marry someone from within his or her own clan. Besides regulating marriages, the practice fostered peaceful interactions between clans, which in most things cared strictly for their own. Clans divided society into manageably sized units that felt loyalty and obligation toward their own members but maintained connections with other clans also. Clans policed themselves, but crimes between clans were dealt with according to a system of retribution.

The custom of blood revenge was perhaps the most important feature associated with clans, and the one most fraught with danger. Blood revenge refers to the right of a clan to avenge the death of one of its own at the hands of a member of another clan. This was not the sort of generational feuding popularly associated with the Hatfields and McCoys, but a system designed to maintain social balance, albeit precariously. When a person in clan A was killed by someone from clan B, it was clan A's right and obligation to kill someone from clan B. Clan A preferred it to be the killer or someone from his or her lineage, but anyone from clan B would do. Because of this policy, killers usually did not try to escape their punishment, though sometimes an older clansperson was put to death for the crime of a younger relative, who could then remain alive.

After the second death, the matter was considered resolved and had to be dropped. When, during the historical period, it was recognized that a death was accidental or unintentional, the two clans involved would sometimes come up with some other way to pay for the death, but such a resolution was not regulated and was left up to the discretion of the dead person's relatives, not the perpetrator of the accident. As for bloodshed within a clan, it was almost unheard of because the penalty for killing one of your own was banishment from the clan. Banishment was a fate worse than death: a person with no clan was laid open to insults and assaults from anyone without fear of retribution.

The Social Organization of Elites

The shift to inheritable power at the beginning of the Mississippian Period led to the permanent ranking of clans, lineages within clans, and individuals within lineages. Ranking was done in accordance with the principle of primogeniture, or "first born is best." In this respect it was much like Old World inheritance. In the Mississippian world, inheritance went to the eldest son of a man's eldest sister, in keeping with matrilineal principles. Everything was ranked according to its nearness to the chief. The intricacies of this ranking system and many of its particular manifestations cannot be known, but enough evidence exists to trace the broad outlines with some certainty.

The ranking of clans was based on when, according to oral tradition, each clan was created. The oldest clan was the highest ranked, and the youngest clan the lowest. Each lineage within a particular clan was ranked similarly, though that hierarchy must have been more contentious and more likely to change with the fortunes or misfortunes of a lineage. Each person within a particular lineage was given a rank based on genealogical closeness to the head of the lineage. That rank could be fluid, altering when lineage heads changed, as they did regularly. There was plenty of room to maneuver within the social realm, and so jockeying for position was common.

Much about the social world of the Mississippian elite is unknown or poorly understood, but it appears that the clan of the chief was held above all others and that all the lineages within it were elite. Within the elite lineages, genealogies were extremely important and were calculated for a number of generations. In fact, it is likely that each elite lineage appointed one or more "genealogical specialists" to keep track of the information and periodically recite it.

Like other members of the society, chiefs were generally replaced by the eldest son of their eldest sister. Metaphorically, the chief and his eldest sister were the "king and queen" because she produced the chiefly heir (though he did not father it). The requirement of exogamy meant, ironically, that the chiefly heir and all other elite children were fathered by commoners. In this way, marriage offered commoners some chance for social mobility. Exogamy meant also that elite men fathered commoner children, since their wives had to be commoners and the children belonged to the mother's clan. The spouses and children of chiefs and other elites did receive the kind of social and economic benefits normally accorded to the elite, despite their being commoners.

The real struggle for position took place within the elite lineages themselves, especially that of the chief. Emphasis was placed on the office of chief, not the person occupying the position. Elite society was thus rife with in-

trigue and contention over who filled the office of chief or who would fill it next. There were a few people who had particularly good claims to the office, particularly the eldest son of the chief's eldest sister, and the chief's nearest brother in age. Other brothers of the chief had legitimate claims, as did all of a chief's nephews. Evidence suggests that women could sometimes become chiefs, or perhaps regents until their sons came of age to rule. Spanish explorers encountered female leaders ruling chiefdoms in South Carolina and North Carolina during the sixteenth century.

A woman of importance being transported on a litter. There is some evidence of female chiefs or regents in the Ancient South. (Beinecke Rare Book and Manuscript Library, Yale University)

At any given time, therefore, numerous persons could potentially and legitimately hold the office of chief. So, like royalty everywhere, the Mississippian elite used marriage, diplomacy, and war to improve the position of their claimants. Some courted the favor of the reigning chief, while others hatched plans to usurp the office. There is evidence that heirs to the chieftainship were sometimes poisoned, and it is easy to imagine similar intrigues occurring as well.

It is still unknown how the chief was able to place himself and his clan above the other clans. It is apparent that some of the organizational capabilities of chiefdoms would have been possible only if the chief stood above clan law. For example, as mentioned already, a chief could demand periodic communal labor and military service from the people of their chiefdom. A chief could require people to take turns working in the fields of the chiefly lineage. The construction and repair of the chief's home, the temple and public structures, defensive structures such as bastioned stockades or moats, and the earthen mounds were undertaken by crews of commoners under the management of the elite. In addition, plazas often required significant earth-moving in order to create their large, level surfaces. That sort of communal labor was episodic and may have often been tied to certain ceremonies. The earthen mounds of the Mississippian world were built one basket-load of dirt at a time, each one weighing approximately forty to fifty pounds. Dirt was usually taken from a nearby riverbank or from borrow pits near the mounds themselves. Borrow pits were excavated for the secondary purpose of creating artificial ponds that were stocked with fish. To carry out such daunting tasks, workers used wooden digging sticks and hoes made of stone, shell, or deer scapulas.

Warfare

The material evidence for conflict in the Ancient South comes in several forms, the most common being defensive fortifications, which made it possible for a small number of warriors to protect a large number of noncombatants while the majority of warriors were away raiding enemy villages. Mississippian stockades were built of closely spaced logs set vertically into the ground and interwoven with smaller lathes. The entire wall was plastered over with daub, both inside and out, which served to slow its deterioration, hinder climbing, and make it more difficult to set on fire. The logs were from secondary-growth trees a few inches in diameter and between twelve and seventeen feet high. Three to five feet of each log was buried in the ground, leaving nine to twelve feet exposed. The top of each log was generally sharpened to a point.

Many of the stockades included bastions or watchtowers that both buttressed the large walls and provided elevated platforms from which archers could defend the town. A series of loopholes were cut into the walls to allow archers to fire out. Stockade "gates" were merely small openings at the corners of the walls; more frequently, walls were overlapped to create a narrow, easily defendable walkway that allowed entry to the town. Most stockades had more than one entrance.

Walls were sometimes fronted by moats, which artificially increased the height of the walls. Moats were generally several feet deep and two to three times as wide. Moats were dry in most of the Ancient South, but in the Mis-

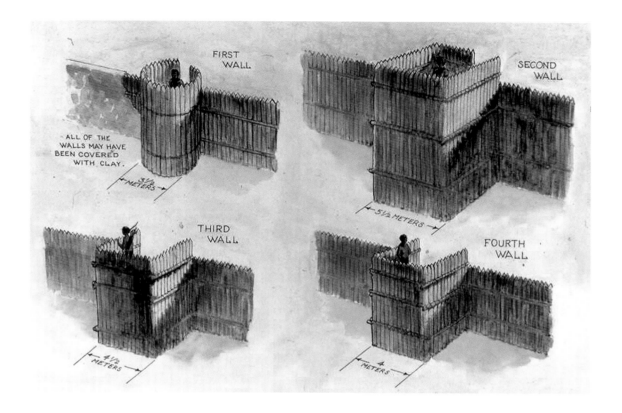

FIRST WALL

SECOND WALL

THIRD WALL

FOURTH WALL

ALL OF THE WALLS MAY HAVE BEEN COVERED WITH CLAY.

5½ METERS

5½ METERS

4½ METERS

4 METERS

sissippi Valley they were often filled with water from connecting bayous or rivers, allowing people to launch their dugout canoes directly into the moats.

The skeletal remains of Mississippian peoples often show the effects of violence. For instance, skeletons have been discovered with stone arrowheads still embedded in the bone. The most common form of skeletal evidence associated with violence, however, is damage from war clubs — generally fractures to the skull, collarbones, and forearms. The breaking of collarbones was likely a deliberate fighting tactic, since a broken collarbone would make it almost impossible to lift a club above one's head and bring it down with any force; to break an enemy's collarbone was to put oneself at great advantage. The bones in the lower arm were often broken as the result of holding up the arm to shield the face from a blow, resulting in what archaeologists refer to as a parry fracture. Cut marks on the skull indicate scalping, though scalping could occur without leaving these marks.

Mississippian peoples were so preoccupied with conflict that their art abounds with imagery of war and violence. Depictions of warriors and weapons play a prominent role, as do images of severed heads and hands and broken long bones. Images of the animals that Mississippian peoples associated with martial prowess, particularly hawks and falcons, were common

Changing bastion styles over time at Cahokia. Bastions, which served as watchtowers for a town's defenders, were a regular feature of Mississippian stockades. (Cahokia Mounds State Historic Site)

LEFT:
A shell gorget depicting a warrior carrying a severed head and mace-like war club. Note the forked-eye design that mimics the markings of a peregrine falcon, a creature highly revered for its martial abilities. (Courtesy, National Museum of the American Indian, Smithsonian Institution [150853.000]; photo by Walter Larrimore)

RIGHT:
A shell gorget depicting two anthropomorphic figures locked in combat. Note the antlers, wings, tail, and talons as well as the columella pendants, earspools, and flint "daggers" displayed by the warriors. (John Bigelow Taylor, Frank H. McClung Museum)

on pottery and shell. In addition, Mississippians crafted artistic representations of a variety of clubs and daggers that were never intended for use, but instead served as powerful visual symbols of warrior might. Many such ritual weapons have been unearthed from throughout the Ancient South, and they are also featured prominently in most depictions of the Falcon Warrior, an idealized combination of the martial capacities of both humans and raptors.

The principal weapon of war was the club. Unlike projectile weapons such as spears and arrows, the club was not used for hunting any animal except humans. Clubs were generally from one to three feet in length and carved from a dense wood such as hickory. Clubs were often individually decorated and quite elaborate. For instance, clubs have been found in Florida that had shark's teeth embedded along their leading edge — a blow from such a weapon would have left teeth in the victim much like a real shark bite. Like a knight's sword, a club served as the ultimate symbol of a warrior.

Mississippian archers used D-shaped selfbows (bows made from a single piece of wood) that were generally made of black locust, though occasionally of hickory, ash, or another suitable wood. By far the most coveted bow wood, however, was Osage orange, which grew in a fairly restricted area near the western edge of the Mississippian world. Although little evidence remains, since wood does not readily preserve in the southern climate, it is clear that staves of Osage orange were traded east. Bows were typically between fifty and sixty inches long with a pull of up to fifty pounds. Mississippian archers were accurate up to about two hundred paces and were capable of firing arrows very rapidly. Stone or cane knives were also carried, principally for collecting trophies of war such as scalps, heads, hands, and, occasionally, other body parts.

Mississippian warriors held in high regard animals that attacked with cleverness and stealth and struck with swift and powerful blows: cougars, falcons, and serpents. Like those creatures, Mississippian warriors relied on speed and agility, fighting nearly naked and with little concern for defensive equipment — though tightly woven cane shields were noted on occasion by the Spaniards.

Chiefs inculcated martial values in young men, whose cooperation they ensured by making war exploits the principal means by which common men could raise their social and political status. Although they were only part-time warriors, just as they were part-time hunters, fishermen, and craftsmen, Mississippian men were eager for war. Many of the skills of hunting, such as tracking, stalking, ambushing, and using a bow and arrow, translated directly to warfare. In addition, men trained to fight with clubs, preparation that included dancing, a practice something like the ritualized movements of martial arts.

Most military encounters were small-scale, generally involving only a few warriors and occurring in the buffer zones. It was common for small groups of warriors to steal quietly into their enemies' territories with the intent of taking people unawares and killing or capturing them. Small, guerilla-style raids could occur at any time, but tended to be more frequent during the warm season after the fields had been prepared and planted and men had more free time. Raids were also carried out to destroy an enemy's fields or set fire to the woods around his village. As the corn grew, it provided cover for a stealthily approaching enemy, and as it dried out on the stalk, it became highly flammable. Although it may have been nearly impossible to completely destroy a town's crop by intentionally burning it, the loss of any significant percentage would have been quite a blow.

Mississippian chiefs could launch large attacks against their enemies, too. Adult men made up about one-fifth of the population, so Mississippian armies could number from several score warriors to a thousand or more. There is evidence that large Mississippian armies sometimes faced each other on open fields of battle.

Although Mississippians built no war engines, they did practice other basic siege techniques. For example, one group used fire arrows against the Spaniards, setting their thatched-roof houses ablaze from afar and driving the Europeans out into the open. They may have used ladders in conjunction with woven cane shields to try to breach an enemy's walls. Throughout the Ancient South, archaeologists find evidence of stockades being burnt. Often the walls were not rebuilt afterwards, and at least in some cases this was due to enemy assault.

If an army did breach the walls of an enemy's capital or secondary mound

center, it appears there was standard protocol for celebrating the victory. Warriors ascended the mounds and stole all the valuables left in the houses or temples. Everything else was ransacked, especially the temple and the mortuary houses of the elite, where the bones of ancestral leaders were kept — these were strewn about the ground, broken, and otherwise profaned. The heads of some of the enemy dead were placed on pikes and prominently displayed outside the doors of the temple. Eventually, the whole town was set on fire, and any prisoners not already executed were taken back to the victorious army's point of origin, where they could be slowly tortured to death for the pleasure of the elders, women, and children.

The torture of war captives was a common aspect of the Mississippian world, and although any prisoner could expect to be tortured, adult men were certain to receive the cruelest and most inhumane treatment. The possible combinations of abuse were endless, but savage beatings and death by fire were usually the outcome. Prisoners were often tied to poles in the plaza and then tortured with firebrands by women and children. Sometimes the tormentors would help a captive recover from such ordeals only to begin them all over again. A common form of torture was known as "little fire," during which large splinters of heart pine were driven into every part of the victim. The splinters were so full of turpentine that they would ignite instantly and continue to burn past the point where they penetrated the flesh. The bodies of the victims who were spared death by fire were sometimes cut into pieces and hung in the trees for the birds to eat. The scalps of torture victims were generally hung from the post in the plaza as a sort of public, collective war honor.

Prisoners who were not executed were generally enslaved, though some were adopted. Children, especially boys, were often brought up as members of their captors' society, and young women were sometimes taken to serve as slaves for the wives of warriors or perhaps as wives themselves. Mississippians did not practice the sort of slavery that was associated with the antebellum South. Instead, they kept a few slaves to perform burdensome or dangerous work and to offer evidence of the warrior prowess of their owners.

Taken as a whole, the Mississippian military tradition that developed over several centuries was quite formidable, but the most impressive Native forces encountered by Spanish explorers were the navies of the Mississippi River Valley. The maze of waterways in the heartland of the Mississippian world hosted a specialized version of Mississippian warfare. Chiefdoms in the region could field navies composed of up to several hundred dugouts, some of which were enormous. A large dugout could hold up to seventy-five warriors sitting three abreast, armed with bows and arrows. The navies showed military discipline greater than that encountered elsewhere in the Ancient South.

It was the organizational capabilities of chiefdom societies and the leadership of chiefs that made such armies and navies possible. Although a chief may not always have led his army into battle, he had to have distinguished himself as a warrior at some earlier time. War leadership may have had more to do with the age of the chief than anything else — that is, elderly chiefs were not expected to lead armies into battle. In all cases, the chief was called on before battle for his war medicine, for only a chief could act as an intermediary with the gods and ensure a victory for the army.

Belief Systems

Very few primary documents record any information about Mississippian chiefdoms, and those that do are mostly silent about native beliefs. How then can anything be known about the Mississippian worldview? Belief systems, like languages, are one of the most conservative aspects of culture. For instance, despite some substantial differences in vocabulary and dialect, an

English speaker of today could, with difficulty, speak with and understand an educated English speaker from several hundred years ago. In the same way, some of the most basic aspects of Western religion have a long history — one God, heaven and hell, divine retribution, eternal life, and so forth. By comparison, other aspects of culture change relatively rapidly. For example, over the past four hundred years English speakers have been part of political systems as diverse as monarchies, commonwealths, and republics. Likewise, Mississippian peoples spoke the same languages as their descendants, such as the Creek and Cherokee, and shared with them some central views and beliefs about the world, yet the Creek, Cherokee, and related tribes organized themselves according to very different political systems.

While the Mississippian belief system cannot be fully reconstructed, its foundations can be understood. Mississippians, like all peoples, sorted and classified the world around them. For instance, they distinguished between male and female, between human and animal, and between birds and four-footed creatures. Mississippians did not have the benefit of written language, and so, like preliterate peoples everywhere, they limited the number of categories they created. They were protective of their categories: they wanted things to fit neatly within their classification system, and they kept things from different categories separate — they would not serve the meat of a four-footed animal on the same plate with turkey or fish, for example.

To emphasize this separateness, Mississippians conceived of most categories in terms of binary opposition — males were opposed to females, the warm season was opposed to the cold season, and so forth. They felt that the mixing of categories would result in a sort of pollution that if left unrectified would result in illness or calamity. Thus, a person who ate venison and fish off the same plate could expect to become ill or suffer ill fortune. It was believed the sexes should remain separate at certain times, namely, when they were exhibiting their most gender-specific attributes. For example, when a woman was menstruating, she would retire to a special hut for the duration; she would not sleep with her husband or cook food for any man, lest she make him sick. Men would refrain from sleeping with their wives and generally sequester themselves from the company of women both before and after hunting or waging war.

Through these and similar actions, Mississippians tried to maintain an ordered existence, a difficult task to accomplish in the face of a chaotic world. Nature was full of things that defied the Mississippian classification system by seeming to belong to more than one category. Instead of ignoring or being dismayed by such anomalies, Mississippians held them up as special. For example, atypical animals were celebrated in art over and over again — the snake, which lacks arms, legs, and wings but can be found in the water, on the ground, and in the trees; creatures that could hunt at night, such as cougars and owls; and those that were equally at ease on land or in the water, such as turtles and frogs. Mississippians invented bizarre creatures too, including several varieties of dragons and supernatural bird beings, both commonly depicted in Mississippian art.

Mississippians conceived of the world as a large island divided into four quarters by the cardinal directions. The directions were in opposition: north opposed to south, and east to west. Each direction was associated with a particular color: black, red, white, and blue or purple. The concept of the earth island and the four directions was commonly symbolized in art by a circle divided by an equal-armed cross. In addition to the island world, two other realms were recognized by Mississippians: the Upper World and the Under World, each connected with the world of humans but accessible to only a few.

The Upper World existed on the other side of the sky, which was conceived of as something akin to an inverted bowl that the sun crept under every morning to follow its path across the sky before sneaking under the opposite edge at dusk in order to travel through the Upper World and return to the starting point. The Upper World was home to all the most powerful beings, such as the sun, moon, thunder, and lightning, as well as the archetypes of all the animals that dwelt below. The Upper World was associated with order, perfection, and all that was sacred. Although Upper World beings were capable of great power, they remained remote, rarely intervening in any understandable way with the world of humans. When they did intervene, the results could be dire, such as a natural catastrophe or disease.

The Under World existed below the island home of humans and was a world of chaos peopled exclusively by anomalous creatures. It was a place of inversion where the seasons were opposite and even mundane events did not occur as expected. Yet the Under World was associated with fertility and creativity as well. The Upper and Under Worlds do not correspond to Western religious ideas of heaven and hell. Instead, Mississippians saw the Upper World as a place of order and regularity and the Under World as a place of chaos and unpredictability, between which humans tried to strike a balance on their island world.

Mississippian chiefs, their close relatives, and presumably all elites were associated with the Upper World to some extent. The chief was considered a living link to the powers of the remote Upper World, and in some cases was seen as a divine figure directly related to the principal deity, whose physical manifestation was the sun. Without exception, the chief and the mother of the chiefly heir were seen as the direct descendants of those who first brought Mississippian ways to the people, commemorated by the paired statues kept in the temple. The current chief and his sister were only the occupants of

Reflections on Three Worlds. The painting depicts the Mississippian conception of the universe, showing the Upper World, Under World, and this world, representations of birds and animals of particular importance to Mississippian peoples, and the mythical creatures of the Ancient South. (Illustration by Andy Buttram, courtesy of the Illinois State Museum — Dickson Mounds, Lewistown, Ill.)

sacred positions that went back directly to the original leaders represented by the statues. Thus, Mississippian chiefs ruled because of the place they occupied in the sacred world order — that was what gave them their power and their ultimate sanction.

Chiefs legitimized their positions by developing rituals designed to promote the continuity of society and the order of the universe. For instance, the chief came out of his house just before dawn every morning to smoke and to greet his brother the sun while pointing out the path the sun was to take across the sky.

The chief's blessing was needed for a successful corn harvest. Sometimes seeds were brought to the chief so that he could utter words of prayer over them. In other cases, the chief would travel the length and breadth of his domain to bless the newly sown fields that stretched for miles along the bottomlands of the rivers and creeks.

Such journeys served also to reassert the supremacy of the chief — especially in large chiefdoms with many subchiefs. Chiefs traveled with large retinues that included their cadres of military specialists and scores of attendants dressed in elite finery. And the chief would have been particularly careful to display the symbols of his office. It is likely that slaves carried the entire retinue's belongings. Each town would send out messengers to greet

the party before it arrived. At the edge of town, the subchief or village head-man would greet the traveling chief with presents, including but not limited to gifts of food. The chief had corncribs in every town the procession visited, and fed his retinue from that supply, which was supplemented with the fresh food contributed by the townspeople. These actions were formal expressions of hospitality.

These were just a few of the rules that set the chief apart from other people and connected him more closely with the gods. The rules probably differed from chiefdom to chiefdom, though some practices were common. Chiefs enjoyed a special residence, the finest of clothes, multiple wives, an assort-ment of servants and slaves, the best food, and an elaborate funeral. (See the box feature Dress and Adornment, pages 58–59.)

Some chiefs expected elaborate rules of protocol to be followed in their presence, such as never walking between the chief and a fire, using special language to address the chief, not allowing one's head to be at the same level as that of the chief, and bowing before and after addressing him. At times, a chief's principal warriors carried him on a litter made of red cedar, to pre-vent his feet from touching the profane earth. At other times chiefs sat under shades and were fanned by their servants while musicians played flutes, rattles, and drums and a chorus sang. All forms of special treatment served the purpose of reminding people of the unique place the chief occupied in the sacred order.

To emphasize a chief's special status, mound centers were treated as metaphorical versions of the cosmos. With their four sloping sides, mounds

A Mississippian chief, surrounded by three attendants, greeting the arrival of the dawn. This is thought to have been a daily ceremony throughout the Ancient South. (Cahokia Mounds State Historic Site)

A feathered cloak, a copper headpiece, shell gorgets, columella pendants, decorated pottery, bow staves (presumably of Osage orange wood), and other objects of Mississippian finery. Reconstruction by Tom Hall. (H. Tom Hall, National Geographic Stock)

symbolically represented the entire universe, with the adjacent plaza representing the human realm between order and chaos. The constant cleaning and sweeping of the plaza was akin to the continual struggle of humans to maintain balance and purity. The pole in the plaza represented a "world tree," or *axis mundi*, which connected the three realms. Above the plaza sat the chief in the Upper World, with the sacred fire in the temple representing the sun providing warmth and life to the world of the plaza below. The sacred Upper World was safe from the ravages of the floodwaters of the Under World. In many cases, mounds and sometimes houses were oriented to the cardinal directions or to the solstices and equinoxes. Unfortunately, many of the subtleties of this re-created sacred landscape are lost to us.

Despite the religious sanction of chiefs' authority, it is clear that their sacredness existed along a scale, as did their economic and military power. Chiefs had to weld together as much power as they could from each of the three sources. The combination was different in each chiefdom, which produced unique societies despite the many shared understandings and practices across the Mississippian world. One chief might have gained much of his power by virtue of his potent blessings and benevolent wisdom in mediating between clans, while the power of another might have come from his military skill or his deft way of helping his people survive a terrible drought.

Instability

Evidence suggests that maintaining a successful chiefdom was not easy. Chiefs faced a number of problems endemic to the Mississippian world, and as a result many chiefdoms were short-lived, lasting between seventy-five and one hundred years on average. Chiefdoms that did last longer, such as those at Cahokia and Moundville, nonetheless underwent major social and political changes during their history.

Climatic factors played a role in the fall of some chiefdoms. For instance, as mentioned earlier, the Little Ice Age reduced the overall area of the Mississippian world, a process that inevitably eliminated a number of chiefdoms. Short-term elements of climate, such as annual precipitation and temperature variation, played a more immediate role in the instability of Mississippian chiefdoms. For example, corn could not be stored indefinitely. It could be stored for a year, perhaps a bit longer, if kept properly, but not for more than two years with any certainty. When supplies of stored corn were low or exhausted, a chiefdom was in peril. Even a seemingly well-stocked chiefdom, one with a year's worth of corn stored and a crop in the fields, was vulnerable to the devastation of a severe drought, especially if it lasted longer than a year. And it didn't necessarily take a severe drought to decimate a horticultural

DRESS AND ADORNMENT

The peoples of the Ancient South wore little clothing, even in winter, and this imperviousness to the vagaries of weather was a cultural trait first developed during youth. Mississippian infants were often strapped naked in a cradleboard (a backpack-like device) with a "diaper" of absorbent plant material such as moss, which would be changed as needed. Toddlers and young children often went about naked or nearly so except when weather demanded a cloak of some sort, although it would have been rare for such youngsters to be out in foul weather in the first place. By adolescence, both sexes began to adopt the dress of adults.

The basic article of clothing for men was the breechcloth or loincloth, a long narrow strip of material that was placed between the legs, with excess material hanging in front and behind, and suspended by a belt or a decorative sash. In good weather, men often wore little or nothing else. Generally, this breechcloth was made of buckskin leather, but woven material was sometimes used as well. When traveling in the woods, men wore moccasins and leggings for protection. Leggings were not tailored pants, but instead came in pairs that resembled long footless stockings. They were pulled up to midthigh, tied to the belt that held up the breechcloth, and gathered just below the knee with a garter. Leggings and moccasins were generally made of deer hide, and thus became stiff and heavy when wet. For this reason they were often removed for river crossings and during heavy rain. Shirts were not employed until Euro-Americans introduced them during the historical period, and mantles or cloaks were used instead to cover the upper body. These too were often made of deerskin, but bears, cougars, and other fur-bearing animals were used as well. Cloaks were sometimes decorated with designs dyed in red, yellow, or black. Men generally went bareheaded but sometimes wore turban-like headgear. Every man carried some sort of pouch attached to his belt or worn over the shoulder in which he carried essential belongings.

A woman's basic garment was a skirt that usually came to about the knees. Like a man's breechcloth and leggings, skirts were sometimes made of deerskin, but sometimes woven plant material, particularly the fibers of the inner bark of the mulberry. Women wore moccasins when traveling but did not use leggings. When in cold or rainy weather, women wrapped a light cloak or shawl around themselves and fastened it above one shoulder in order to keep their hands free. The cloaks were made of buckskin or woven mulberry fiber. Women used heavier mantles in colder weather, just like men, but always went bareheaded. They carried a small bag for essential items when traveling away from the village, and in most such cases, a burden basket for gathering.

Women tended to wear their hair long and straight, while men wore theirs in a wide variety of styles, though most of them incorporated a scalp lock in some manner. Men and women sometimes wore feathers in their hair; brightly colored ones as well as those collected from raptors such as eagles, falcons, hawks, owls, and buzzards were particularly sought after. Both sexes grew their fingernails long and plucked the hair from their bodies, excepting head hair, in most cases. All people, regardless of sex or age, rubbed oil and fat onto their skin and into their hair. Tattooing and body paint were also common to both sexes. Men paid more attention than women to hair and makeup—especially during times of war. In some parts of the Ancient South, people stained their teeth black, but the practice does not seem to have been widespread. Both men and women wore an array of jewelry, including necklaces, bracelets, arm and leg bands, pendants and gorgets, earrings, earspools, earplugs, and nose rings. These items were made of shell, bone, or copper.

Mississippian elites wore the same types of clothing and jewelry as commoners, but theirs was of the highest quality and often incorporated exotic materials. For instance, earspools worn by elites were often covered in copper, and their necklaces and bracelets were generally made of marine shell, while commoners had little access to copper and used local freshwater shells. Elite mantles were sometimes made of the skins of river-dwelling mammals such as otter and mink. In addition, they wore cloaks made by attaching feathers to a sort of netting. Turkey feathers were commonly used, but the feathers of the Carolina parakeet were prized as well.

Two elite Mississippian males being dressed and painted by a number of their attendants. Note the copper headpieces, beaded forelocks of hair, earspools, and columella pendants. (H. Tom Hall, National Geographic Stock)

surplus: a series of below-average harvests would have had the same effect over a few years that a severe drought had in one or two catastrophic seasons. In addition, Mississippian farmers had to worry about early and late frosts, flooding, and agricultural pests.

Chiefdoms were expansive, a feature that put nearly constant pressure on the environment. In most areas there was a population limit beyond which the available arable land could not be rotated frequently enough to prevent soil degradation. The incompatibility between a chief's desire for a larger chiefdom and the decreased fertility of soil used for corn cultivation often created a vicious cycle: the need for more food led to less frequent crop rotation or the cultivation of marginal land, both of which resulted in decreased yields, which then sped up the cycle until calamity struck.

Soil degradation, however, was probably less a concern in most cases than wood depletion. Wood was used for more than fuel; it was the most important building material and was needed for the manufacture of many tools. It was not possible to fell large trees and cut them into logs, so people used small limbs, many of which fell to the forest floor naturally, and larger ones that washed downstream during floods. Smaller trees could be brought down and processed with stone axes. New fields provided a source of easily gathered fuel as the standing skeletons of dead trees dropped their limbs. Corncobs, when properly dry, provided another source of fuel, but it wouldn't have taken very long for a large population to put quite a strain on wood availability in an area.

Environmental stresses could be greatly aggravated by Mississippian politics, particularly regarding the size of buffer zones and the effects of violence on the settlement patterns within a chiefdom. Dispersed farmsteads decreased the environmental stress of large populations on the land, reducing the possibility of soil degradation and wood depletion. Thus, it would have been relatively easy to maintain the stability of a chiefdom over the long term in a political environment allowing for a dispersed settlement pattern. Conversely, a political atmosphere that demanded a nucleated settlement pattern — that is, one marked by recurring violence — would likely have shortened the life span of a chiefdom from the combination of resource stress and external conflict.

Sometimes, however, the greatest threats to political stability came from within. Internal conflicts in a chiefdom involved both those between elite factions and those between elites and commoners. If a particular chief became too demanding, it may have been possible for commoners to seek membership in another chiefdom. In volatile regions, that sort of transfer would have been nearly impossible, though, because enemies were more likely to torture, kill, or enslave strangers than adopt them as full-fledged members. It seems more likely that disgruntled commoners encouraged and helped bring about a change of power rather than abandoning the chiefdom altogether.

If a legitimate claimant to the office of chief was particularly skilled and ambitious, intrigue was almost inevitable. Political infighting probably reached a fever pitch when a chief died while his heir was too young to assume office, or when a new chief was poorly qualified for the office. A chief who suffered a recent military defeat might find himself in the middle of an internal power struggle, as would a chief whose blessings appeared to be unsuccessful — droughts, floods, and other natural events might well be blamed on a leader who had fallen out of favor with the gods.

Of course even a chiefdom with no serious internal disputes, located in a favorable environmental area that had not experienced any recent climatic setbacks, could still be vulnerable to the depredations of other chiefdoms. Open conflict between chiefdoms could make it difficult to maintain a smoothly running society. There is evidence of military defeats that effectively ended the existence of particular chiefdoms. But conflict short of military defeat could disrupt the movement of elite goods, thereby making the maintenance of sacred chiefly authority more difficult. It should be pointed out, however, that in the Mississippian world, slow declines were more common than quick defeats, and that no single factor would likely have been enough to end the existence of a chiefdom.

CHAPTER THREE
THE EMERGENT AND EARLY
MISSISSIPPIAN PERIOD,
AD 800–1200

THE MISSISSIPPI VALLEY region around modern St. Louis was the heartland of the Mississippian way of life. During the tenth century, people there came to depend on corn supplemented by squash and other minor domesticates as the staple of their diet (beans were not widely used in the Ancient South until the thirteenth century). In addition to this new crop, people accepted the leadership of certain lineages that had come to be seen as closely connected with the gods. Under the direction of members of these elite lineages, the rest of the population began construction on the town of Cahokia, which soon grew into a city centered on large public plazas bordered by earthen platform mounds on which the ruling elite lived, literally and figuratively, above the world of normal humans.

The people accepted this new social and political arrangement for more than ideological reasons. The chiefly elite collected part of every harvest and kept it in public trust as insurance against the vagaries of corn agriculture. In addition, the elite lineages were able to draw enough people into their new system that they managed to create a wider area of peace than had been enjoyed before the rise of chiefdom organization. Peace was of great importance in part because the relatively recent development of the bow and arrow (circa 400–500) allowed people to be much more efficient and effective killers of humans. In the decades before 900, many people in the region had been forced to live behind stockade walls because of endemic violence. After the rise of the chiefly elite, stockades stopped being built until the middle of the twelfth century. In fact, it appears as though the rulers at Cahokia not only maintained peace in the region, but also began to spread their way of life beyond Cahokia's borders.

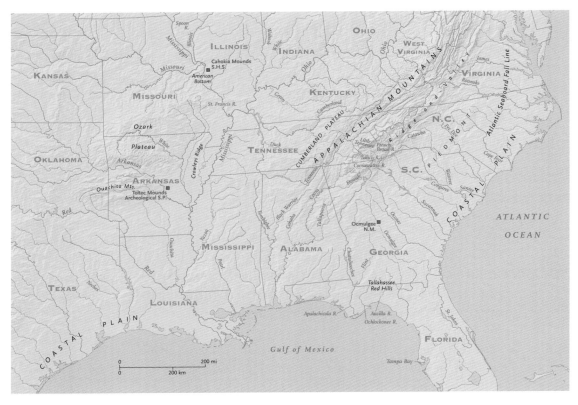

EMERGENT AND EARLY MISSISSIPPIAN SITES

In addition to the bow and arrow and corn agriculture, people affected by Cahokia's rise adopted new techniques in the manufacture of pottery, in particular the use of burned and crushed mussel shell as a tempering agent. They began using stone hoes in their fields, especially hoes made of Mill Creek chert. A new game, known to us as chunkey, which was intimately associated with the emerging elite (see the box feature Chunkey, page 65), quickly became important in the Mississippian world. Perhaps of more significance was the razing of the old village along Cahokia Creek and the erection of a new one based on a plan that envisioned Cahokia as a city. The people of Cahokia even changed the nature of the houses they built, adopting a new construction method that would eventually spread throughout the Ancient South.

One of the most important mechanisms for spreading the Mississippian way of life was trade. Cahokia's elite imported raw materials, some from quite far afield, and exported both manufactured items and new ideas. Salt and buffalo products probably entered the city from the west, copper was brought in from the Great Lakes region, and marine shell was traded north from the

Chunkey, which was played by two males at a time, was a game that required little in the way of equipment—a long pole like a spear without a sharp point for each player and a single chunkey stone between them. The round, thin stones varied in circumference, up to a few inches in diameter, and often had concave sides. Chunkey stones were used to play a variation of the "hoop and pole" game that was common throughout North America. In chunkey, however, the hoop was made out of stone, whereas most variants played outside the Ancient South used wood. Players took turns rolling the chunkey stone, and each time it was rolled both competitors tossed their poles after it, the object being to land closest to the stone. The scoring system varied, and many of its intricacies are now lost to history. During the early historical period, some of the poles had marks on them that were used in scoring. Players would run after their poles once they were cast, as if trying to influence their movement. Players and spectators took the game very seriously and bet heavily on the outcome. The matches were played in public at the town's chunkey yard—a flat area about one hundred feet long and of varying widths made of well-packed, carefully maintained earth or sand. The chunkey yard was used also for events such as dances, and it usually contained a tall pole that could be used in other games or as a display pole for enemy scalps, heads, and other body parts.

If material culture is a good indicator, then chunkey was certainly the most important game played during the Mississippian period. Chunkey players are commonly depicted in Mississippian art—an honor bestowed on no other athletic endeavor—and were often depicted on shell drinking cups and statuary pipes carved from stone. Hundreds of chunkey stones have been found, some of them as finely crafted and highly polished as works of art. Chunkey stones have been found also in burials, particularly elite burials. In fact, evidence suggests that chunkey played an integral role in the ideology that helped legitimize the ruling elite. Only a handful of chiefdoms had any of their stories recorded, but among these was a myth explaining that chunkey was created and played by the gods and the progeny of gods, who are identified as chiefs. The protagonist of the story is Niko Watka (lightning), whose name was used as the title of a social position: a warrior who had slain seven other warriors and three other warriors of rank. The story can thus be seen as a kind of charter explaining the nature of the position and its association with the chiefly elite. In the early historical period, chunkey stones were often "owned" not by individuals but by clans—in the Mississippian world, the stones may have belonged exclusively to the chiefly lineages.

A few of the finely crafted chunkey stones unearthed at Cahokia. Chunkey, the most important game played in the Ancient South, is commonly depicted in Mississippian art. (Cahokia Mounds State Historic Site)

Gulf Coast. Mica and other minerals came east from the southern mountains, and a host of other resources were gathered closer at hand. Among the many items sent out from Cahokia in return were Mill Creek hoes, chunkey stones, and shell-temper pottery. In addition, a number of flint clay statues, many of which were pipes, appear to have been sculpted in Cahokia and exported. The scenes depicted by these statues were central to the Mississippian way of life, beliefs, and cosmology, and included chunkey players; Earth Mother with corn, squash, and sunflowers; and the so-called long-nosed god. Some of the copper that came into the city may have left the region as finished plates, embossed with images of the so-called Falcon Warrior.

Not everyone fully accepted these new developments. While the population of Cahokia was developing the Mississippian way of life, the people who lived farther south in the Mississippi and Arkansas Valleys, known to archaeologists as the Plum Bayou and Coles Creek cultures, were conducting their own experiments in social stratification. The peoples of these cultures built ceremonial centers that included large earthworks, but they were not organized into chiefdoms with hereditary rulers. Eventually, Coles Creek peoples came to accept the Mississippian way of life and altered their towns and villages accordingly, but the Plum Bayou people of the Toltec site abandoned their homes and left the central Arkansas Valley. During the twelfth century, Mississippian technology and ideology spread beyond the Mississippi Valley as well, affecting people in places as far apart as eastern Oklahoma and Georgia. The exact mechanisms by which Mississippian practices spread remain to be fully elucidated.

For example, did immigrants from Cahokia establish colonies beyond the boundaries of the chiefdom? Did missionaries accompany Cahokian trade goods to the far corners of the Ancient South, or did people simply imitate the traders from whom they were obtaining the Cahokian items? Did the rulers of Cahokia expand their influence militarily, enforcing at least an outward acceptance of Cahokian hegemony? Was it a combination of these scenarios, or perhaps something altogether different? It is apparent that "colonial" outposts were established by immigrants from Cahokia, with the clearest case being that of Aztalan in southern Wisconsin. But it seems unlikely that colonists were the driving force behind the spread of the Mississippian way of life, which instead seems to have been closely tied to trade. There is also some evidence to support the idea that Cahokians subjected the areas immediately north and south of the chiefdom to military strikes. In any case, events at Cahokia were ultimately responsible for spawning the Mississippian world.

Cahokia Mounds State Historic Site

By any measurement, Cahokia is one of the most important pre-Columbian sites in the New World, and is without question the largest Native American site north of Mexico. Occupied between 900 and 1350, Cahokia contained up to 120 earthen mounds (more than 100 of which have been described), including magnificent Monks Mound, the largest earthen structure ever built in North America. Three types of mounds are found at Cahokia: platform mounds, conical mounds, and ridge-top mounds. Platform mounds, which represent the majority of mounds at the site, served as bases for a variety of buildings. Conical mounds, which tended to be smaller than platform mounds, may have served as repositories for burials, though not much is known about them because of limited excavations. There are nine examples of conical mounds paired with platform mounds. Ridge-top mounds vary greatly in size, and their purpose is not well understood, but they appear to be markers or engineering tools of sorts. They have been shown to contain burials also. Many of the mounds have been severely modified or even destroyed, but a surprising number are still extant — amazingly, seventy are currently preserved within the boundaries of the historic site. The site also includes a reconstruction of one of Cahokia's famous sun circles, a large open-air celestial calendar, or "woodhenge." More than six and a half miles of trails wind through Cahokia's 2,200 acres of mounds, plazas, and borrow pits, all of which seem to appear as if by magic out of the urban sprawl of nearby St. Louis. The site boasts a large museum that includes a vast array of spectacular artifacts, wall-sized murals, and even a reconstructed village.

Geography

Cahokia is located toward the northern end of the American Bottom across the Mississippi from modern St. Louis, about eight miles east of the city. The American Bottom, which stretches south from Cahokia for about seventy miles, is the name given to the floodplain created by the confluence of the Missouri, Illinois, and Mississippi Rivers. This area was a large wetland up to twelve miles wide in places, containing a maze of waterways connecting oxbow lakes, chutes, and tributary streams to the main channel of the Mississippi, which flooded much of the valley each year. Most floods took place between April and June; the river tended to be lower between August and February. Cahokia is far enough away from the main channel (about eight miles) that it would have taken a big flood to seriously inundate the site, and the water from such a deluge would have taken quite some time to drain. There were plenty of reasons, however, to live in such a wet place. The American Bottom sits at the confluence of several eco-zones that offer easy

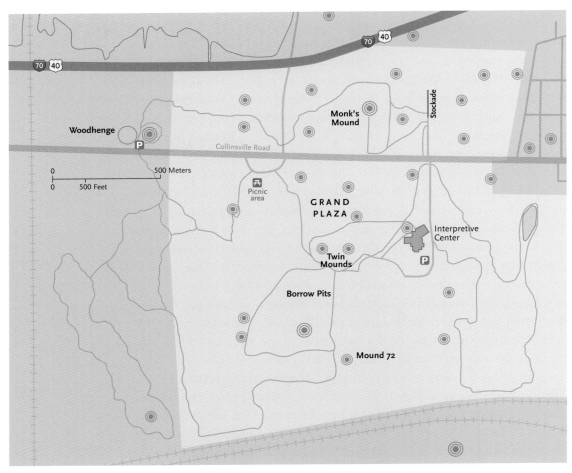

DOWNTOWN CAHOKIA

access to a wide variety of resources: the Ozarks to the west, prairie to the north and east, woodlands to the east and south, and the lower Mississippi River Valley to the south. The area was a natural nexus for travel, trade, and communication.

Generally rising to no more than ten feet above the level of the river, the topography of the valley is known as ridge and swale. Created from deposits laid down by previous river channels, the valley consisted of parallel curving ridges and swales (or depressions), some of which were barely noticeable, while others were prominent features of the landscape. Ridges were composed of silty, sandy soil, while the soil of a swale had a high clay content, which inhibited draining. The higher areas, including ridges and natural levees, were therefore the best places to plant crops. Although floods could devastate crops at times, they also replenished the nutrients in the soil. The

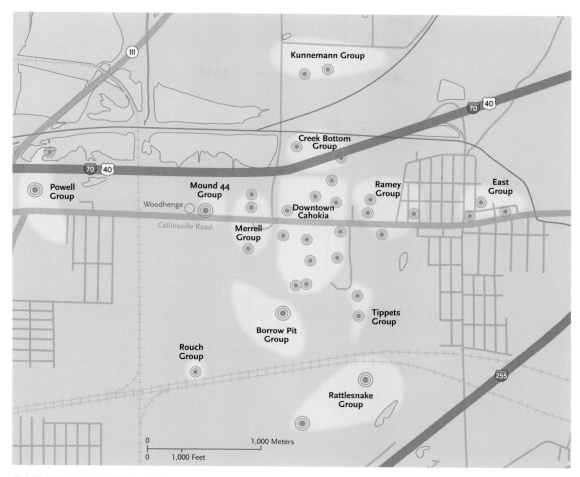

CAHOKIA MOUND GROUPS

floodplain of the Mississippi was separated by these high and low areas into minibasins with their own creeks, oxbows, swamps, prairies, and woods. Much of the floodplain was bordered by wooded bluffs that ranged from steep to nearly vertical, and were up to two hundred feet high. There were numerous lakes and swamps along the base of the bluffs; the bottomland forest that bordered the floodplains was broken not only by wetlands but also by bottomland prairies, including a large prairie near the Cahokia site.

Today, however, Cahokia looks much different. The prairie near the site is gone, and much of the area has been drained and now lies behind a series of man-made levees. The bottomland forest is gone too — the victim of human endeavors that also eliminated many bird and animal species that once thrived here. Not all of the changes at Cahokia can be traced to human activity. For instance, during the Medieval Warm Period, bald cypress grew

The three distinctive types of mounds constructed at Cahokia: ridge-top, conical, and platform. The majority were platform mounds, upon which buildings were erected. Conical mounds may have been repositories for burials, and ridge-top mounds appear to be markers or engineering tools. (Cahokia Mounds State Historic Site)

in the area and rice rats were common residents, but those southern species are no longer found that far north. For a few hundred years, the American Bottom was an ideal place to grow corn and, coupled with the other benefits of the area, allowed Cahokia to emerge as the most dominant political and ideological entity in the eastern United States.

Features

MONKS MOUND. Monks Mound stands about one hundred feet tall, nearly the height of a ten-story office building, with a base of about fourteen acres. The mound, which includes four terraces, was built between 950 and 1200 in fourteen to eighteen stages and used about twenty-two million cubic feet of dirt (the equivalent of more than 407,000 pickup trucks full of dirt). A ramp that originally included log stairs ascends forty feet to the first and largest terrace. On the left side of the first terrace in the southwest corner, a small platform mound supported a succession of at least nine buildings that appear to have been periodically burned and rebuilt. The second terrace, which is slumping and inaccessible to visitors, is on the west side of the mound and rises sixty-five feet above the ground. Little is known about this section of the mound, but recent research suggests it may have once been the same height as the summit but then collapsed in a major slump sometime during the Mississippian occupation. Log stairs originally led from the first to the third terrace, ninety-five feet above the ground. Wooden stairs were built in 1980 to allow access for visitors, but they became unstable because of erosion beneath them, and were replaced in 1998 with a more permanent concrete set. The third terrace originally contained a conical mound in the southeast corner. Just a few feet above the third terrace was the summit, which was originally surrounded by a wooden stockade and supported a building along the back edge of the mound. The building was quite large: 48 feet wide, 104 feet long, and perhaps 50 feet tall. A large post was erected on the summit directly in front of the building.

There is still much to learn about the raising of Monks Mound, but some things are relatively clear. Based on the interpretation of soil corings made in the 1960s and later, the original construction stage resulted in a mound twenty feet high, with the second stage adding six feet and the third ten more. The third stage may have included an additional eight-foot terrace on the back side of the mound. At some point it appears that the rest of the mound was raised to the level of the back terrace. The next stage of construction added a full seventeen feet to the mound. Again, there may have been a raised terrace along the back edge. A recent reanalysis of the core data and carbon dating suggests the mound may have been built in fewer stages over a shorter period of time, but more analysis is needed to confirm the new interpretation.

The building of Monks Mound was an engineering feat, since the clay used for much of the construction doesn't drain well and shrinks and swells in accordance with the moisture content of the soil. It appears the mound was designed in such a way that water was drawn up into the mound to a height of about thirty feet. That moisture kept the inner clay core in a constant state of expansion and helped stabilize the continually growing mound. In fact, part of the slumping problems seen today may be related to a change in groundwater levels and the accumulation or pooling of water inside the mound, perhaps trapped by dense clay layers. It is likely that the construction plan was developed by a single, early engineer or group of engineers, since later additions seem less sophisticated. Despite the stability provided by the internal drainage system, the mound was so large that the first terrace was probably added fairly late as a buttress to prevent slumping of the front of the mound. A layer of rock of unknown dimensions and unknown purpose was recently discovered beneath the second terrace.

TWIN MOUNDS. Twin Mounds, also known as Fox and Round Top, are located directly across the Grand Plaza from Monks Mound. Fox Mound is a platform mound, and Round Top is a conical mound, both about forty feet tall. It appears the two mounds were originally erected on a shared low platform, which is no longer extant. No excavations have been conducted on these two mounds, but it is believed Fox held a mortuary house that served as a staging area for burials in Round Top, perhaps the burials of members of the chiefly lineage living on the terraces of Monks Mound.

MOUND 72. Measuring about 6 feet tall, 70 feet wide, and 140 feet in length, Mound 72 is one of six ridge-top mounds discovered at Cahokia, the largest of which (Powell Mound) has been destroyed. Mound 72 is composed of three smaller mounds covered by a ridge-top mantle. Nearly three hundred burials were discovered below this small mound, all of which appear to have taken place between 950 and 1050 in six burial incidents. The most famous burial yet discovered at Cahokia, the so-called Bird Man, was part of the fourth set of burials. The ridgeline of Mound 72 is oriented to sunset on the summer solstice and sunrise on the winter solstice, and the mound is located on the north-south centerline of the site. The spot was marked by a succession of large posts, two placed before the mound was built and one, which penetrated the mound itself, afterward.

STOCKADE. Starting in the second half of the twelfth century, the people of Cahokia built a series of four log stockades around the central section of the city. The wall was about two miles long and enclosed Monks Mound, Twin Mounds, the Grand Plaza, and fifteen other mounds — nearly two hundred acres of land. The stockade included bastions spaced approximately eighty-five feet apart, clear evidence that the walls served a military purpose. The design of the bastions changed with each new wall, the last two versions apparently designed to save wood, which may have been becoming scarce by that time. (See figure on page 47.) Each stockade required between 15,000 and 20,000 trees at least a foot in diameter and perhaps twenty feet tall. The wall was probably plastered with mud and certainly included loopholes through which archers could send their arrows flying at the enemy.

SUN CIRCLES. The so-called woodhenge or sun circle of Cahokia represents one of the most amazing and unique finds in the history of North American archaeology. Discovered about half a mile west of Monks Mound during a highway project in the early 1960s, the woodhenge was a sequence of five circles constructed of evenly spaced, upright logs. The first sun circle was built around 1000, and the others seem to have been built and used through the middle of the thirteenth century. The original sun circle seems to have consisted of twenty-four logs, including one placed exactly at each of the cardinal directions. A twenty-fifth post may have been placed in the center. When the circle was rebuilt, twelve additional posts were added, and each successive circle added twelve more. Over time, the diameter of the circles increased from 240 to 480 feet. The posts, made of red cedar, measured up to two feet in diameter and were probably twenty feet in height, although each post was buried to a depth of more than four feet. The third circle has been most fully excavated. The model of the reconstruction, it consists of forty-eight posts set around a circle with a diameter of 410 feet. The circles could be used to determine the solstices, equinoxes, and other important dates on the agricultural calendar. The engineers of Cahokia were sophisticated

ABOVE: Construction of one of the five so-called sun circles or woodhenges west of Monks Mound. These large circles of upright posts could be used to determine the solstices and equinoxes, which were important dates on the agricultural calendar. (Cahokia Mounds State Historic Site)

LEFT: A reconstruction of the third sun circle, viewable at Cahokia today. It consists of 48 posts and has a diameter of 410 feet. (Cahokia Mounds State Historic Site)

enough to understand that an accurate calendar at their latitude required the center post to be placed five and a half feet east of the exact center in order to align it properly with the solstice sunrises. Several exotic artifacts have been found near the solstice posts of these circles, including a beaker with a sun image, marine shells, red ochre, quartz crystals, and wolf teeth. Very little of the massive site of Cahokia has been excavated, so the idea must be entertained that the sun circles described above were not the only ones at the site. The circles may have been used in conjunction with the other posts at the site as an engineering tool to help lay out the community, in which case we might expect to find a sun circle in each quadrant of the site. In accordance with this theory, it has been proposed that the post associated with Mound 72 was part of a sun circle, and some evidence has been found to support that contention.

GRAND PLAZA. The Grand Plaza was located between Monks Mound on the north and Twin Mounds to the south. The aptly named plaza covers about forty acres, or nearly thirty football fields. The area encompassed by the plaza was originally ridge and swale topography and therefore had to be leveled by human labor, an earthmoving project that required an average of more than two feet of soil to be added across the entire area of the plaza. The plaza, which was kept clean and treeless, was defined by mounds on each of its sides. The Grand Plaza appears to have been constructed early in the occupational history of Cahokia. Four smaller plazas have been found at the site as well; each is associated with a group of mounds located outside the perimeter of the stockade and to the east, north, and west of Monks Mound. They vary in size, but the largest is no more than a third the size of the Grand Plaza.

A bird's-eye view of the Grand Plaza, depicted in a mural at Cahokia. Note Fox Mound and the shadow of Round-top in the foreground; Monks Mound is in the upper right-hand corner. (Cahokia Mounds State Historic Site)

BORROW PITS. Borrow pits are by-products of mound construction. At least twenty borrow pits have been discovered at Cahokia, the largest of which covers about seventeen acres and is located south of Twin Mounds near Mound 72. At one time it was probably about six feet deep but is now much shallower, though it holds water throughout the wet season. The ponds formed by borrow pits hosted populations of fish and turtles and attracted waterfowl as well. They were probably too stagnant to be used for drinking water, but the wetland prairie grasses that grew along their edges, and throughout the marshy areas of the American Bottom, would have been harvested to make thatch for Cahokia's roofs. Some of the smaller borrow pits were filled with trash and covered over.

CAUSEWAYS. Causeways at Cahokia are small, elevated, man-made ridges that sometimes connected the bases of mounds to each other or led from mounds to borrow pits. They may have been used also as pathways to facilitate movement across low-lying areas of the site. Although a number of causeways have been recorded at Cahokia, they are now mostly gone. Although little is known for sure about their use or meaning, similar earthworks have been found at other Mississippian sites, though they may not have been common.

Research

The ruins of Cahokia, named after an unrelated group of Illiniwek (Illinois) Indians who had migrated to the area from the Great Lakes during the early seventeenth century, were seen by early Euro-American explorers and traders, but no written description of the site appeared until after the region was acquired by the United States in 1803 as part of the Louisiana Purchase. It did not take long for scientific and recreational interest in Cahokia to grow. Henry Brackenridge visited the site in 1811 while on a presidential commission to explore the area, and his written description of the trip called the public's attention to the mounds. Brackenridge mistakenly believed Cahokia had been built by people who were later driven out by the ancestors of Native North Americans, after which they moved south and erected the pyramids of Mesoamerica. The first detailed account of the mounds appeared as a result of the Missouri River expedition of Major Stephen H. Long in 1819. He described Monks Mound as "so overgrown with bushes and weeds, interlaced with briars and vines, that we were unable to obtain an accurate account of its dimensions."

It was not until 1832 that the first accurate illustration of Monks Mound was made, by Karl Bodmer. Bodmer, a Swiss artist and member of Prince Maximilian von Wied's expedition, drew several mounds at the site when his party stopped at St. Louis after its two-year exploration of the American West. In the years between 1865 and 1876, an industrious fellow named John Patrick commissioned a map of the entire Cahokia site. It was the most accurate map of the site until a new one was made in 1966. Patrick's map, which was drawn before the area had been intensively cultivated, depicted the mounds close to their original proportions. Because of its accuracy, Patrick's map is still useful today. The number system he used to identify the mounds is still in use as well. In the 1880s, Patrick built a three-dimensional model of Monks Mound and worked with Frederick Ward Putnam of Harvard's Peabody Museum on a scholarly description of the Cahokia site.

In 1893, William McAdams of the Bureau of American Ethnology displayed many artifacts from Cahokia and other sites in the region at the World's Columbian Exposition in Chicago. During the St. Louis World's Fair in 1904, an electric railway took sightseers out to Monks Mound, though unfortunately they liberally removed artifacts from the site. The first local person to write about the site was John Francis Snyder, who was born in 1830 and lived on a farm that included the Pulcher Mounds. A lifetime of interest induced Snyder to publish about thirty articles on Cahokia during the nineteenth century. Snyder was also one of the first people to support the idea of preserving the mounds for posterity, founding the Monks of Cahokia, an organization dedicated to obtaining state protection for the site.

Early in the twentieth century, a Harvard professor named David I. Bushnell published a short report that examined a number of the important sites in the American Bottom, including Cahokia. In 1922, he published a second report, which included aerial photographs, the first of many taken of Cahokia and the first taken of a North American archaeological site. Warren K. Moorehead, who investigated many of the most famous Mississippian sites, worked at Cahokia throughout the 1920s, producing a number of reports detailing his excavations in several mounds. Like Snyder, Moorehead sought to protect the site and open it for public viewing. Archaeological investigations continued sporadically at Cahokia in the ensuing decades. The Works Progress Administration began excavations at the site in 1941 and ended in mid-December of the same year. Several survey and test excavation projects were undertaken in the 1950s by a number of institutions, including the University of Michigan and the Thomas Gilcrease Foundation, but it was not until the next decade that extensive excavations were conducted at Cahokia.

Major interstate construction in the area prompted a number of salvage archaeology projects at Cahokia beginning in 1960, including ones developed in conjunction with the Illinois Archaeological Survey and the Illinois Department of Transportation. In addition, the Illinois State Museum excavated two tracts west of Monks Mound (one led to the discovery of the

woodhenges); the University of Illinois worked at the Powell Mound group at the west edge of the site; and Southern Illinois University at Carbondale oversaw investigations north of Cahokia at the Mitchell site. Those projects provided invaluable information about domestic architecture, daily life, and population numbers at Cahokia. Investigations were done on a number of mounds, including Monks Mound, which was the subject of numerous excavations between 1964 and 1971. Melvin Fowler of the University of Wisconsin–Milwaukee was responsible for producing the first accurate map of the entire site since John Patrick's from a century before. He and his students excavated Mound 72 between 1967 and 1971, unearthing the Bird Man burial. Much of the archaeological work at Cahokia since 1971 has been associated with the development of the site for public use, reexamining old excavations, answering new research questions, and conducting remote-sensing scans of the site, all conducted by university and public field schools and through independent research.

During the course of these scientific inquiries, Cahokia underwent a number of drastic changes. A dozen railroad companies had tracks running throughout the six-mile extent of the site. It was not easy to maintain tracks through the low, swampy area, so the railroad companies often took dirt from

Monks Mound at Cahokia under a dark and foreboding sky. (Photography by Daniel Seurer, Seurerphoto .squarespace.com)

the mounds to fill in the low places. By 1860, the expansion of St. Louis was spelling destruction for large numbers of mounds, including the St. Louis Mounds and the East St. Louis Mounds. With the help of the Ramey family, who owned much of the land within the boundaries of Cahokia, and others like them, Cahokia Mounds State Park was created in 1925 after many unsuccessful attempts to gain legal protection for the site. One hundred forty-four acres surrounding Monks Mound were included within the boundary of the park, which was mainly used for picnics during the summer, sledding in the winter, and sometimes for camping in the spring and fall.

A subdivision called State Park Place was built near Monks Mound around the time of World War II. A drive-in theater constructed in the 1950s within sight of the mound wasn't torn down until 1983. The Downtown Air Park, a small airport, was built on the edge of the site during the 1950s and remained in operation until the 1970s. Cahokia was finally declared a National Historic Landmark in 1964, and by the late 1970s it had become a state historic site, thanks in no small part to the efforts of the archaeologists Jim Anderson and William Iseminger. They and others helped implement a long-term plan that shifted the focus at Cahokia from recreation to cultural interpretation and led to Cahokia being named a UNESCO World Heritage Site in 1982. The State of Illinois began to buy the land surrounding the historic site property, including the airport, drive-in, and subdivision. By 1989, it had completed

the task, increasing the size of the park to twenty-two hundred acres. The same year saw the opening of Cahokia's new interpretive center, bringing to fruition the farsighted vision of Iseminger and his colleagues.

City Plan

Cahokia was the most densely populated site in Native North American history. If the population was around 30,000 as some of the higher estimates claim, then Cahokia was comparable to some urban areas in other parts of the world during the twelfth and thirteenth centuries — the United States did not have a city as big until the beginning of the nineteenth century. Even if the lower estimates of several thousand people are correct, Cahokia can still be rightly referred to as a city when compared with other communities in North America at the time. The city of Cahokia was the capital and cultural center of a society that was distributed throughout the entire American Bottom, though we know more about the northern sites than the southern.

Cahokia can be separated into "downtown" Cahokia and the surrounding "suburbs." Downtown Cahokia refers to the two hundred acres of land that were enclosed within the stockade, an area that at its height contained eighteen mounds and scores of houses arranged into elite neighborhoods. The suburbs of Cahokia included more than eighty mounds and many hundreds of residences within five miles of downtown. Most of the mounds were included

Downtown Cahokia, seen from above in an artist's reconstruction. Note Monks Mound and Twin Mounds (Fox and Roundtop) with the Grand Plaza between them, the stockade wall, a sun circle, and a number of barrow pit ponds. (Cahokia Mounds State Historic Site)

within one of eleven clusters that formed two concentric circles around the central precinct of the city. The eleven mound groups are the following:

CREEK BOTTOM GROUP. Creek Bottom includes five mounds and a plaza, but only three mounds are still partly visible; the level they were built on is more than six feet below the current ground surface, covered by deposits from Cahokia and Canteen Creeks.

RAMEY GROUP. The Ramey group includes twenty-one mounds and a ten-acre plaza. Many of the mounds are paired platform and conical mounds. This group alone is larger than most other Mississippian sites built in the Ancient South.

TIPPETTS GROUP. This group includes three mounds, one of each type, located on the banks of a borrow-pit lake. A man-made peninsula extended from the base of the conical mound out into the lake and terminated in a large area that measured more than one hundred feet on a side. It served as the community's plaza.

BORROW PIT GROUP. The Borrow Pit group was composed of five mounds, including a group of three mounds similar to the Tippetts group and Mound 72, but had no clearly defined plaza.

MERRELL GROUP. This group was composed of seven mounds. Five mounds were arranged so that a plaza was formed between them, and the plaza contained a sixth mound. The seventh mound was built to the north of the plaza configuration.

MOUND 44 GROUP. This mundanely named group of four mounds around a small plaza was built adjacent to the sun circles discovered to the west of Monks Mound.

KUNNEMANN GROUP. Kunnemann was composed of seven mounds but lacked a plaza. The mounds were arranged linearly along the north bank of Cahokia Creek and included two sets of paired conical and platform mounds, each with a connecting causeway. This group included what appears to have been a workshop for the production of shell beads.

EAST GROUP. Very little is known about this group, which was originally composed of five mounds, some of which may be associated with a former small golf course.

RATTLESNAKE GROUP. Rattlesnake included eight mounds that formed two subgroups, neither of which included a plaza. One of the group's mounds, Rattlesnake Mound, is the largest ridge-top and southernmost mound at

Cahokia; it marked the north-south axis of the site. It appears that this mound group may have been reserved as a special-function area without a residential neighborhood, perhaps making it unique among the eleven groups.

ROUCH GROUP. This group included three mounds and possibly a plaza. One of the platform mounds in the group is quite large — about thirty feet tall now, it once stood as high as forty-five feet.

POWELL GROUP. The Powell group was composed of four or possibly six mounds (two seem isolated and may not have been included in the group). Powell Mound itself was a large ridge-top mound located at the western boundary of the city of Cahokia and connected to the downtown area by a long ridge, which was a broad natural levee formed by a long-abandoned channel of the Mississippi River.

THUS CAHOKIA FORMED a rough diamond shape marked by four ridge-top mounds, with Monks Mound located roughly at the center. The city was about three miles wide along its east-west axis and measured more than two miles along its north-south axis — about five square miles. The stockaded central precinct was the domain of the highest order of elite families, with lower-ranked elite lineages living around each of the eleven mound groups in the suburbs. The villages of the commoners who built the walls and mounds were scattered throughout the rest of the site among hundreds, perhaps thousands, of fields and old fields.

The city and its people did not live in a vacuum; Cahokia had significant relationships with other sites throughout the American Bottom. Although the exact nature of those relationships is debated, Cahokia had significant influence over, maybe even outright control of, nearby chiefdoms. Within fourteen miles of the city there were four large multimound sites of more than 120 acres, whose people added several thousand more to the overall population of the chiefdom of Cahokia. The elites living at those mound centers were probably connected to the chief of Cahokia through marriage, political alliance, the military dominance of Cahokia, or perhaps some combination of the three. The four mound centers are the following:

EAST ST. LOUIS MOUNDS. This group was composed of at least seventeen mounds, as mapped by Patrick in the 1870s, but perhaps as many as forty-five, as estimated by Brackenridge in 1811. The ridge between downtown Cahokia and Powell Mound continued all the way to the East St. Louis group, forming a direct connection between the sites. The mounds were mostly destroyed, but the bases of many of them remain beneath the city's rubble and fill.

ST. LOUIS MOUNDS. The St. Louis group was located about eight miles from downtown Cahokia, across the Mississippi River from the East St. Louis group. This group, which led to St. Louis being nicknamed "Mound City," included at least twenty-six mounds, all of which have been destroyed because they were located within the boundaries of the modern city of St. Louis, Missouri.

MITCHELL MOUNDS. This group was located seven miles north of Cahokia's central district on a long lake formed from an old channel of the Mississippi River. The site was composed of at least ten mounds and, being located adjacent to the confluence of the Mississippi and Missouri Rivers, was ideally situated to take advantage of trade from the north.

PULCHER MOUNDS. The Pulcher Mounds were located about fifteen miles south of downtown Cahokia near the modern town of Dupo, Illinois. This set of about ten mounds was once known as "Snyder's group," after John Snyder.

Political Organization and Elite Status

There has been an enormous amount of debate on the topic of political organization at Cahokia, most of which revolves around the defense of one of two positions: Cahokia was qualitatively and quantitatively different from other Mississippian societies, or it was only quantitatively different. There are a handful of things on which both camps agree. Cahokia was the largest and most important site in the region, and some organizational force was required to build the city, which some believe may have been laid out using a standard unit of measure known as the "Cahokia yard" (1.03 meters). Some people at Cahokia had access to exotic goods, and some craft specialization existed. Sites throughout the American Bottom were linked socially and politically to the elite lineages of Cahokia, who built an impression of themselves as occupying a crucial position in the natural order of the universe. Not everyone accepted the idea, since the society experienced at least some conflict.

On one side of the debate over political organization at Cahokia, scholars see the leaders of Cahokia as having had coercive power over an extensive regional system that included elite-controlled religious, military, and artistic specialists. They believe Cahokia itself to have had a population of ten to thirty thousand, with thousands of others throughout the region under the sway of Cahokia's leaders. To increase their power, the elite of Cahokia used their far-flung exchange network to help expand Cahokian hegemony. Scholars on the other side of the debate believe everything that occurred at Cahokia occurred at other places in the Mississippian world, only on a smaller scale. In this view, the leaders of Cahokia had control over the five-square-mile site, the population of which they estimate at only three to eight thousand, but wider political relations were much more unsettled. Although the elite funded part-time specialists, each community within the Cahokia area was self-sufficient as far as the daily needs of life were concerned, and participated in the regional system for subtle social and political reasons, but not because they were forced to do so by Cahokia's elite.

There is clear evidence at Cahokia of a distinction between elites and commoners, and one of the primary forms of evidence comes from burials. Frequently, elites were interred in mounds with numerous artifacts made of nonlocal material, marine shell being most common. Most goods buried with the elite appear to be merely indications of wealth, but some were clearly crafted to serve as symbols of office and were reserved exclusively for Cahokia's leaders. In addition, sometimes members of Cahokia's elite were interred with loved ones, servants, and war captives, all of whom were killed specifically for the occasion.

Mound 72, beneath which the famous "Bird Man" burial was discovered. (Photography by Daniel Seurer, Seurerphoto .squarespace.com)

Common people, on the other hand, were interred in cemeteries located throughout Cahokia. Generally, a commoner was buried in a separate grave in an extended position, often with utilitarian objects and less frequently with shell of mediocre quality. Occasionally, a person found in a commoner cemetery was buried with a number of artifacts made from exotic material. Usually these persons are male, and it is believed they came to their elevated position through service to an elite lineage — most likely as a warrior. At the other extreme, some commoners were dumped in the trash, though the bodies may have been the corpses of Cahokia's enemies.

The most spectacular burial yet discovered at Cahokia is a stunning testament to the social and political inequalities that existed within the city. Sometime between 950 and 1050, two elite males in their early forties were buried in Mound 72. The men were laid to rest one below and one above a bed of 20,000 whelk-shell beads that were placed in the shape of a falcon. Both the whelk shells and the man lying atop them — the Bird Man referred to above — were further supported by a litter made of red cedar. Besides the man beneath him, three more men and three women, perhaps related to the chief, were buried with this important personage. Nearby, a number of artifacts were buried on top of those seven men and women, including a roll of sheet copper, stacks of mica, fourteen chunkey stones, and more than eight hundred finely crafted arrowheads made from high-quality stone from many midwestern sources. To the northwest of the beaded burials were four men without their heads or hands, almost certainly prisoners of war, and fifty-three women between the ages of fifteen and twenty-five, who were buried two-deep in two rows, ready to serve the elite in the next realm as well.

Artisans and Laborers

Cahokia's leaders imported copper from Lake Superior; mica from the Southern Appalachians; galena, hematite, and ochre from Illinois and Missouri; fluorite from Illinois, Tennessee, and Kentucky; shell from the Gulf and Atlantic coasts; and chert from Illinois, Missouri, Oklahoma, Tennessee, Wisconsin, and other regions. Most things traded into Cahokia came in the form of raw materials, and much of it went out again as finished products. Cahokia pottery has been found in small amounts throughout the midcontinental region, as have hoes made of imported Mill Creek stone, which were universally used by the city's farmers and may have served as a symbol of the region to outsiders. Some of the most spectacular exports from Cahokia were large statuary pipes made from a kind of soft stone known as Missouri flint clay. Scholars have speculated that many of the greatest artistic treasures found throughout the Mississippian world, such as Missouri flint clay

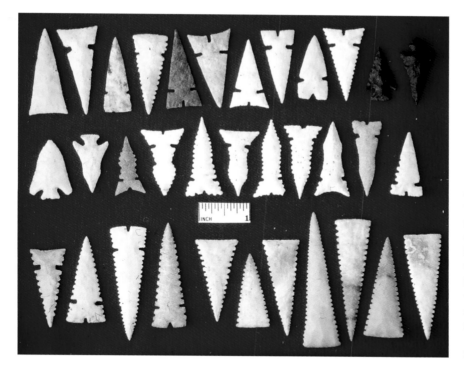

A few dozen of the more than eight hundred projectile points unearthed in the Bird Man burial in Mound 72 at Cahokia. The stone used in their production came from places as far away as Oklahoma, Tennessee, and Wisconsin. (Cahokia Mounds State Historic Site)

The Birger figurine, depicting a kneeling female holding a large snake with her left hand while striking it with a stone hoe held in her right. Squash vines and gourds cover her back. (Courtesy of the Illinois State Archaeological Survey, University of Illinois)

figurines, the copper work discovered at Etowah in Georgia, and some of the shell work found at Spiro Mounds in eastern Oklahoma, were crafted in Cahokia. It is likely that most of the artwork was produced in the winter months by specialists supported by the chief.

In addition to the work of artisans, Cahokian elites were able to periodically demand labor from all commoners. Attempts to calculate the communal labor requirements at Cahokia have concluded that work crews numbering in the hundreds or low thousands would have been sufficient to build and maintain the city. Moreover, labor demands varied with each type of project —mounds were not built all at once, stockades were repaired no more often than every twenty-five years, and chiefly residences and temples were rebuilt only slightly more often.

Some projects required an enormous amount of work. Leveling the ridge-and-swale topography to create the Grand Plaza was incredibly labor intensive. The first stockade, however, was probably the largest single building event undertaken at Cahokia; workers started from scratch and almost certainly erected the entire wall as part of a single, continuous project. Thousands of logs had to be felled and carried or floated to the site, and most of them came from bluffs about four and a half miles away. Subsequent walls could have made some use of logs from the previous stockade, and new sections would have been built up as others were torn down. In general, mound and plaza construction dominated Cahokia's early history, whereas more effort was put into the erection of walls as Cahokia's star waned.

History

Despite some disputes, scholars have begun to formulate a developmental history of the occupation of Cahokia.

900–1050. The beginning of Cahokian history is marked by the adoption of maize as the primary crop. Many small, nucleated farming communities were spread throughout the American Bottom, and the hamlets were organized by kin groups who built their houses around small courtyards that included posts like those that later adorned Cahokia's plazas. One of the largest settlements in the region was located along Cahokia Creek, the northern boundary of what would later become the city of Cahokia. Certain lineages there began extending their influence to other kin groups through economic and ideological means. Using their prime geographic location to underwrite the development of a political-religious cult, the emerging elites built Cahokia into the most influential and, presumably, most powerful society in the region. Construction was begun on Monks Mound and three hundred burials occurred on Mound 72 between 950 and 1050. The first sun circle was built during this period as well, but a stockade was not erected. The population of the entire American Bottom was probably no more than a few thousand at the time, though that soon changed. Shortly after 1000, people began to spread out from their small, nucleated villages to inhabit scattered farmsteads, clear evidence that the leaders of Cahokia were creating a new, region-wide area of peace.

1050–1150. The inception of this period is referred to by the archaeologist Timothy Pauketat as Cahokia's "big bang." Several classic Mississippian traits were evident by this time, including shell-tempered pottery, semi-subterranean houses with attached ramadas or separate outdoor kitchens, and corncribs for the efficient storage of produce. There was an emphasis on public works within the city, the centerpiece of which was the construction of the Grand Plaza. Other projects included the erection of woodhenges and the conversion of former residential areas for ritual use. During this period, Cahokia's commoners lived better than they ever had before or ever would again. Political conflict, environmental degradation, and health problems were in the future, and the feasts held by the leaders were still grand events. Pauketat describes one such feast as involving the "cooking, consumption, and discard of select portions of over 2,000 individual white-tail deer, the use and breakage of perhaps more than 7,000 pots, the smoking of great amounts of tobacco, the production of craft objects, and the ritual use and disposal of red cedar branches and quartz crystals." The region's population increased both naturally and through migration as people drawn to the city's glamour and success established a number of new mound centers in the vicinity. The most reasonable population estimates for Cahokia at its height range between 10,000 and 16,000 people in the city, with another 15,000 to 35,000 living in nearby mound centers and spread throughout the rural areas in between. It was during this period that colonists from the city helped found towns remote from Cahokia, such as Aztalan in Wisconsin. (See the box feature Aztalan State Park, pages 88–89.) In addition, Cahokia sent traders (or at least trade goods) and perhaps missionaries to regions throughout the Ancient South. As the chiefdom expanded, however, opportunities arose for lesser chiefs and lineages to begin jockeying for power.

1150–1275. By 1150 the rulers at Cahokia found it necessary to enclose the central district with an enormous wall, which had to be rebuilt three more times before the city was eventually abandoned. Although the wall had social implications, its primary purpose was military, though it is unclear whether the threat was internal, external, or both. The construction of the stockade included Cahokia's version of urban renewal — a former residential neighborhood was destroyed and the wall built through it. Similar changes

AZTALAN STATE PARK

Aztalan State Park is located about fifty miles west of Milwaukee, Wisconsin, on the Crawfish River near the township of Aztalan. The twenty-one-acre site included three platform mounds, a plaza, and two residential areas contained within a stockade wall. The wall enclosed a spring that would have been indispensable during a military siege. Two of the platform mounds have been reconstructed, as have small sections of the stockade wall, although the site lacks a museum and park interpreters. Aztalan was one of the northernmost Mississippian villages, and the only one in the Crawfish River region. When the site was first recorded by Euro-Americans, in 1836, the remains of the walls were visible, and it became known as the "Citadel." It was later officially dubbed Aztalan, based on the erroneous idea that Wisconsin was the northern homeland from which the Aztecs emerged to conquer Mexico. Archaeological research at the site began in the nineteenth century, and all three mounds, parts of the plaza and walls, and sections of the residential area reserved for commoners have since been investigated. In 1948 the state acquired 120 acres surrounding the site, and opened the park in 1952. Aztalan State Park is a National Historic Landmark and is listed on the National Register of Historic Places. Despite a chronic lack of funding, locals have fought to keep the site open over the years, and it remains an often-visited park despite the lack of interpretative aids.

The Crawfish River is a tributary of the Rock River, which is a tributary of the Mississippi. Aztalan is located on the western bank of the river at an ideal fording point where the remains of a stone fishing weir have been found. Although there were fewer frost-free days at Aztalan than was ideal for a Mississippian farmer, the soil itself was quite good, and the area had a flourishing deer population. Aztalan sat at the crossroads of two major Indian foot trails, and its founding at that location indicates that its primary purpose may have been trade. It is certain that copper from quarries to the north as well as some local tool stone and lead (which was used in making white paint) was traded south to Cahokia. It is also likely that deer meat, skins, and wild rice were traded as well. Some of the stone traded south was fashioned into arrow points that ended up in the famous Mound 72 burial at Cahokia, while Mill Creek hoes and two copper maskettes of the long-nosed god have been unearthed at Aztalan.

The northeast mound (no longer extant) was erected in a single building episode and served as the foundation for a temple that measured 45 by 90 feet. The southwest mound was a two-tiered mound with a base of 185 by 130 feet, with the second tier rising to a height of 16 feet. The mound was built in several stages, at least three of which supported structures that were approximately 42 feet square and served as the chiefly residence. The top tier of the mound was covered with white clay, which must have created a stunning visual image each morning as the chief greeted the rising sun. The northwest mound, another two-tiered mound built in multiple stages, was nearly 10 feet tall with a base of 105 by 92 feet and was crowned by a 12-by-5-foot structure that was almost certainly a mortuary house for the elite.

The mounds were enclosed within a tall stockade wall that included thirty-two evenly spaced bastions for archers. The stockade at Aztalan was unusual in that it divided the town into three major areas: the residence area of the commoners, which included the northeast mound; the plaza, which occupied the middle of the site; and the residence area of the elite, which included both the southwest and northwest mounds. The elite neighborhood was located at the high end of the site as a protection against floodwaters, while the commoners built their houses right along the river. The stockade climbed the face of the southwest mound in two places, forming a narrow, open corner through which the chief could descend to the plaza. Several gates led into the plaza area from both the elite and common residential areas, and a few gates led from outside the walls into the commoners' residence area, but only one outside gate led directly into the elite residence area. The plaza, which had to be leveled when built, was L-shaped in order to give direct access to the river. The northern end of the plaza contained at least seventy pits, which were originally used for storage but ultimately for refuse. Overlooking some of the town's fields from a nearby bluff was a series of thirty conical mounds, nine of which remain today. Some of these mounds covered what were once large posts. Only one burial has been recovered from the bluff—a young woman covered with thousands of beads.

Aztalan was first occupied about AD 900 by non-Mississippian peoples, who nevertheless became involved in the trade network that ultimately led back to Cahokia. Around 1100, a group of Mississippians came to the site and settled with the people already living there, as evidenced by the contemporaneous use of both peoples' pottery and house-construction styles, and together they erected the mounds and stockade. The Mississippian "ambassadors" may have come from someplace in northern Illinois but could just as easily have come from Cahokia itself. They were intent on controlling a trade that had previously been handled by non-Mississippian middlemen, but they appear to have met some resistance. Aztalan was permanently abandoned about 1200, and the stockade was burned. Could the Mississippians and their allies have been driven away by force, and if so, who were their enemies? They may have been one of a group of societies known collectively as the Oneota culture. The groups appear to have adopted both corn and shell-tempered pottery around 1050, but never built platform mounds and were not ruled by hereditary chiefs. The Oneota culture developed virtually everywhere the Mississippian influence intruded into the northern regions of the continent, and the Mississippian influence was tenuous and short-lived there.

Village life at Aztalan, one of the northernmost Mississippian towns, located on the Crawfish River in Wisconsin. (Courtesy of the Kenosha Public Museum, Rob Evans, Artist)

occurred regularly throughout the city's history, including at its inception, when residential neighborhoods were turned into ceremonial areas by the newly ascended rulers. During the thirteenth century, the population at Cahokia began to decline as people, presumably commoners, moved back to the uplands on the border of the city and perhaps beyond. Mitchell Mounds to the north of the city was still a thriving multimound community, but the East St. Louis and Pulcher Mound sites went into steep decline.

1275–1350. In the last quarter of the thirteenth century, mound centers began to appear on the fringe of Cahokia's territory, fourteen miles or more from the city, and the leaders at Cahokia found themselves less able to control the people of the chiefdom. Multicommunity cemeteries were abandoned in favor of small plots near residences, possibly indicating an increase in local autonomy. Mound enlargement at Cahokia decreased during this period and then finally stopped altogether. Some ceremonial districts, such as the woodhenge area, were converted to residential use. The flow of goods in the larger regional exchange system was disrupted, exacerbating the problems faced by Cahokia's leaders. The city undoubtedly showed signs of decay — overgrown mounds and a rotting wall. Though the population continued to decline, it may not have been as low as generally believed. During the nineteenth century there was significant evidence of late thirteenth- or early fourteenth-century occupation lying on the surface, but much of it was picked up or destroyed within a few decades of the twentieth century.

In contrast to its meteoric rise, Cahokia's decline was long and drawn out. The city was abandoned for several reasons, though the weight to be given to each continues to be debated. Wood was not plentiful in the American Bottom, because of the nature of the active floodplain, so much of it used in Cahokia had to be brought in from as far as fifteen miles away. As distant political relationships became unsettled, it may have become difficult to collect wood, which was in high demand for fuel and construction. Once the forests on the bluffs to the east of Cahokia were severely depleted, runoff would have silted in channels, ultimately leading to devastating floods. The worst of such floods would have come in the late summer and ruined young crops while also making it more difficult to catch fish.

With the onset of the Little Ice Age at the beginning of the fourteenth century, Cahokia's farmers began to suffer more setbacks. It would not have taken much to tip the balance of survival against such a densely settled society — even a series of subpar harvests without a major crop failure would have put too much strain on the system. The nutritional stress that resulted from poor harvests exacerbated other health problems. The people of

Cahokia did not have beans for protein, and though they had access to fish, did not eat much meat unless they were elite. The hunting pressure in the American Bottom was intense, and so commoners there ate much less deer than in other parts of the Mississippian world. Human waste disposal may also have been a problem.

Human conflict surely contributed to the abandonment of Cahokia. Although the sources of conflict were probably both internal and external, there is little physical evidence of conflict beyond the stockade itself. One can imagine rival chiefs growing powerful enough to disrupt regional trade, attempt to co-opt the legitimacy of Cahokian rulers, or perhaps threaten the city militarily. In another likely scenario, subchiefs within Cahokia could have garnered enough support to break away from the main leaders through religious or military coups. Untimely deaths or incompetent rulers might have made the chiefly lineage particularly vulnerable. In any case, during the 1300s mighty Cahokia became a shadow of its former self, and before 1400 the city was abandoned and never reoccupied.

Toltec Mounds Archeological State Park

Toltec Mounds Archeological State Park protects what remains of a large village that thrived between 700 and 1000 near present-day Little Rock, Arkansas. The people who lived at Toltec belonged to the Plum Bayou archaeological culture. While Cahokia and its distinctly Mississippian way of life developed in the central Mississippi Valley, alternative ways of life were developing in other parts of the valley. Eventually, Mississippians dominated the region, but Toltec provides a fascinating glimpse of one of Cahokia's powerful early neighbors. At one time, Toltec included eighteen mounds arranged around two plazas, all of which were contained within an earth embankment enclosing about ninety-nine acres. The embankment and the ditch that fronted it surrounded the mounds on three sides, the fourth side being defined by an oxbow lake. Almost the entire northern half of the site has been destroyed, the victim of rice cultivation in the 1960s. Only three of the mounds are still prominent, though the remnants of others remain, and two small sections of the embankment and ditch are preserved — yet the site is still spectacular. Visitors to Toltec can see the remaining mounds, including forty-nine-foot-tall Mound A, while traversing the site's two short trails. Toltec is one of the few remaining sites located adjacent to an oxbow lake that can be accessed easily by the public. A boardwalk built around Mound A allows visitors to enjoy that aspect of the park. Guide booklets available for both children and adults enhance the experience available at Toltec.

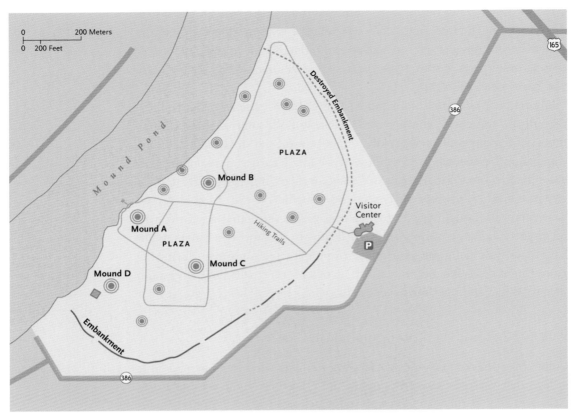

TOLTEC MOUNDS ARCHEOLOGICAL STATE PARK

Location

Toltec is located fifteen miles southeast of Little Rock on Plum Bayou, an ancestral channel of the Arkansas River. The site is directly adjacent to Mound Lake, which formed about two thousand years ago, long before the occupation of the Toltec site by peoples of the Plum Bayou culture. The Arkansas River is currently about three miles west of the site, but was only about a mile away when Toltec was occupied. Toltec is located within the Arkansas River lowland physiographic province, an area composed of the drainage basins of three bayous occupying what were once active channels of the Arkansas River. In addition to Plum Bayou, they are Bayou Meto and Indian/Bakers Bayou. The Arkansas River lowland is about sixty-two miles long and up to thirty miles wide. Toltec, which occupies the extreme northern extension of the province, is adjacent to four other physiographic provinces, all of which were exploited by the residents of Toltec.

Toltec was situated within a bottomland hardwood forest with a diverse array of trees, including several species of oak and hickory along with cotton-

wood, elm, and cypress. Persimmons, maypops, several varieties of grapes, and numerous types of berries were abundant, as were nut-bearing trees. The environment around Toltec was varied enough to provide a wide range of fish, mammal, and bird species suitable for consumption. Deer, turkey, and passenger pigeon were regularly eaten at Toltec, along with turtles and fish taken from the lakes, bayous, and rivers. Unlike their emerging Mississippian neighbors to the northeast, Plum Bayou peoples did not become corn farmers. Instead, they cultivated several species of plants indigenous to the eastern United States, including little barley, maygrass, Chenopodium, sumpweed, knotweed, sunflower, squash, and bottle gourds. Most of the resources used by the people of Toltec could be obtained from within eighteen miles of the site, but they did import some material from the Ouachita Mountains to the west.

A view of Mounds A and B at Toltec from adjacent Mound Lake. (Courtesy of Elizabeth Horton)

Features

MOUND A. Mound A is relatively intact and, at forty-nine feet, is the tallest mound in Arkansas. It has not been tested or excavated, and to preserve it as a sacred monument of the past, there are no plans to do so in the future. Archaeologists do not know exactly when it was built or how many construction episodes it took to complete the project. It is certain, however, that Mound A figured prominently in the ceremonial rites conducted at Toltec.

MOUND B. Mound B, a platform mound on the northeastern edge of the main plaza, rises to a height of about thirty-nine feet, with a base well more than two hundred feet on each side. During the late nineteenth century, cotton was cultivated on top of it. Later, the upper two-thirds of the mound was excavated, revealing five construction episodes that seem to have capped the platform of earlier stages without adding additional earth to the sides. Mound B was probably used for the entire time Toltec was occupied.

MOUND C. Mound C is a conical mound on the eastern edge of the plaza. It stands just over thirteen feet high, making it the third tallest at the site. Two burials, an adult male and an adult female, were recovered from Mound C during limited professional excavations. Pothunters uncovered burials in and around the mound, too, making it likely that it served as one of the primary mortuary areas of Toltec. No further excavations are planned for Mound C.

MOUND D. The most comprehensive mound excavation undertaken at Toltec occurred on Mound D, though much of the mound had already been removed in the 1950s and used for road fill. Although this platform mound is now hardly discernible, at one time it measured five feet tall, ninety-five feet long, and seventy-nine feet wide at the base. Excavations over three seasons, 1977, 1978, and 1979, identified at least four construction stages, and it appears that the mound was lengthened and widened, though not raised in height. Mound D, which sits on the southwestern edge of the main plaza, was almost certainly used as the base for a building, and large trash deposits were found on the southwestern side, facing away from the plaza. A building underneath the mound dates to 850, so mound construction began after that date and appears to have continued until at least 1000.

PLAZAS. The Toltec site once included two plazas, but they are not clearly distinguishable today. The main plaza was surrounded by ten mounds, including Mounds A, B, C, and D. The smaller plaza was surrounded by seven mounds. Mound B was the only one adjacent to both plazas.

EMBANKMENT AND DITCH. The embankment and ditch were more than a mile long and enclosed the site on three sides. At one time, the embankment was eight to ten feet tall, with a base about fifty feet wide and up to three small entrances. It does not appear to have supported a stockade wall and may have been a boundary between the sacred and secular instead of a defensive construction. If the embankment was built in one episode it would have been quite an undertaking. The ditch was more than sixty feet wide, though its depth seems to have varied, and part of it was formed from an empty channel scar. The only date associated with the ditch is much earlier than other dates at the site and is thus suspect.

Research

A Frenchman named Louis Bringier wrote the first account of Toltec, a description of his visit to the site in 1812:

> This fortification is tolerably regular, covering an area of about twenty-five acres; the trenches remain about eight feet high, and the ditches which are nearly filled up, seem to have been very deep, and about twenty-five feet wide. There are two gateways, in the inside of which there is a large well, which probably was a covered way; and in the centre there are two mounds about eighty feet in height, whose bases are about three hundred feet in diameter, with a truncated summit offering a surface of about ninety feet across. Both are artificial, and perhaps were formed from the dirt of the ditches. The country around is perfectly level. (Quoted in Martha Ann Rolingson, "The Toltec [Knapp] Mounds Group in the Nineteenth Century," 123)

The site was a regional landmark throughout the nineteenth century, and although it was described briefly in other accounts, it failed to garner much scientific interest, despite its grandeur, until the wife of one of the landowners took an interest in Indian "curiosities."

In 1876, Mrs. Charles Knapp wrote two descriptive letters concerning the earthworks then known as the Knapp Mounds; her accounts eventually reached the Smithsonian Institution, where they prompted two archaeological investigations of the site. Edwin Curtiss of Harvard's Peabody Museum visited the site in 1879, but made only a sketch map of its layout after some hasty test excavations. Edward Palmer of the Smithsonian visited the site three times as a member of the Division of Mound Exploration of the Bureau of American Ethnology, the first in late 1882, when he was accompanied by an African American artist from Pine Bluff, Arkansas, named Henry J. Lewis, who made several sketches of the mounds and embankment. Palmer came back in early 1883 and excavated eight mounds, and then returned in 1884 to check his earlier measurements of Mounds A and B. The results of Palmer's work, later published by the Bureau of American Ethnology, have been invaluable to modern researchers.

It appears the site on the Knapp family farm began to be referred to as "Toltec" within a few years of Palmer's visits. Whether the name was based

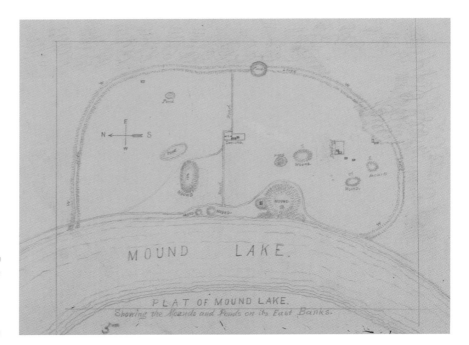

PLAT OF MOUND LAKE.
Showing the Mounds and Ponds on its East Banks.

Toltec Mounds as drawn by Henry J. Lewis for the Smithsonian Institution in 1882. (National Anthropological Archives, Smithsonian Institution)

on the speculations of Mrs. Knapp, Edward Palmer, or a combination of the two remains unknown; however, the appellation "Toltec" was applied to a post office, a small community, and a stop on the railroad line — all because of a mistaken association between the Arkansas site and the Toltec empire of Mexico. Despite the allure of its outlandish new name, Toltec received very little archaeological attention in the following decades. Clarence Moore, a lawyer and amateur archaeologist from Philadelphia, visited the site briefly in 1908 but chose not to conduct excavations. Later, both the Works Progress Administration and the Lower Mississippi Valley Survey failed to investigate Toltec.

The first modern, professional archaeology conducted at the site was not undertaken until 1966, when Charles R. McGimsey led a nine-day excavation of Mound C with the help of the University of Arkansas Museum and the Arkansas Archeological Society. Toltec was placed on the National Register of Historic Places in 1973, and two years later the site was purchased by the state, to be developed as a park jointly managed by the Arkansas Department of Parks and Tourism and the Arkansas Archeological Survey. In 1978, Toltec was declared a National Historic Landmark after a long-term research plan for the site had been implemented by Martha Ann Rolingson, who began by recording the remaining features at the site. Between 1978 and 1981, extensive excavations were undertaken in several areas of Toltec, and this information, together with what had been recorded about the site in the nineteenth century, has provided insights into the history of this early contemporary of Cahokia.

History

Toltec was an important ceremonial center and the primary site of a local settlement hierarchy that included smaller mound sites and nonmound hamlets and homesteads. As few as fifty to one hundred people lived at Toltec. The majority of the chiefdom's population lived in the surrounding area, in the floodplain and in the higher country along the tributaries of the Arkansas River. People lived in scattered homesteads, but often built several houses together in order to pool their resources and provide an extra measure of security for their family members. A few clusters large enough to be considered small towns included one or more mounds. There seems to have been a chiefdom associated with each of the three bayous that drained the basin, and a similar pattern likely was in place for the rest of the culture area, though Toltec was by far the largest multimound site built by Plum Bayou peoples.

Toltec exhibited definite signs of social stratification, but unlike their emerging Mississippian neighbors, the leaders of Toltec were not buried with a great display of exotic grave goods, though Toltec chiefs did possess small amounts of copper, marine shell, and galena. In addition, a variety of mineral pigments, platform pipes, and deer-bone gorgets and hairpins have been found. It is apparent that although the site was populated only by elite lineages, it served a ceremonial purpose for the surrounding communities. The labor used to construct the mounds, ditch, and embankment (more than was needed to erect all the rest of the Plum Bayou mounds combined) was drawn from those communities, though it does not appear that the engineers at Toltec had any coercive power over the laborers. Instead, it is likely that the elite served as religious leaders and were thought to possess esoteric knowledge from which the rest of society could benefit.

The space delineated by the earth embankment at Toltec was considered sacred, and the man-made landscape within was not only an impressive engineering feat, but also an expression of the inhabitants' conception and understanding of the universe. The mounds were arranged in correspondence with certain celestial events. As Martha Rolingson so concisely stated, "A person standing on Mound A saw the sun rise over Mound B on the summer solstice, June 21, and rise over Mound H on the equinoxes, March 21 and September 21. Standing on Mound H, an observer saw the sun set over Mound B at the summer solstice and Over Mound A on the equinoxes. From Mound E, the North Star could be seen directly above Mound A." The mounds were not used as a calendar, however, but as a kind of "map" that served as a physical reminder of the sacred order of the universe and the elites' place within that sacred order. The mounds and plazas at the site were laid out with a standard unit of measure, 47.5 meters (approximately 154 feet), though it is not known how that unit was arrived at or what symbolic meaning it held, if any, for the people of Toltec. (The unit has come to be called the Toltec Module.) In any case, much foresight and planning went into the design of what was clearly the most important and influential site within the Plum Bayou culture area.

Plum Bayou culture, which lasted from approximately 650 to 1050, was found within the Arkansas and White River basins and is a distinct northern variant of the Coles Creek culture, which predominated in the lower Mississippi Valley. Both Plum Bayou and Coles Creek were contemporaneous with the emerging Mississippian culture of the American Bottom. Although Plum Bayou peoples shared many characteristics with their northern neighbors, the people resisted a wholesale adoption of Mississippian ways. They did not become dependent on corn agriculture, aggrandize their leaders with great displays of wealth, or adopt technological advancements such as shell-tempered pottery. They were also different from their Coles Creek cousins to the south, among which no equivalent of Toltec ever emerged.

Toltec reached its maximum size, and presumably the height of its regional influence, around 900. In the ensuing century and a half, Cahokia rose to prominence and began to exert a strong influence throughout the greater Mississippi Valley. Toltec's neighbor to the west, a polity that became the Mississippian chiefdom known as Spiro, was heavily influenced by the developments at Cahokia, and that development may have altered its relationship with Toltec. Cahokia's influence was evident also to the northeast, just beyond the boundaries of Plum Bayou culture on the far side of Crowleys Ridge in the Mississippi Delta portion of Arkansas. Yet for unknown reasons, the people of Toltec were less inclined than their neighbors to welcome the influence of Cahokia. Ultimately, the ceremonial centers of the Plum Bayou area were abandoned, and the people who occupied them migrated to unknown destinations. After a hiatus during which the area was virtually uninhabited, Mississippian peoples settled in the region.

Ocmulgee National Monument

Ocmulgee National Monument is a large, sprawling, wooded site near the heart of Macon, Georgia, bordered by the Ocmulgee River and one of its tributaries, Walnut Creek. The park features the remains of the earliest recognized chiefdom in the state, as well as those of later Creek Indians who lived near an English trading post that was erected on the site in the late seventeenth century. Approximately two miles south along the Ocmulgee

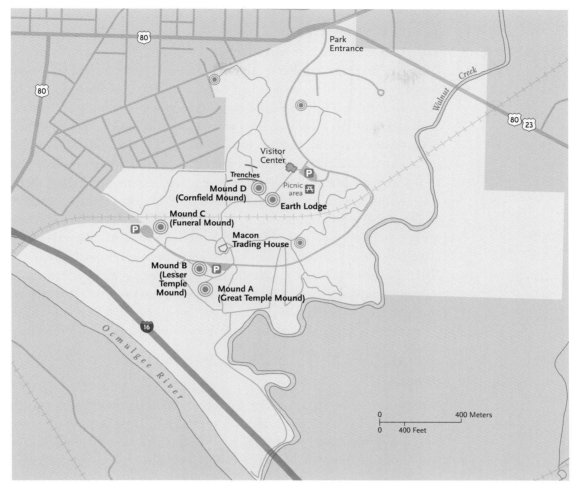

OCMULGEE NATIONAL MONUMENT

River, the monument includes a tract of land that contains the Lamar site, the capital of a chiefdom encountered by Hernando de Soto and his army in 1540. The main attraction at the park is the Mississippian site referred to as Macon Plateau, a 173-acre town that was occupied from approximately 1100 to 1200. The Macon Plateau site contains a significant number of mounds, several of them quite large. Nearly all appear to have been built in multiple stages, but a detailed chronology of mound use and construction at the site remains to be worked out. Eight mounds have undergone some degree of excavation, and most have yielded evidence of summit architecture. Those mounds as well as the other features of the site can be viewed along a series of paths that begin at the park's museum. Highlights include the opportunity to enter the reconstructed earth lodge and to climb to the top of the Great Temple Mound.

Location

The Macon Plateau site is located on a geographic feature of the same name, a relatively flat area of the normally hilly Piedmont that sits directly on the fall line of the Ocmulgee River. Above the fall line, the river channel is more constricted than below, where the floodplains reach a width of about two and a half miles. The people of Macon Plateau had easy access to the resources of both the Piedmont and the Coastal Plain. The Piedmont section of the river and nearby creeks contained shoals that were exploited for fish such as channel catfish, largemouth bass, and gar. Freshwater mussels and turtles were eaten as well. The upland hills of the Piedmont provided excellent hunting grounds for deer, bear, and raccoon as well as turkey, bobwhite, and passenger pigeon. A number of important wild foods were gathered from the woods, including pecans, hickory nuts, and persimmons. The wide plains just below the site offered abundant stands of river cane, the most productive farming soils in the vicinity, and a climate well suited for taking advantage of the topsoil (up to three feet deep) that lay along the margins of the river. In addition, the Macon Plateau site sits atop a forty-nine-foot escarpment from which the people of the town were safe from flooding and could more easily defend their houses from attack.

Features

MOUND A. Also known as the Great Temple Mound, Mound A measures 979 square feet at its base and is 49 feet tall; it appears much larger because it sits on the edge of the escarpment. Thus, from the perspective of the floodplain the mound rises more than ninety feet. Originally, the Great Temple Mound included a terrace on its western side and three ascending ramps, but today the summit is reached by means of a wooden staircase that offers an excellent view of the floodplain below, especially in the late fall and winter. Testing has yet to be done, but as its name suggests, Mound A presumably served as the foundation for both chiefly residences and temples. In addition, it appears as if the summit edge may have included an earthen berm, a small curb whose purpose is unknown. Similar "curbs" were sometimes built up around the edge of plazas as a result of sweeping them clean. Limited testing has suggested that the mound was built in at least five stages.

MOUND B. Mound B, known as the Lesser Temple Mound, is a ten-foot-tall platform mound located approximately 295 feet north of Mound A. Most of the mound was destroyed in 1834 by one of the four railroad cuts that pass through the site, though it has since been reconstructed. Little is known about Mound B beyond its having been built in four stages. It is assumed that summit architecture existed.

MOUND C. Mound C is a flat-topped conical mound located northwest of the Great Temple Mound. Mound C, also known as the Funeral Mound, was built in seven stages, each stage containing burials as well as evidence of architecture. It appears as if each summit was crowned with a mortuary house. When first recorded in the late nineteenth century, the Funeral Mound was thirty-nine feet tall with a summit diameter of about eighty-two feet, which could be reached via a ramp on the western side of the mound.

MOUND D. Mound D, 6.5 feet tall with a base of 220 feet by 51 feet, is located well to the north of the Great Temple Mound and is not visible from its summit. It appears as though Mound D was built in a single construction episode and was capped with a thick layer of clay. The mound's oval-shaped summit was crowned with multiple buildings. One referred to as Terrace House was rebuilt at least once and seems to have been coupled with a structure referred to as the Granary. The remains of a building were discovered under the mound, and the building rested on top of what had previously been an agricultural field, which is why Mound D is more commonly referred to as the Cornfield Mound.

Great Temple Mound at Ocmulgee National Monument. It measures 979 square feet at its base and is 49 feet tall, but appears even taller because it is located on the edge of an escarpment above the floodplain of the Ocmulgee River.

The reconstructed Earth Lodge at Ocmulgee National Monument, which visitors may enter.

EARTH LODGE. One of the most prominent features at Ocmulgee National Monument is the reconstructed Earth Lodge. Visitors can enter the Earth Lodge and view the excavated interior, which includes a clay bench encircling the room as well as a central fire hearth and a raised clay platform shaped like a bird of prey with a forked-eye design. Discovered underneath a three-foot-tall circular mound in the 1930s, these features were interpreted to be the remains of a sod-covered earth lodge that had burned and collapsed. That interpretation now seems mistaken. Many Mississippian structures were earth embanked, and their walls and ceilings were regularly plastered with clay, which explains the presence of the earth and burnt clay that was interpreted as the remains of a complete earthen mantle. Sod, however, was not readily available in the region. Further, the southern climate was too wet for sod to have been an effective roof covering. It is still a magnificent structure, however, and the remains on the inside clearly indicate that it was an important ceremonial feature of the Macon Plateau site.

MACON TRADING HOUSE. The Macon Trading House was a small stockade enclosing a handful of structures built by the English for the purpose of conducting trade with the Creek Indians. All the datable artifacts associated with the trading house are from 1690 to 1715, part of the earliest period of trade between the Creek and the English. Trade such as this was partly responsible for the destruction of the Mississippian world, a subject covered in chapter 6.

Research

The earliest known written reference to the mounds at Ocmulgee is found in a 1736 report by one of James Oglethorpe's Rangers, who patrolled the Georgia frontier in the decades following the colony's founding. The famous naturalist William Bartram penned a much fuller description in his *Travels*. He passed the site in 1774 while traveling along the Lower Creek Trading Path:

> On the east banks of the Oakmulge, this trading road runs nearly two miles through ancient Indian fields, which are called the Oakmulge fields: they are the rich low lands of the river. On the heights of these low grounds are yet visible monuments, or traces, of an ancient town, such as artificial mounts or terraces, squares and banks, encircling considerable areas. Their old fields and planting land extend up and down the river, fifteen or twenty miles from this site.

Charles C. C. Jones, a Savannah lawyer turned archaeologist, included the first "scholarly" account of Ocmulgee in his book *Antiquities of the Southern Indians*, published in 1873.

Modern archaeological research at Macon Plateau began in the early 1930s as a government-funded work-relief project. The work at Ocmulgee was made possible by a number of prominent Macon citizens along with Carl Vinson, a Georgia congressman who lobbied vigorously for the government to include Macon in its Works Progress Administration plans. Among the Macon citizens who promoted the idea was General Walter Harris, who not only wrote letters to the Smithsonian Institution in Washington concerning the possible importance of the Macon Plateau site, but also helped form the Georgia Society for Archaeology.

Soon after its founding, the society was instrumental in obtaining the status of national monument for Ocmulgee, an honor bestowed in 1934. After the site officially became the Ocmulgee National Monument, plans were begun to develop the monument for the public. In 1937, a Civilian Conservation Corp workforce of 250 men was assigned to Ocmulgee, and among the projects they completed was the reconstruction of the Earth Lodge, still a centerpiece of the monument. After World War II, the development of Ocmulgee continued with the building of a museum, which has been updated several times since it first opened. In addition, stairs were added to the Great Temple Mound, numerous trails were constructed, and several markers were erected.

The Earth Lodge at Ocmulgee, which was excavated in the 1930s and reconstructed by a Civilian Conservation Corps crew. Visitors can enter the lodge today and view the uncovered remains of the original building. (Courtesy National Park Service, Southeast Archeological Center)

Archaeological work at Ocmulgee took place under the direction of Arthur Randolph Kelly, a Harvard-trained archaeologist who had previously worked at Cahokia. Kelly was given one undergraduate assistant, James Ford (who would later become a famous southeastern archaeologist), and about two hundred untrained workers, though eventually he would have up to seven hundred, many of whom were former textile mill employees. With so many available workers, Depression-era archaeology crews could excavate large areas and amass huge collections of artifacts that, along with the field notes, have been preserved and are available for modern scholars to study. Such large-scale archaeology, however, presented difficulties with organization and efficiency. Kelly tackled this problem by selecting a number of men he deemed particularly suitable and then training them in archaeology during the early evening hours after work. These men were given larger responsibility for the excavation, becoming crew foremen and laboratory assistants. Throughout the 1930s, Kelly and his workers excavated many of the features at Ocmulgee, including the Macon Plateau site and the Lamar site, and investigated several other sites in the vicinity.

Archaeological work at Ocmulgee was halted with the onset of World War II. Kelly went on to become head of the Anthropology Department at the University of Georgia in Athens, and relatively little archaeological work has been done at the site since. Some excavation was done in the 1960s as a result of the construction of Interstate 16, and a small area was tested in 1974

The Southeastern Archaeological Conference at Ocmulgee National Monument in 1939. The site's lab and collections were among the most important in the South during the mid-twentieth century. (Courtesy National Park Service, Southeast Archeological Center)

when air-conditioning was installed in the Earth Lodge. Perhaps the most interesting find since the days of the Depression was a cache of unworked shell of the variety used to make cups for use in black drink ceremonies. The cache was discovered near Mound C before the installation of utility lines.

Despite the cessation of fieldwork, Ocmulgee continued to play a prominent role in southern archaeology. The lab and collections at Ocmulgee were among the most important in the South during the mid-twentieth century. The national monument was the original home of the Southeastern Archaeological Center, which was eventually relocated to Tallahassee, and has hosted several annual meetings of the Southeastern Archaeological Conference and the Society for Georgia Archaeology. In 1986 the lab at Ocmulgee was renamed the Charles H. Fairbanks Memorial Lab in commemoration of the archaeologist who excavated the Funeral Mound. Today, the site continues to host many educational activities for schools and private groups.

History

One of the most intriguing aspects of Ocmulgee is the origin of the Macon Plateau peoples. The Lamar site, which was occupied in the Late Mississippian period, and the Macon Trading House, which was built about 1690 by English deerskin and slave traders, are both clearly related to the historic Creek peoples. The Macon Plateau site, on the other hand, seems to have been occupied by a completely different group. It was once believed that the Mississippian way of life spread throughout the Ancient South as a result of a wave of conquest and migration originating from the Mississippi Valley. It has since become clear that the Mississippian transformation was the result of a spread of technology, organizational principles, and ideology rather than a spread of people. The Macon Plateau site, however, may represent a case of long-distance migration, though not necessarily of conquest.

The pottery discovered at Macon Plateau and its affiliated villages is unlike pottery found anywhere else in Georgia. Instead, it appears to be related to the ceramics of eastern Tennessee, which may indicate that the Macon Plateau peoples either came from that area to found their chiefdom or migrated there after they abandoned Ocmulgee. It is also important to note that after its abandonment in the early thirteenth century, the Macon Plateau site was never reoccupied during the Mississippian period, something counter to normal Mississippian practice. The Late Mississippian Lamar site was established in the fifteenth century, two miles south of Macon Plateau in an inferior location in the floodplain of the Ocmulgee River. Why was the long-abandoned Macon Plateau site not used, since it was clearly a better-suited location? Perhaps the peoples of the Lamar site recognized it as the remains of an alien culture and avoided the place.

No matter the origins of its people, the Macon Plateau site was first occupied around 1100, and it appears that construction began on Mounds A and B, the Great Temple Mound, and the Lesser Temple Mound when the site was founded. As Mounds A and B were enlarged in the following decades, Mound D, the Cornfield Mound, and the Earth Lodge were begun. In addition, a stockade and moat surrounding the mounds and a residential district — a total area of about thirty-seven acres — were constructed sometime early in the site's history. It seems that Mounds A and B formed one ceremonial precinct, presumably with a plaza, and Mound D and the Earth Lodge formed another.

Despite the apparent architectural grandeur of its capital, the Macon Plateau chiefdom was small in size and regional influence. Seven sites within about five miles of Ocmulgee contain Macon Plateau pottery and are clearly subordinate villages. It follows that Macon Plateau was a simple chiefdom exerting control over a handful of villages with a total population somewhere between a few hundred and perhaps two thousand. Population is difficult to estimate because most of the excavation at Macon Plateau has been related to the mounds; very little is known about the site's domestic structures. It is clear, however, that substantial community labor could be mobilized, as evidenced by the mounds, stockade, and moat. Yet the level of wealth seen at places such as Cahokia, Etowah, and Moundville is missing at Macon Plateau.

One hundred fifty burials have been recovered from the site, representing both prehistoric and historical occupations. This small sample set, which was studied in the early 1980s, has yielded some tantalizing clues to the health and the wealth of the Macon Plateau peoples. The most elaborate burials occurred in Mound C, the Funeral Mound. Some of the earliest burials were contained within log tombs and may have been for members of the chiefdom's founding lineage. One of the burials included the most fascinating artifact yet discovered at the site — a headpiece made out of native copper and the jaw of a mountain lion. Perhaps it was even worn by the first chief of Macon Plateau. The majority of burial goods were unremarkable, however — mostly shell beads but also a few gorgets, spoons, cups, and hairpins.

The prehistoric burials contain little evidence of nutritional stress, despite the people's lack of beans to complement their corn and squash. It is thus possible that the apparent lack of differentiation in wealth was reflected in a more equitable division of nutritional resources as well, something one might expect in a relatively small chiefdom. It is equally plausible that the prehistoric burials recovered so far represent only the elite members of the chiefdom and that nutritional stress was widespread in the general populace, a common occurrence in the Mississippian world before the introduction of beans in the thirteenth century. In either case, healed fractures evident in some of the burials, along with the presence of a stockade and moat, indicate a level of endemic violence.

At some point during the site's occupation, the stockade wall was taken down or allowed to deteriorate without being rebuilt. Three mounds were built outside the wall, most likely after it stopped being used. The mounds within the stockade, including Mounds A and B, fell into disuse, but it is not known whether that neglect occurred before or after the construction of the other mounds. All that is certain is that about a century after its founding, the Macon Plateau chiefdom foundered for unknown reasons, and by 1200, its seat of power had been abandoned and would not be reoccupied until the late seventeenth century.

During the sixteenth century, the Lamar site, just to the south of Macon Plateau, served as the capital of a small chiefdom known as Ichisi. When Hernando de Soto's expedition entered the territory of Ichisi, it was greeted with a protocol that was encountered repeatedly on the journey. The one-eyed chief sent messengers bearing gifts to greet the army before it reached the capital town, including mulberry fiber shawls, suede leather made from deerskins, and food in the form of cornbread and wild onions. The people of Ichisi ferried the Spaniards across the Ocmulgee River, and at the capital the chief presented Soto with additional food and fifteen prisoners of war to serve as porters. He also provided the army with a guide, who led them farther east.

CHAPTER FOUR
THE MIDDLE MISSISSIPPIAN
PERIOD, AD 1200–1400

T HE THIRTEENTH AND fourteenth centuries have justifiably been referred to as the high point of Mississippian culture, the period of its greatest geographic extent. Cahokia attained its peak near the beginning of this period, as did many other large and impressive Mississippian chiefdoms, including Etowah, Moundville, Spiro, and Winterville. Mississippian artwork, including a set of "international" symbols based on the cosmology of Cahokia, reached the height of its development between 1200 and 1400 as well. In addition, one of the common problems of the previous period was somewhat mitigated — the adoption of beans added much-needed protein to the diets of commoners, especially where large populations were densely settled.

Although the rulers of Cahokia managed to maintain an uneasy peace in the American Bottom and surrounding regions for more than two hundred years, Cahokia's political strength began to wane during the thirteenth century, and new polities developed near the confluence of the Mississippi and Ohio Rivers and in the Missouri Bootheel region to the south. (See the box feature Towosahgy State Historic Site, page 111.) In stark contrast to the political character of the eleventh and twelfth centuries, which one archaeologist has referred to as the "Pax Cahokiana," Middle Mississippian chiefdoms developed in a political atmosphere of conflict and violence. For example, between 1200 and 1400 at least twenty-five large, fortified towns were founded in extreme southeast Missouri, and there is clear evidence that several were sacked and burned. Even the rulers of mighty Cahokia were forced to live behind walls; they continued to export the idea of Cahokia despite the fact their hegemony was beginning fail. They may even have pursued this "missionary" work with increased intensity.

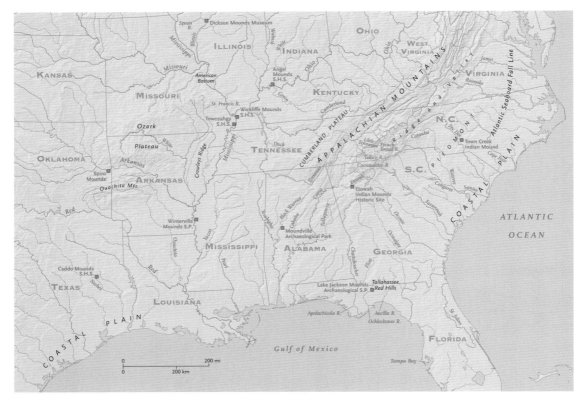

MIDDLE MISSISSIPPIAN SITES

The Mid-South was dominated during the Middle Mississippian period by the chiefdom at Etowah, which appears to have used Cahokian cosmology to legitimize its rulers. In fact, the famous Rogan plates recovered from Mound C at Etowah were probably crafted at Cahokia, perhaps reaching Georgia as part of a standard diplomatic package. (See figures on page 153.) Etowah in turn attempted to impose its hegemony in the region — the copper plates unearthed at Jackson Mounds in Florida may well have been made at Etowah. (See the box feature Lake Jackson Mounds Archaeological State Park, page 112.) In the Deep South, Moundville was clearly the most important polity, its political dominance extending almost three hundred kilometers east and west. To the west there were no large chiefdoms before reaching the territory of Winterville in the Yazoo Basin, and to the east the first formidable polity was Etowah. The relationships that existed between these chiefdoms remain to be worked out.

The adoption of the Mississippian way of life throughout the Ancient South led to an increase in competition between chiefdoms, perhaps in part as a way to control trade. Evidence of the increasing level of violence is

PHOTO, PAGES 108–9: Mound A at Winterville, which rises to a height of fifty-six feet. (Mississippi Department of Archives and History)

The Towosahgy site is near East Prairie, Missouri, in Mississippi County. It includes remains from the Early and Middle Mississippian periods (approximately 900 to 1350) and was originally known as Beckwith's Fort, named for a nineteenth-century owner of the property. Towosahgy, which contains the remnants of seven mounds, was once surrounded by a ditch, an earthen embankment, and a wooden stockade. The site seems to have been the capital town of a small chiefdom that included two smaller administrative centers and a population spread throughout the area in homesteads. Today Towosahgy is maintained as a state historic site and is on the National Register of Historic Places. The sixty-four-acre site, reached by a gravel road, nestles amid a broad expanse of fields. A series of ten kiosks helps explain the site and its history. Although Towosahgy was first excavated in the nineteenth century and has been the focus of many archaeological digs between the 1960s and 1980s, no comprehensive account of the site's archaeology has been published.

Towosahgy is located in the Missouri Bootheel region in an area known as the Cairo Lowlands, an alluvial plain near the confluence of the Ohio and Mississippi Rivers. During the Mississippian period, the area was very swampy and habitation sites were invariably located on the highest ground available. Towosahgy sits atop Pinhook Ridge, a six-mile-long point-bar deposit from an old channel of the Mississippi. It was the only place within miles that was not inundated by the great flood of 1882. The eastern boundary of the site was a bluff overlooking the cypress swamps that once surrounded Towosahgy, and the southeast corner sloped down to a slough connected to a bayou. Today both the slough and the bayou have been drained, and because of road construction, the bluff no longer appears as high as it once did. Towosahgy is near Big Oak Tree State Park, one of the few places left where old-growth bottomland forest and cypress swamps can still be seen.

The most imposing remnants left at Towosahgy are the mounds. Of the seven mounds at the site, four retain a measure of their original stature. Mound A is a platform mound that rises to a height of about twenty feet. Mound B is a smaller platform and, unlike the others, is oriented to the cardinal directions. Mounds C and D, located to the west of A and B, are both conical mounds. Mounds E, F, and G form a line along the eastern edge of the site, but all three have been severely diminished in size over the years. Near Mound A was a borrow pit that held water almost continually before canals were added to drain more of the surrounding area for farming. There were likely some smaller borrow pits that have since been filled to form level fields. The embankment, bastioned wall, and moat that protected Towosahgy surrounded the town on three sides, with the bluff forming the fourth. They were expanded at least two or three times to accommodate a growing population.

View from the summit of twenty-foot-tall Mound A, looking across the plaza of Towosahgy to the smaller Mound B. (Towosahgy State Historic Site, Missouri State Parks, Missouri DNR)

Lake Jackson Mounds Archaeological State Park in northern Florida contains three of the original seven mounds that composed the capital town of the Apalachee chiefdom. The site is located in the Red Hills of the Florida Panhandle, an upland area between the Aucilla and Ochlockonee Rivers. Although the region has little in the way of developed bottomlands, it boasts many small patches of excellent soil and is well watered. Visitors to the park can climb all three mounds; the largest two have decks on their summits that can be reached by staircases, and the other is too small to need stairs. A number of kiosks explaining a little about the site have been installed, along with picnic tables and a quarter-mile nature trail. There is no interpretive center. In addition to the mounds, the remains of a gristmill dam and a dyke that date to the antebellum period can be seen.

The Lake Jackson site was occupied between approximately 1100 and 1500, when it was the pre-eminent town within a large chiefdom that comprised a 1,600-square-mile territory bounded east and west by the Aucilla and Ochlockonee. Lake Jackson was populated by elite lineages and their retainers. The commoners lived in small homesteads spread throughout the chiefdom wherever a suitable patch of soil was found. It is evident that the chiefdom feared no outside foes — not even the mound sites were walled — and in fact, all of the surrounding societies respected the military might of the Apalachees. By the time Hernando de Soto passed through the area in 1539–40, Lake Jackson's star had faded, and the site had been abandoned in favor of a new capital. In its heyday, Lake Jackson was composed of six platform mounds and one conical mound located around one or possibly two plazas. The largest remaining mound is 278 feet by 312 feet at its base, and rises to a height of 36 feet.

Very little archaeology has been done here except on one of the mounds, so the precise details of its occupational history are unknown. In 1975, Mound Three was being sold for fill dirt, but B. Calvin Jones of the Florida Bureau of Archaeological Research managed to perform a salvage excavation of the mound before it was destroyed. Jones discovered it had been built and used between 1240 and 1476. The mound eventually rose to a height of fifteen feet in a series of twelve construction stages, each of which was crowned by a building. The floors of the buildings were used to bury twenty-four people, children and adults, along with a single dog. Bodies were placed in pits three to six feet deep, with split-log "lids." At least some of those buried were placed on litters and were interred with a fantastic array of grave goods. Those items were made of local and imported raw materials, and some of the artifacts were almost certainly imported as finished products.

Shell and pearl beads were common, as were columella pendants and gorgets. Two gorgets were engraved with birdlike creatures akin to the Falcon Warrior. Other artifacts included bone hairpins inlaid with copper, shark-tooth spangles, a galena belt fastener, copper and stone celts, all types of pipes (including a variety of effigy pipes), whelk-shell cups, a stone palette and ochre, chunkey stones, a mica mirror backed with galena, and copper pendants and hair ornaments. Perhaps the most impressive artifacts found at the site were the repoussé copper plates made by cold-hammering copper ore into thin sheets that were riveted together, embossed, and backed with split cane. (The designs were beaten into the plates; hence the description "repoussé," or "pushed back.") Four were found in three burials. One burial contained two plates: one featuring a twenty-one-inch Falcon Warrior lay over a plate embossed with a foot-long image of a bird. The other two plates were buried separately, one a twenty-inch Falcon Warrior and the other a seventeen-inch Falcon Warrior. At the head of another burial was a stack of five copper cutouts of falcons.

found in the common practice of fortifying towns, especially mound centers, and the high prevalence of war motifs on artifacts of the period. Although violence was depicted on artwork of the Early Mississippian period, the increase in its use is obvious to even the most casual observer. At the same time, images of women and horticultural products were reduced to almost nil. The most successful leaders of the period surrounded themselves with exotic riches, some of which likely came directly from Cahokia. Sometimes they donned their finery and cloaked themselves in the image of the Falcon Warrior, a powerful symbol of leadership and warrior might in the Mississippian world. (See the right figure on page 48.) In fact, representations of the falcon warrior are found throughout the Ancient South during this period, as images in art and as artifacts worn by chiefs. When these chiefs died, they were buried with their riches in the most ostentatious displays of wealth discovered outside of Cahokia. Although little exists in the way of indisputable proof, it seems likely that the Middle Mississippian period represented the zenith of a chief's ability to wield military power and coerce subjects with the implied threat of force.

As the period wore on, internal and external stresses began to take their toll on the chiefdoms. When the trade network was disturbed by war during the fourteenth century, chiefs may have had too much difficulty maintaining their elaborate displays of wealth and perhaps the confidence of their subjects as well. Adding to these difficulties was the climatic downturn referred to as the Little Ice Age, which resulted in unpredictably early and cold winters that played havoc with crops. After a slow decline, Cahokia was abandoned by 1350, and Etowah was deserted about 1375 as the result of a military attack that left the capital in ashes. Other impressive Middle Mississippian chiefdoms such as Spiro and Moundville continued to operate into the fifteenth century, but in a much reduced form.

Angel Mounds State Historic Site

Angel Mounds State Historic site in Evansville, Indiana, was once home to a population of up to three thousand Mississippian peoples who lived within the stockade wall of the 100-acre town between approximately 1200 and 1450. During the course of many archaeological investigations, almost 4 percent of the site has been excavated, and more than two million artifacts have been unearthed. The remains of eleven earthen mounds are preserved at the site, though many had been damaged before coming under the stewardship of the state. In addition to the mounds, the site includes a partial reconstruction of the wall that once enclosed the town. Visitors can view artifacts excavated from the site and learn the story of Angel Mounds by touring the excellent

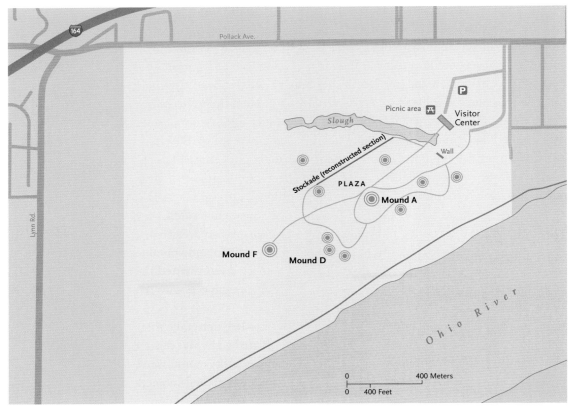

ANGEL MOUNDS STATE HISTORIC SITE

on-site museum. Highlights include the negative-painted pottery produced there during the Mississippian period. (In negative painting, a design is left uncolored, and the surrounding area is painted or pigmented.)

Location

Located just upstream from the confluence of the Green and Ohio Rivers in southwestern Indiana, the Angel Mounds site sits on a terrace above the Ohio but is separated from the river by a "slack water chute and a narrow island" known as Three-Mile Island, which is today part of the state of Kentucky. A slough surrounds the other three sides of the D-shaped town, which was regularly subjected to floods if the historical record is any indication. In ninety-one years, the first terrace (where few houses were located) flooded sixty-three times, the plaza and adjacent residential areas nineteen times, the highest areas of the site six times, and the entire site with the exception of the top of Mound A, which stands forty-two feet tall, twice. Most floods in the area occurred between December and March, when no crops were

planted in the fields. Despite the inconvenience of seasonal inundations, the site was favorable for Mississippian settlement for several reasons.

Angel was the northernmost extension of the range of several southern plant and animal species, including pecan trees, cottonmouth snakes, alligator snapping turtles, bald cypresses, persimmons, and Carolina parakeets. Large canebrakes grew close to Angel Mounds, and the people had access to prairies like those near Cahokia. In addition, southwestern Indiana is the only place within the surrounding region where the rivers — the Wabash, White, and Ohio — have a pronounced meander belt. Another appealing characteristic of the Lower Ohio Valley was the abundance of salt licks and saline springs. The people of Angel exploited several of those locations and probably traded salt to the south in return for foodstuffs to supplement the produce of their own fields.

Located on the periphery of the Ancient South, Angel received an average of only 186 frost-free days a year and forty-five inches of rain — not ideal for Mississippian farming, but acceptable. Even minor fluctuations in rainfall or the timing of early and late frosts, however, could put the people of Angel at great risk. Wild foods such as pawpaws, cherries, persimmons, and nuts were an important supplement to agricultural crops. Yet in spite of their easy access to the river and to sloughs and ponds to the north, the residents of Angel do not appear to have relied heavily on fish. On the other hand, freshwater mussels were gathered in abundance five miles upriver at shoals adjacent to a small village allied to the Angel chiefdom. Hunters pursued deer and small mammals as well as turkeys, passenger pigeons, and a variety of waterfowl — the standard fare of the Ancient South.

Features

MOUND A. Forty-two feet high, Mound A is the largest at the site and one of the largest north of Mexico. Test excavations were conducted on the mound in the summer of 1955, but relatively little is known of the massive earthwork. There are no borrow pits near Mound A, and the earth used in its construction may have been taken from Three-Mile Island. The base of the mound is 644 by 415 feet, from which rise two terraces. Evidence suggests that a mortuary house for the preparation of the dead was built on the first terrace, and the chiefly residence stood atop the upper terrace, which measured 270 by 130 feet — about 30,000 square feet. In addition to the house of the chief, the second terrace contained a conical mound that rose 14.5 feet from the southeast corner, the highest point on Mound A.

MOUND D. Mound D was probably never taller than three feet, but it did contain noteworthy artifacts — twelve skulls arranged in a circle within a three-foot-diameter stone cist (burial chamber). A thirteenth skull was placed in the center of the circle, along with two thighbones. The purpose of the feature remains unknown.

MOUND F. Mound F, the second-largest mound at the site, was completely excavated and rebuilt by Works Progress Administration (WPA) laborers beginning in 1940. It stood to the west of Mound A, and the intervening space was used as a public plaza. Despite having had crops cultivated on its surface, Mound F was fairly well preserved at the time of its excavation, and investigators were able to discover much about this particular earthwork. It was constructed in three or four stages, eventually reaching a height of thirteen feet. The summit of each mound stage served as the foundation for a temple. In fact, the results of the excavations on the summit of Mound F have given scholars one of their clearest archaeological views of the multiroom Mississippian temples described in the accounts of early Spanish explorers. The mound was erected over what had originally been the location of a substantial ground-level building from early in the occupational history of the site.

STOCKADE. The Angel Mounds site was surrounded on at least three sides by a stockade that measured approximately 7,300 feet, with bastions placed every 120 feet. The town wall was rebuilt or repaired two or three times, so defense appears to have been a periodic concern throughout the occupation of the town. For much of Angel's history, an interior wall branched from the main stockade and enclosed much of the eastern side of the site, including eight of the eleven mounds. Evidence of other interior walls has recently been found, but their exact dimensions and use are still unknown. The wall at the southeast corner of the village stood at a right angle to the flow of the river and was reinforced, presumably to support it in times of flood.

The main mound and plaza at Angel Mounds State Historic Site
in Indiana. (Courtesy of the Glenn A. Black Laboratory of Archaeology
and the Trustees of Indiana University)

PLAZA. There may have been multiple plazas at Angel. One was located west of mound A, and recent work has discovered another possible plaza on the east side. Archaeologists are unsure whether they were used at the same time or at different times. In addition, there may have been a small, third plaza north of Mound F and a fourth associated with Mound B.

Research

The region surrounding Angel Mounds became part of the United States in 1804 with the signing of the Treaty of Vincennes, and was first surveyed by Americans the next year. Over a century and a half later, archaeologists used a marker stone placed by the surveyors from 1805 while conducting their own mapping of the site. Although the original surveyors noted the mounds, professional investigation at Angel did not begin until much later in the nineteenth century when an Evansville, Indiana, physician sent a letter concerning the site to the Smithsonian Institution. Soon afterward Cyrus Thomas, an archaeologist at the Smithsonian, visited Angel Mounds. He published the first map of the site in 1890, showing six of the mounds and the remains of part of the stockade. A fuller and more accurate description of Angel was penned by A. H. Purdue and published in 1896.

Nothing more was written about Angel until 1937, when Eli Lilly, who had visited the site at least twice, included it in his book about the Native peoples of Indiana. In 1938 with Lilly's help, Angel was purchased by the Indiana Historical Society. Professional excavations were undertaken at the site the following year and have continued intermittently to the present day. The investigations that began in 1939 were part of a WPA project that lasted until America entered World War II. During the thirty-seven months, 277 men were employed at Angel — none of whom started with any archaeological experience. After removing fences and old buildings from the property,

Works Progress Administration (WPA) crew, Mound F excavation at Angel, 1941. Governmental work programs such as this one provided a tremendous amount of labor for archaeological projects throughout the South in the 1930s and early 1940s. (Courtesy of the Glenn A. Black Laboratory of Archaeology and the Trustees of Indiana University)

crews surveyed the site and undertook a number of projects, including test excavations on the stockade and village and an extensive investigation of Mound F.

Glenn A. Black, the archaeologist whose name is synonymous with Angel Mounds in professional circles, led the WPA project. After the war, Black began teaching at Indiana University and conducted field schools at Angel each summer from 1945 to 1954 and again each year between 1957 and 1962. Black conducted investigations of Mounds A and K in 1955. Black died in 1964; his two-volume report on Angel Mounds, which continues to be considered the quintessential work concerning the site, was published in 1967. Most of the artifacts recovered from Angel are housed at the Glenn A. Black Laboratory of Archaeology at the University of Indiana, a fitting tribute to a pioneering archaeologist. Recent research has helped sharpen our understanding of what happened at Angel between the thirteenth and fifteenth centuries, but much remains to be discovered about this chiefdom on the northeastern frontier of the Mississippian world.

History

Angel is the only mound site associated with this society, and although it was clearly home to the chiefly lineage, commoners lived within the walls of the town as well. The eastern portion of the site was the most densely occupied area at Angel, containing as many as two hundred houses at a time. The cultural remains there were found at a depth of two feet on average and were significantly thicker in some places, indicating an occupation that lasted many decades. Another habitation area was situated north of Mound A, probably an elite neighborhood, which also had a relatively thick layer of cultural debris. Other residential sections of the site had much thinner cultural deposits, and were thus likely to have been used later in the occupational history of the town and for a shorter duration. Angel was oriented in relation to the cardinal directions — a common characteristic among Mississippian towns and mound centers.

The Angel Mounds site was founded around 1200, and over the next century Mound A and its primary plaza were constructed in their entirety. Mound F and the plaza between it and Mound A were also likely begun during the first century of Angel's occupation. The eastern half of the town was given over to residential structures in two neighborhoods, one for commoners and one for elites. Angel seems to have been walled at an early stage in the site's history, perhaps from inception. The most extensive use of the Angel site, at least spatially, occurred in the fourteenth century, when many of the mounds were fully constructed and residential areas expanded, though, curiously, Mound A fell into disuse. The stockade wall was rebuilt for the final

Statue of a kneeling man carved from fluorite, discovered at Angel Mounds. Statues such as this, made of a variety of materials and usually accompanied by a female, have been found throughout the Ancient South. (Courtesy of the Glenn A. Black Laboratory of Archaeology and the Trustees of Indiana University)

time about 1325, but during the final decades of Angel's existence the site may not have been walled at all.

The chiefdom at Angel included many satellite communities within several miles of the capital town, with the farthest about twenty-five miles up-river to the east. To the west of the site was an area of sloughs and ponds cut through by former river channels, and on the high places throughout the wetland were farmsteads, the occupants of which gave allegiance to the chief at Angel. Small villages and hamlets were common in the area as well. In fact, Mississippian societies flourished throughout the region adjacent to the confluence of the Wabash and Ohio Rivers, though to the east and north lived people organized according to different principles from those of their Mississippian neighbors. Known as the Fort Ancient peoples, these societies grew corn, squash, and, eventually, beans and built plazas and walled towns, but did not erect platform mounds or enshrine sacred leaders. Despite their lack of regional, hierarchical organization, the Fort Ancient peoples (like the Oneota peoples on the periphery of Cahokia) had enough military sophistication to present a threat to Mississippian towns — the wall at Angel was likely a protection against Fort Ancient raids.

Angel was one of four known Mississippian mound sites in the Lower Ohio Valley region, the others being Kincaid, Tolu, and Wickliffe. Of those, Kincaid, located about eighty miles away in Illinois, was most similar to Angel, though larger. Despite the suggestion of some scholars, it is highly unlikely that Kincaid and Angel were part of the same chiefdom, since they were separated by 150 river miles. On the other hand, it seems quite possible that they were trading partners, or perhaps enemies. Angel received exotic items in trade — copper from the Great Lakes, fluorite and galena from Illinois, flint from Tennessee, and marine shell from the coast. Although such materials were rare at Angel, it is clear that the ruling lineage sought to justify their position in ways common to other Mississippian chiefs. Elite burials included such items as coal earplugs; human-effigy pipes, including "prisoner" pipes; perforated canine teeth, especially those of bears; and a great deal of effigy pottery. The classic Mississippian statue form of a kneeling man has also been found at Angel, carved from fluorite. It seems clear, however, that contact with Cahokia was rare or nonexistent at Angel, which may have been founded to develop a trade in salt. Whatever its political history, the chiefdom did not last into the second half of the fifteenth century, perhaps undone by the climatic upheaval of the Little Ice Age.

Wickliffe Mounds State Historic Site

Wickliffe Mounds State Historic site in Ballard County, Kentucky, protects the remains of a six-acre Mississippian village that was occupied from approximately 1100 to 1350. The village probably had a population of around three hundred people at its peak, and at one time contained at least eight mounds, four of which are still preserved. Evidence recovered from the site indicates the people of Wickliffe had at least indirect contact with Cahokia, but the nature of the relationship is unknown. Wickliffe was one of the first Mississippian villages to be founded near the confluence of the Ohio and Mississippi Rivers, an area that did not become densely populated until after Cahokia began to decline. Although Wickliffe is currently administered by the state of Kentucky, it has had a long and colorful history as a public site, opening in the 1930s as one of the first Mississippian sites to be marketed as a tourist attraction. It is also one of the rare sites where excavations can be viewed by the public. Each of the two areas at Wickliffe is protected by a building erected over the open excavation pits. Being able to view artifacts and features in situ, that is, exactly where they were located when archaeologists uncovered them, affords visitors a unique perspective on the kinds of evidence scholars use to arrive at their conclusions.

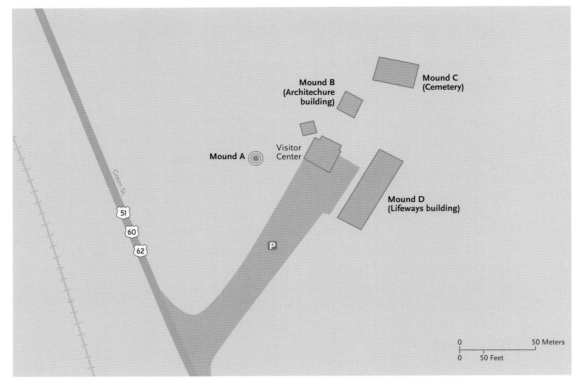

WICKLIFFE MOUNDS STATE HISTORIC SITE

A portion of the museum at Wickliffe featuring the open excavation of a domestic area at the site. Note the mural in the background. (Courtesy of Wickliffe Mounds State Historic Site)

Location

Wickliffe sits near the edge of a bluff almost fifty feet above the floodplain of the Mississippi River, which lies about a quarter of a mile away, three miles south of its confluence with the Ohio. Many things recommended this location, including proximity to the fields in the floodplain below without the danger of being flooded when the river rose. The bluff location would have been easily defensible, an important consideration, since most of the towns in this region were fortified during the thirteenth and fourteenth centuries. In addition, the bluff itself may have had an important symbolic meaning. One archaeologist has suggested the bluff may have been a "geoglyph," a landform that resembles a human creation — in this case, the head and wings of a thunderbird that, perhaps not coincidentally, pointed toward Cahokia to the northwest.

In any case, the residents of Wickliffe took advantage not only of the floodplain but the oxbow lakes and extensive bottomland forest as well. They grew corn and squash, but no evidence of beans has been recovered, presumably because they were not introduced to the area until after the site was abandoned. The early occupants of Wickliffe relied heavily on fish, particularly backwater species available in the river bottoms, where they also hunted for waterfowl. Within a century and a half, however, the residents began to rely more on the resources of the upland oak-hickory forest. Riverine fish species and freshwater mussels were still taken from streams feeding the Mississippi, but deer, turkey, and raccoon were more heavily exploited. The reason for the shift in emphasis from bottomland to upland resources is unknown, but may have been related to a change in the course of the Mississippi or, perhaps more likely, an increase in population in the area

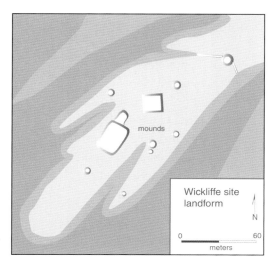

mounds

Wickliffe site
landform

N

0   60
meters

Diagram of the bluff upon which Wickliffe sits. One archaeologist has suggested the site is a geoglyph, that is, a landform that resembles a human creation, in this case the head and wings of a thunderbird. ("Diagrammatic Plan of the Wickcliffe landform," figure 6.6, as it appears in Timothy R. Pauketat, *Chiefdoms and Other Archaeological Delusions* [Lanham, Md.: AltaMira Press, 2007], 161) beginning in the thirteenth century that led to violent competition over floodplain resources.

Features

MOUND A. Mound A, also referred to as the Ceremonial Mound, is located on the west side of what was the plaza but today is occupied by the visitor center and parking lot. This platform mound was built in at least six construction stages, all of which appear to have included buildings on their summits. Because the structures lacked the domestic trash of everyday living, it is assumed they were either temples or mortuary houses where the privileged were prepared for the afterworld. Mound A is the largest remaining mound at Wickliffe. It was used throughout the site's existence, and the artifacts recovered from it have been instrumental in defining the occupational history of Wickliffe.

MOUND B (ARCHITECTURE BUILDING). The Architecture Building covers what remains of Mound B, a smaller platform mound on the north side of the visitor center. Two construction stages have been identified, but there may have been more. Evidence of buildings and domestic trash were found on both the identified summits. It is likely these structures were used by the ruling family of Wickliffe, not only because they were located on top of a mound but also because they have yielded evidence of an extraordinary number of serving dishes and only the choicest cuts of venison. Within the Architecture Building is a partial reconstruction of a wattle-and-daub house. The inside walls of the building are painted to show mound stratigraphy (the soil layers of which the mound was composed), and displays discuss construction techniques and household furnishings.

MOUND C. Mound C appears to have been a complex of three closely spaced mounds containing burials both within and between them. Most of the burials occurred between 1175 and 1250. Some people were buried soon after death in an extended position; others had their bones defleshed and bundled together; and still others may have been cremated. Some of the bodies were placed in large baskets, and others in wood or bark containers that remind scholars of the stone-lined graves found in the Cumberland region of Tennessee and in southern Illinois. Few of the estimated eight hundred to nine hundred burials had associated artifacts, though one adult female burial contained rich grave goods, including several large mussel shells, a large, well-made bowl, a squash-effigy bowl, and an owl-effigy bottle.

MOUND D (LIFEWAYS BUILDING). The Lifeways Building preserves another excavation, that of Mound D, which may have been paired mounds

connected by an earthen "saddle." Elite burials were concentrated here, and a large number of infant burials unassociated with the mound have also been recovered from this area of the site. A number of shell cups and effigy pots were recovered from Mound D, as was a cache of projectile points and chunkey stones. The presence of red cedar may indicate a burial litter. Taken together, this suite of artifacts reminds one of a provincial replica of Mound 72 from Cahokia. Mound D was completed in the period 1250–1350 and was built in a place that had previously been used as a residential area. The Lifeways Building contains a large mural depicting activities that took place at Wickliffe. In addition the building contains a large collection of displayed artifacts and a number of impressive tool replicas.

Village life at Wickliffe, a Mississippian mound site occupied between 1100 and 1350 and located in Ballard County, Kentucky, near the confluence of the Ohio and Mississippi Rivers. (Courtesy of Wickliffe Mounds State Historic Site)

Research

The Wickliffe site was part of the region included in the Jackson Purchase, which procured Chickasaw land in western Kentucky and Tennessee for the United States in 1818. The site was first investigated by R. H. Loughridge, in 1888, but it garnered little interest until the twentieth century. Wickliffe came to the attention of the general public when the southern half of the site was disturbed during a highway construction project in 1930. Fain King, an archaeological enthusiast and entrepreneur from Paducah, Kentucky, bought the site in 1932 and developed a tourist attraction that was known by

King Mounds, the name by which Wickliffe was advertised to the public for many years. The site was as much a sideshow attraction as a public archaeological site and museum. (Courtesy of Wickliffe Mounds State Historic Site)

a variety of names over the years, including King Mounds and Ancient Buried City. King exaggerated some aspects of the site and fabricated others. His attractions included not only Indian skeletons and artifacts, but also strange, Ripley's-style exhibits.

Using Don Dickson's work at Dickson Mounds in Illinois as his inspiration (see the box feature Dickson Mounds Museum, pages 128–29), King undertook an archaeological investigation of Wickliffe, conducting a number of excavations at the site between 1932 and 1939, eventually accumulating more than eighty-five thousand artifacts from his digs.

After visiting a University of Chicago field site and meeting the archaeologist Walter B. Jones (who is most famous for his work at Moundville), King began work at Wickliffe in September 1932 with the help of some of Jones's students. For unknown reasons, Jones withdrew his help shortly after the project began. This was the first of many conflicts between the archaeological establishment and King, who, despite sometimes attempting to do what was necessary to carry on "professional" work, was regarded with suspicion by contemporary archaeologists. King continued, however, to seek the advice and guidance of professionals.

In 1934, King spent part of the year studying with Faye-Cooper Cole at the University of Chicago and was soon implementing what he learned there at Wickliffe. He divided the site into a grid of five-by-five-foot squares, labeled artifacts according to their location in the grid, made drawings of the site, and took field notes. Over the next few years King and his wife, Blanche, who had also become interested in archaeology, investigated six of the mounds at

An example of human-effigy pottery discovered at Wickliffe. (Courtesy of Wickliffe Mounds State Historic Site)

Wickliffe and excavated tens of thousands of artifacts. Thus, most of what King recovered from the site was removed and labeled "professionally," though his field notes have disappeared, unfortunately, and he never wrote a site report.

In 1939 King, still feeling slighted by professionals despite all his efforts, ended his collaboration with Cole and sent home two of Cole's students who were at Wickliffe studying pottery remains. King soon gave up his attempt to become a respected archaeologist and tried unsuccessfully to give the Wickliffe site to the University of Chicago in 1941. After the war he put the site up for sale, but finding no one interested, he donated it to Western Baptist Hospital in Paducah, Kentucky. The hospital kept the site open between 1946 and 1983, but virtually no archaeology was done during that time, and no improvements were made to existing displays. In 1983, after the death of Fain King's wife, the hospital gave Wickliffe and its collections to Murray State University, in Murray, Kentucky, ushering in a new era of investigations at the site.

The university founded the Wickliffe Mound Research Center (WMRC) to study and curate the collections, and between 1984 and 1996 it tried to make sense out of the previous excavations at Wickliffe. In addition to mapping the site, the WMRC reinvestigated King's work on four mounds and undertook new excavations in the village area. Building on the limited archaeological survey work done in adjacent areas of the Ohio-Mississippi confluence and a small number of excavations at nearby mound sites, the WMRC has begun to place Wickliffe within the regional context of the Mississippian world.

DICKSON MOUNDS MUSEUM

Located near the town of Lewistown, Illinois, the Dickson Mounds Museum is adjacent to three archaeological sites: the Dickson mounds, the Myer-Dickson village site, and the Eveland village site. The museum's third-floor observation deck affords views of the Dickson mounds, but they are hardly discernible as man-made in their current form. Inside, the museum features the natural and human history of the area, with a special emphasis on the Mississippian period. The museum includes an auditorium and other meeting rooms intended for small conferences and educational outreach, along with a discovery center aimed at hands-on learning for children. The 235-acre grounds include picnic tables and a playground as well as some preserved excavations from the Eveland village site—a portion of the excavation has been left "open" for viewing and is protected by a building constructed around the excavation itself.

The mounds are located on a ninety-foot bluff above the floodplain near the confluence of the Illinois and Spoon Rivers in the central Illinois River Valley. This was the best-suited place within the vicinity to implement Mississippian subsistence practices. The valley is about four miles wide, bordered on both sides by bluffs. The soils are excellent, and oxbow lakes and other wetlands are more numerous here than in other parts of the valley. During the Medieval Warm Period, the area enjoyed a climate akin to that of the modern South. Many of the plants and animals relied upon by the people of Dickson Mounds were the same as those used in the rest of the Mississippian world, including pecans, catfish, freshwater mussels, turtles, and passenger pigeons. Today, however, the area receives only 127 frost-free days and thirty-four inches of rain a year on average, hardly conducive to the Mississippian style of life.

During the late nineteenth and early twentieth centuries, the mounds were exploited by people intent on selling their contents. Starting in 1927, however, the mounds came under the care of a well-respected amateur, Don Dickson, who was a doctor and the son of the owner of the property. Eventually, Dickson excavated and analyzed more than 250 burials. Throughout the years, the site was visited by many professional archaeologists, and Dickson's investigations generated media attention. The site was opened to the public as a tourist attraction even as research continued. Between 1960 and 1968 more than eight hundred burials were excavated, pushing the total to more than one thousand. The site, which has been under the protection of the state since 1945, has had a park and museum for decades, though the current facilities are modern.

The Dickson mounds are an overlapping series of ten burial mounds and an additional platform mound. They were used off and on over the course of four hundred years, during which time about three thousand persons were interred in the mounds. The loess soils of the area lacked the acidity normally found in southeastern soils, resulting in good bone preservation. Most of the grave goods were local

Ogden-Fettie Mound Group at Dickson Mounds. (Courtesy of Matt Hucke, used under the Creative Commons license 3.0)

and utilitarian; some were exotics: copper-covered earspools, bi-pointed knives, a Ramey knife, a three-foot-long copper rod, and marine-shell artifacts found within burials associated with the Eveland village occupation. Many common Mississippian symbols were employed, such as the forked-eye design, the long-nosed god, and the cross-in-circle motif.

Eveland, the first Mississippian village in the central Illinois Valley, was founded about 1050. It was small site, only about three acres in extent, built at the base of the bluff. Eveland was occupied for only a few decades; then a village of more than twenty acres with a population of about four hundred people was built adjacent to the Dickson mounds on the bluff top. That site is known as the Myer-Dickson village and was occupied between about 1250 and 1350. The contemporaneous Larson site, a walled village located about a mile away, was associated with the Dickson Mounds also. The decline of Myer-Dickson and Larson coincided with the decline of Cahokia, which is consistent with the idea that the sites were important components in the city's northern trade, perhaps having even been founded for that purpose.

After years of conducting its own field schools and public-outreach projects, Murray State formed the Middle Mississippi Survey in 1991 with the help of Southeast Missouri State University and others, and passed the administration of the Wickliffe site over to the state of Kentucky.

History

There was no substantial occupation at the Wickliffe site before 1100, but after 1200 the valley's population increased, and with it competition. There are several small, compact mound sites about every five to six miles along the Mississippi River in the area, apparently without buffer zones between them. Temporal data in the region are not precise enough to determine which mound sites were occupied at any given time. Thus, it is not yet possible to tell whether Wickliffe was an independently functioning chiefdom or part of a larger, regionally organized chiefdom. There is clear evidence of at least one elite lineage at Wickliffe, but it does not appear to have been greatly set apart from the rest of society, with the exception of enjoying slightly better food and pottery and slightly more elaborate burials.

A few items that marked the Mississippian elite in other parts of the Ancient South, such as chunkey stones, whelk-shell cups, and copper-covered earspools, are present in small numbers. While excavating the remains of a structure near Mounds B and C, the WMRC uncovered a painting of the cross-and-circle motif on the floor. Three shell gorgets displaying the classic Mississippian themes of the spider, woodpecker, and chunkey player have been found at Wickliffe, the styles of which hint at far-flung relationships. In addition, a Ramey-incised potsherd from Cahokia has been found at Wickliffe, along with a local imitation of the Ramey-incised style. Although no concrete evidence supports the idea that Cahokia had direct contact or control over the Wickliffe chiefdom, there are historical precedents of chiefdoms controlling territories that large. Wickliffe was founded during Cahokia's "big bang" period, and like Cahokia, it had been abandoned by the middle of the fourteenth century.

Despite uncertainty concerning the relationship between Wickliffe and Cahokia, researchers have begun to develop some understanding of the occupational history of the site.

EARLY WICKLIFFE PERIOD (1100–1175). During the Early Wickliffe period, a small settlement was clustered around the plaza. By the end of the period, the beginning stage of Mound B had been erected; it served as a platform for an elite household, presumably that of the chief. No other mounds seem to have been constructed until the Middle Wickliffe period, though important buildings likely stood where mounds were later raised. Infants from the period have been found buried in the village area, but no adult burials dating to this period have been discovered, suggesting they were interred in cemeteries located outside the town.

MIDDLE WICKLIFFE PERIOD (1175–1250). The Middle Wickliffe period saw an expansion of the village to the north and south, presumably to accommodate a growing population. Earth was added to Mound B during this period, and Mounds A and C were constructed. It was in deposits from this period that the Ramey-incised potsherd from Cahokia was discovered, and the importation of Burlington chert for the production of stone tools peaked then as well. On the summit of Mound B, the leader of Wickliffe and his family feasted on the choicest cuts of venison and enjoyed a level of prestige that would not last past the end of the period.

LATE WICKLIFFE PERIOD (1250–1350). During the Late Wickliffe period, only one mantle of earth was added to Mounds A and B, and Mound C was not used at all. Conversely, the population of the site and the area of the village expanded to their maximum sizes. Mounds D, F, and H were built, which may indicate increased competition between elite lineages, though little status differentiation is evident in Late Wickliffe burials. In any case, during the century between 1250 and 1350 the residents of the site found themselves embroiled in the fallout from the decline of Cahokia, and eventually abandoned the area altogether.

Winterville Mounds State Park

The Winterville site lies in the heart of the Mississippi Delta region near Greenville, Mississippi. It is believed to have contained as many as twenty-three mounds, but reliable information is currently available for only seventeen, eleven of which still exist within the park boundaries — the most of any of the featured sites in this book except Cahokia and Moundville. While those two sites and others such as Etowah and Spiro included dozens of examples of magnificently crafted Mississippian artifacts, Winterville has produced virtually none. This explains in part why the site has been left somewhat undisturbed by pothunters. One of the foremost reasons Winterville is still around to enjoy is the devastating flood of 1927, which deposited a huge layer of sand over the entire area, turning prime agricultural land into pasturage. Of course, the mounds were ravaged to a certain degree by the cattle, but they might have been destroyed altogether if modern farm and earthmoving equipment had been employed in the area.

Winterville appears to have been a ceremonial center used by the peoples of the surrounding region, with only the elite lineages and their servants

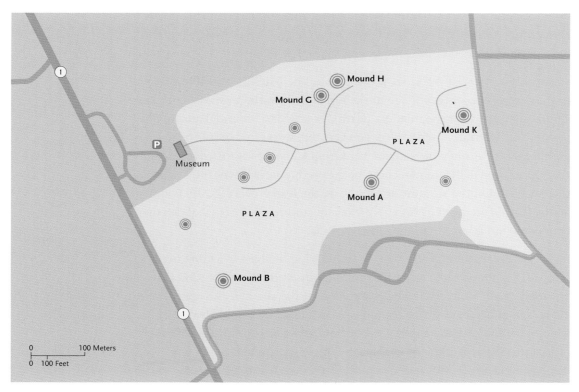

WINTERVILLE MOUNDS STATE PARK

residing permanently at the site. The majority of the population of the chief-dom lived in small homesteads scattered throughout the area on natural levees and along secondary streams. Winterville Mounds State Park, which includes a small museum, covers forty-four acres, but the boundaries of the site were larger when it was occupied by Mississippians. Today Winterville is hemmed in by roads and man-made bayous and drainage ditches. During the Mississippian period, the area surrounding the site was a maze of waterways twisting through old-growth bottomland forest the likes of which no longer exist in the Mississippi Valley, and the people of Winterville were well adapted to this watery world.

Location

Winterville is located in the Yazoo Basin about four miles north of Greenville, Mississippi, and about three miles east of the Mississippi River. The river was closer to the site when it was occupied, and the residents could access it directly by water by following a series of local creeks and bayous. In fact, the area was so wet and swampy that people rarely traveled by foot and instead relied on dugout canoes as the main mode of transportation. Like

The historic flood of the Mississippi River in 1927 inundated the Winterville site, leaving nothing but roofs and the top of mounds exposed. (From the Special Collection of the William Alexander Percy Memorial Library)

An aerial view of Winterville showing the site hemmed in by modern fields and roads. The site would have looked much different when it was occupied by Mississippians. (Mississippi Department of Archives and History)

virtually all other sites in the region, Winterville was located on a relatively high natural levee, the only suitable agricultural sites near the river before the Army Corps of Engineers began attempting to control the Mississippi. Living along natural levee ridges protected people and crops from many floods and allowed people to take advantage of the 240–300 frost-free days and 50–60 inches of rain the region enjoyed each year.

In addition to growing corn and beans in abundance, the people of the Winterville chiefdom exploited a wide variety of other plant resources, including river cane and several species of nuts and berries. Deer and turkey were hunted along the ridges, though swamp rabbits represent an unusually large percentage of the faunal remains at Winterville. The reliance on these small mammals has yet to be adequately explained. The people of Winterville regularly ate many backwater species such as catfish, alligator gar, buffalo fish, and turtles. Waterfowl such as the pintail duck played a prominent role in the diet, which is not surprising given the huge flocks of these birds and other migratory species that were available along the Mississippi flyway.

Features

MOUND A. The tallest mound at the site, Mound A rises to a height of fifty-six feet and is flanked by two plazas, an unusual arrangement in the region, seen again at only the Lake George site. There may have been two ways to reach the summit of Mound A: a ramp leading up from the northeast plaza, and perhaps a ramp leading down the northwest slope. The latter connected at ground level to a low, earthen causeway linking Mound A to the smaller Mound F.

MOUND B. Mound B, twenty-eight feet tall, formerly included a ramp descending to the plaza adjacent to the backside of Mound A. Two-thirds of the mound was erected in the initial construction stage, and the rest was added quickly in a small number of episodes. Mound B was connected by causeways to a number of smaller mounds. Sixteen burials have been recovered from Mound B. Both primary and secondary burials were represented, along with isolated skulls, and half of the deceased were interred with grave goods — fancy pottery, and stone palettes and grinders used in the production of pigment. Mounds B and S and the area between them contained more evidence of habitation than other surveyed areas of the site.

Mound A at Winterville, which rises to a height of fifty-six feet. (Mississippi Department of Archives and History)

MOUNDS G AND H. These closely spaced mounds were connected by a causeway similar to others at the site. Mound H was a standard platform mound, but Mound G appears to have been oval in shape, perhaps reminiscent of the paired mounds of Cahokia. The ground surface between the mounds was rich in cultural debris.

MOUND K. Mound K, located on the opposite side of the northeast plaza from Mound A, rises to a height of eighteen feet and was erected in as few as two construction episodes. The summit of Mound K has been tested extensively, and the remains of a number of structures were excavated, the upper levels of which contained significant cultural remains.

CAUSEWAYS. Several pairs of mounds at Winterville seem at one time to have been connected by low ridges known as causeways. The causeways were probably constructed of cultural refuse produced by the occupants of the mounds. The use and meaning of the causeways are unclear, but they may have had practical as well as symbolic functions, serving as slightly elevated walkways in an often-wet environment. They were all destroyed in the nineteenth century, as were the causeways at other Mississippian sites such as Cahokia.

PLAZAS. Winterville contained at least two plazas, one on either side of Mound A. Together these plazas measured approximately thirty-eight and a half acres, which means much of the land within Winterville Mounds State Park was part of the plaza area. Like other Mississippian plazas, the ones at Winterville were swept clean regularly, and few artifacts have been recovered from them.

Research

One of the first American plantations in the Yazoo Basin included the Winterville site within its boundaries. The plantation, established soon after the area was acquired from the Choctaws in 1820, was known as Montrose but was referred to as "Mount Rose" in the local vernacular. Following the Civil War, the plantation was aptly renamed Mound Place. The earliest written account of the site appeared in 1852, but the first lengthy description and an accompanying map were made by Ephraim Squier in 1860. Squier's map and written account are the only sources indicating the presence of the causeways mentioned above. It should be noted that Squier was a credible observer and that low causeways would not have lasted long on a working plantation. The causeways that appear twenty years later on James Hough's map of the site were probably copied from Squier, the causeways themselves having already become the victims of plowing. The first known excavations at Winterville occurred in 1869 when a riverboat captain unearthed at least forty burials; he left no written description of his work.

Clarence Bloomfield Moore, an amateur archaeologist from Philadelphia, excavated for six days at Winterville in 1907. He and five of his associates dug 150 holes (three by six by four feet) — 45 in the plazas and the rest in fifteen mounds. Moore, who had already made a name for himself by unearthing hundreds of fancy artifacts, was very disappointed with what they found at Winterville. It was probably Moore's time at Winterville that led many folks in the area to believe there was nothing of value in the mounds. Not all the locals believed the mounds were empty, however, as evidenced by a legend claiming the mounds had chambers within them. The story may have developed as the result of a former landowner digging a dairy cellar into Mound A in the late nineteenth century.

There were quite a number of WPA archaeological projects in the South during the 1930s and 1940s, in part because it was possible to work outside year-round. Winterville was not among them, though it was designated a city park in 1939. The first professional investigation of the site occurred in 1940 when both the National Park Service and Harvard University excavated at Winterville. James Ford, whose work with the pottery of the valley led to the first temporal framework for the region, Philip Phillips, and James Griffin led Harvard's Lower Mississippi Valley Survey. They surveyed the upper two-thirds of the Yazoo Basin, and their findings were included in a report released in 1951. Phillips later published an article on further investigations he undertook in the region between 1949 and 1955, and the first accurate contour map of Winterville was completed in 1949 by Albert Spaulding under the direction of Phillips. The Lake George site, another multimound and plaza town not far south of Winterville, was investigated between 1958 and 1960, helping shed light on the regional context in which Winterville developed.

In 1964, the Mississippi Archaeological Association in conjunction with the Mississippi Department of Archives and History (MDAH) sponsored a small excavation at Winterville, during which test pits were dug at the foot of the largest mound. The most thorough excavation of the site to date was undertaken by Jeffrey Brain in 1967–68, and much of what we know of Winterville is contained within the report he published on his work in 1989. Among the projects he undertook was the placement of twenty-three excavation units (roughly six by six feet each) in nine mounds, by far the most comprehensive testing done on the earthworks at Winterville. Recently, the site has received archaeological attention in the form of summer field schools. Winterville was administered by the Mississippi Department of Wildlife, Fisheries, and Parks beginning in 1960, but has been under the direction of the MDAH since 2000. Prime objectives of both agencies have been to restore the

Thick vegetation covers one of the mounds at Winterville in Mississippi.

mounds to something approaching their original form and to protect them from further damage. The site was designated a National Historic Landmark in 1993.

History

Winterville developed along the northern frontier of the territory inhabited by people belonging to the Coles Creek culture, which predominated in the Lower Mississippi Valley between approximately 700 and 1100. Unlike later Mississippian chiefdoms, Coles Creek societies did not cultivate corn, engage in large-scale exchange networks, or participate in hierarchical regional polities. They did share some characteristics with their Mississippian neighbors, however, most notably the construction of platform mounds and plazas around which villages were oriented. Coles Creek mounds were not used as foundations for temples or elite residences, but as the sites of great feasts and elaborate mortuary rituals. Eventually, the Mississippian way of life prevailed in the Lower Mississippi Valley, but vestiges of Coles Creek culture remained evident.

The first recognized occupation at Winterville began sometime around 1000 when a group of Coles Creek peoples moved into the area from the south, perhaps from Lake George, and occupied the southwestern edge of the site. The early village was small but probably included the first stage of at least one mound. Some components of Mississippian material culture, such as shell tempering and the use of bottles and jars, became intermixed at this time with traditional Coles Creek material, though the Mississippian influence appears to have been indirect. Beginning in 1200, Winterville expanded according to a design reminiscent of Cahokia — multiple plazas dominated by large platform mounds but delineated by small house mounds. The Mississippian occupation of Winterville lasted from approximately 1200 to 1350, with the majority of mound construction occurring during the thirteenth century. In fact, compared with the process at other sites, the mounds at Winterville were fully constructed in a relatively short period and then were used without much modification for a long time.

Before 1200 there is some evidence of small migrations of people settling to the north of Winterville, perhaps having migrated from the Cahokia region. In any case, influence from Cahokia is clearly present at Winterville from its founding to its abandonment, including pots made in Cahokia and projectile points made from Illinois chert. Pottery and projectile points made in the Yazoo Basin have been found at Cahokia as well. The people of Winterville did not live behind walls, an indication that internal strife in the region was low and that their relationship with Cahokia was peaceful. The exact nature of the interaction between the two is unclear, but places that showed the most evidence of contact with Cahokia tended to be located at important river junctures along the length of the Mississippi Valley, perhaps because the rulers at Cahokia were interested in preserving their trade in Gulf Coast marine shell and other exotic raw material.

After 1350, Winterville went into steep decline. Only the northeast corner of the site, including the northeast plaza, was still in use. All mound construction at the site ceased, though other mound centers were founded in the area, perhaps even by former members of the Winterville chiefdom. The peace previously enjoyed in the region dissipated with Cahokia's fall and the abandonment of Winterville, and by the sixteenth century the largest and most militarily sophisticated chiefdoms in the Ancient South were located within the Mississippi Valley.

Spiro Mounds

The Spiro Mounds site, which was occupied between approximately 850 and 1450, includes twelve mounds, a reconstructed Mississippian winter home, and a small museum in an area of about 155 acres. Most of the mounds are arranged around a plaza located on an upper terrace of the river, but the largest mound and two others were located several hundred feet away on the Arkansas River bottoms. The two tallest mounds located adjacent to the plaza are platform mounds on the summits of which stood temples. The other mounds near the plaza ranged in height from two to five feet and served as platforms

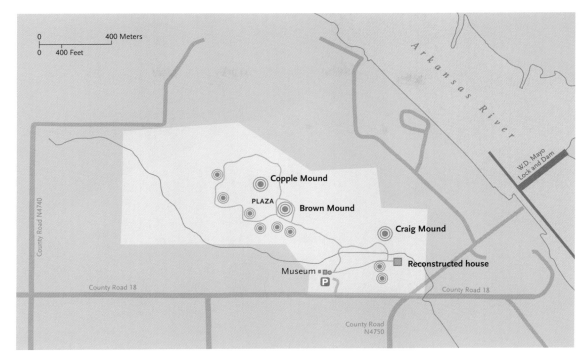

SPIRO MOUNDS

for the houses of the elite and occasionally as mortuaries. One of the three mounds distant from the plaza area was used as a burial mound, and the other two were house mounds. The artifacts recovered from the burial mound are why Spiro is famous throughout the archaeological community. This mound, known as Craig Mound, has produced a plethora of exotic material and exquisite artwork — the most complete collection of Mississippian artwork and exotic goods ever unearthed. The existence of this trove was due in large part to an accident of preservation — the vast amounts of copper and shell buried in the Craig Mound helped preserve material that would normally have decayed, such as wooden masks, wooden statues, and textiles of all kinds.

Location

Spiro is located in Leflore County on the south side of the Arkansas River in eastern Oklahoma, about seven miles north of the town of Spiro and about fifteen miles from Fort Smith, Arkansas. The site lies at the extreme western edge of the Ancient South at an important nexus point for east-west trade, and its involvement in the Mississippian world appears to have been based largely on the exchange of exotic materials such as copper and marine shell. The people of Spiro took advantage of their strategic location in the Arkansas

ABOVE: Reconstructed house at Spiro in Oklahoma. (© iStockPhoto.com / Alan Tobey)

RIGHT: Red cedar statue of a cross-legged male figure. Wooden statues like this one were probably quite common in the Ancient South, but have been rarely preserved in the archaeological record. (Department of Anthropology, Smithsonian Institution [A448892])

River corridor between the southern plains and the Mississippi Valley (which continues to be an important economic route) to broker goods between the Mississippian chiefdoms to the east and the tribal societies to the west.

Spiro sits in a bend of the Arkansas River in an area referred to as the Arkoma Basin, between the Ouachita Mountains to the south and the Ozark uplift to the north. The village occupied the second terrace of the river floodplain in a very productive bottomland reminiscent of preferred sites throughout the Mississippian world. In fact, the valleys of rivers such as the Arkansas and the Red could be considered narrow western extensions of the Ancient South, and their inhabitants pursued much the same subsistence strategies as their Mississippian cousins to the east. Although more research remains to be done, available evidence points to the use of corn and squash as well as deer, turkey, and a variety of fish. Geese were taken seasonally during their migration, and the upland oak-hickory forests were exploited for a variety of wild foods. Unlike their counterparts in the heart of the Ancient South, the people of Spiro continued to rely on some of the species cultivated in the region before the adoption of corn, such as *Chenopodium*, and they relied on bison for some of their meat.

Features

BROWN MOUND. Before it was severely damaged by digging, Brown Mound stood eighteen feet tall with a base of 175 by 200 feet, its platform summit accessible by a ramp on the western slope. It was built in at least five separate construction episodes, and in each of its incarnations, Brown Mound presumably served as the platform upon which the main temple of Spiro was erected. Clear evidence of this is lacking because looters dug out a large pit on the mound's surface, destroying what might have remained of the structures.

COPPLE MOUND. Copple Mound, a platform mound, was located on the north side of the plaza, opposite Brown Mound, and once stood about eight feet tall and sixty feet square. It seems to have been built in at least two stages, but perhaps more. The platform summit of each stage was crowned by a structure that is thought to have served as the residence of the chief.

CRAIG MOUND. Craig Mound is actually four conjoined conical mounds ranging in height from 10 to 34 feet and extending more than 250 feet along a northwest-southeast axis. Over the course of at least nine construction episodes, the four mounds were slowly built up until they joined and took on the appearance of a single earthwork. Craig Mound contained hundreds of burials, and several mortuary houses were erected on the spot before construction was begun on the mound. Of all the burials recovered from Spiro, the richest were contained within what has come to be known as the Great

Mortuary, located in the heart of Craig Mound. There, Spiro's elite were laid out on cedar litters, or their defleshed bones were placed in split-cane baskets for interment, surrounded by a nearly indescribable wealth of material.

Among the items taken from Craig Mound were red, yellow, black, gray, and green mineral pigments stored in plain whelk bowls; 500 pounds of small galena balls and about 1,000 pounds of unworked galena ore; many stone and clay pipes, including human- and animal-effigy pipes; more than 40 red cedar masks that ranged from full size to less than 3 inches high — all of which had eyes, teeth, and earspools of inlaid shell, and 2 of which had antlers; exquisitely made stone maces, swords, and monolithic axes; more than 30 copper axes with wooden handles, some inlaid with shell and mica; scores of chunkey stones; 2 gallons of freshwater pearls; many preserved textiles, including bags woven of buffalo hair; more than 1,000 pounds of shell beads; 500 columella pendants; almost 100 incised shell cups; about 30 shell gorgets; approximately 250 copper plates, 70 of them embossed; and more than 400 earspools.

PLAZA. The plaza at Spiro measures approximately six hundred by nine hundred feet and is delineated by the placement of a number of low platform mounds along with the larger Brown and Copple Mounds. Unlike other Mississippian plazas, the one at Spiro seems to have been oval, though the rea-

ABOVE: Chipped-stone mace recovered from Craig Mound at Spiro. Objects such as these were too fragile to use except for ceremonial purposes. (Courtesy, National Museum of the American Indian, Smithsonian Institution [207099.000]; photo by Photo Services)

RIGHT: Wooden mask of a "deer-man" recovered from Craig Mound at Spiro. (Courtesy, National Museum of the American Indian, Smithsonian Institution [189306.000]; photo by Ernest Amoroso)

sons behind the configuration are unknown. Whatever its shape, the plaza served similar functions to those found throughout the Ancient South.

RECONSTRUCTED HOUSE. Spiro also includes a reconstructed house like those excavated from the site. Spiro houses were one-room dwellings of between two hundred and six hundred square feet. The house is distinctly Mississippian in style and quite different from the houses built by many of Spiro's neighbors.

Research

After Spiro's abandonment in the fifteenth century, the site remained unused and apparently undisturbed. It became covered (and protected) by a dense canebrake that stood until the late 1870s or early 1880s, when it was cleared by Choctaw Freedmen and Choctaw Indians. For many years the Choctaw farmers who worked the land around Spiro left the mounds alone, and local tales spread about a blue flame that could be seen engulfing the mound at night and about animals that became frightened if brought near the earthwork. The area was included in the Indian land allotments of 1905 and 1906, which abolished the so-called Indian Territory in favor of private land ownership — a barely disguised attempt by the United States government to disenfranchise Native Americans. In what can only be considered the bitterest of ironies, Spiro was first "owned" by an Indian Freedman woman, Rachel Brown, after which it passed to an African American man related to Ms. Brown, whose surname became attached to Craig Mound.

One of the first written accounts of Spiro appeared in a history of Oklahoma published in 1916; it described excavations of two of the house mounds by Joseph Thoburn and included a photo of Craig Mound taken no more than two years before. Three years after Mr. Craig's death in 1930, the property was leased for two years to pothunters — local men who called themselves the Pocola Mining Company — for fifty dollars. Half a dozen men ravaged Craig Mound in 1934 and 1935 with the help and guidance of some unemployed miners they hired. The men set up a camp at the foot of the mound and uncovered thousands of artifacts, many of which they sold to collectors at reportedly high prices. Despite the fact that they dug "carefully," since only whole items could be sold, the men still broke countless artifacts and destroyed about a third of Craig Mound, though they had not yet dug into its largest section.

In the wake of these excavations, a Kansas City newspaper compared Spiro to the tomb of King Tut, and a rumor began circulating that Tiffany's in New York would pay half a million dollars for a quart of Spiro pearls. Such fervor resulted in the Oklahoma State Legislature passing an act in 1935 that required those conducting archaeological work to obtain legitimate licenses. Unfortunately, the Pocola Mining Company ignored the law, continuing its operations at an accelerated pace, leaving the mound badly damaged. What remained of Craig Mound was described by Forrest Clements of the University of Oklahoma, who visited the site in the fall of 1935 after the company had been shut down for good:

> The great mound had been tunneled through and through, gutted in a frenzy of haste. Sections of cedar poles lay scattered on the ground, fragments of feather and fur textiles littered the whole area; it was impossible to take a single step in hundreds of square yards around the ruined structure without scuffing up broken pieces of pottery, sections of engraved shell and beads of shell, stone, and bone. The site was abandoned; the diggers had completed their work.

The first professional work done at Spiro took place between 1936 and 1941 when the University of Oklahoma worked in conjunction with WPA crews for twenty-four and a half months and recovered more than six hundred burials from Craig Mound. They investigated eight of the other eleven mounds at the site and mapped the locations of those and other site features. Originally, the material recovered during the WPA project was sent to the University of Oklahoma, but parts of the collection are now housed at a number of institutions, including the University of Tulsa (displayed at the Thomas Gilcrease Museum), the Woolaroc Museum (southwest of Bartlesville), and the Oklahoma Historical Society, in recognition of their financial help on the WPA excavations.

The National Park Service considered creating a park at Spiro before World War II, but never did. Spiro Mounds was bought in the mid-1960s by the Army Corps of Engineers, which also had plans for developing a national park that never came to fruition. In 1969, the site was listed on the National Register of Historic Places, and in 1978 the interpretive center opened. Since 1970 the site has been leased from the Corps of Engineers. The Oklahoma Tourism and Recreation Department, in cooperation with the Oklahoma Archaeological Survey, was instrumental in promoting the preservation of the site. Spiro's new designation spurred another round of archaeological work in the late 1970s and early 1980s, including a reexamination of the WPA records, but much remains to be discovered. The Oklahoma Historical Society took over management of Spiro in 1991, but like many sites in this book, the park struggles to find the financial support it needs to adequately interpret the Spiro story.

History

Spiro was occupied between 850 and 1450, and for much of its history served as the ceremonial center of the largest chiefdom in the Arkansas River Valley. The site contained a village and a number of elite houses surrounding the town plaza. From its inception, Spiro was a nexus for the exchange of eastern and western commodities, first with members of the Plum Bayou culture and then, between roughly 1100 and 1350, as one of the most important centers of trade in the Mississippian world — only Etowah and Moundville have produced comparable material.

The rulers at Spiro collected raw material and finished items from throughout the entire Mississippian exchange network — Gulf and Atlantic marine shell; Lake Superior copper; a number of minerals, including mica, from the Appalachian highlands; and stone from a number of sources, including Kansas, Texas, Arkansas, Illinois, and Tennessee. In return, Spiro sent buffalo products such as robes, dried meat, and tallow; wood from the Osage orange tree, the best wood available for the making of bows; and salt, a product greatly desired and needed throughout the Mississippian world. In addition, Spiro exported a number of finished products, such as T-shaped pipes made of local sandstone, engraved shell cups, embossed copper plates, and other classic Mississippian artifacts.

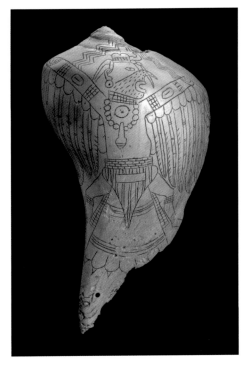

Shell cup discovered in Craig Mound at Spiro and engraved with a Bird Man image. Note the tail, wings, and beak as well as the beaded forelock, columella pendant, and earspools. (Courtesy, National Museum of the American Indian, Smithsonian Institution [189121.000]; photo by Ernest Amoroso.)

Among the items recovered from Spiro are a number of impressive artifacts that may have originated in Cahokia, including a number of copper plates, long-nosed god maskettes, and several platform pipes made of Missouri flint clay. Spiro eventually developed its own distinctive versions of Mississippian themes and depicted them on copper and shell. In fact, certain images, such as the world tree, and certain manufacturing techniques, such as carving shell in bas-relief, have been found only at Spiro, though scholars are unsure whether the images and techniques were unique to Spiro or whether their occurrence is due strictly to the fortuitous preservation mentioned above.

There is a great deal scholars do not know about the Spiro chiefdom. For example, we are not sure who their descendants were. It has long been held that they were a Caddo, Keechi, or Wichita people, but it has recently been postulated that they were a Tunican-speaking people instead. In any case, by the end of the eleventh century, Spiro had gone from being one of several small farming communities along the Arkansas River to having leaders that were preeminent in the region. By the second half of the twelfth century, Spiro had become an important ceremonial center, and construction had begun on Brown and Copple Mounds. The two mounds, along with seven structures that became house mounds, delineated the almost seven-acre plaza. The southeastern lobes of Craig Mound had been erected by this time, and the burials within it were more elaborate than any previous interments at the site. The chief at Spiro designed the new ceremonial center using the Toltec Module of 47.5 meters (just more than 154 feet) and aligned the mounds with the solstice and equinox sunsets. Some scholars have postulated that the mounds and mortuary houses at the site were placed to mirror the image of the Pleiades constellation.

Many people were drawn to the happenings at Spiro, and by 1200 its leaders commanded the fealty of up to ten thousand people in dozens of villages and hamlets in Oklahoma and Arkansas, and they influenced societies as far away as Kansas, Missouri, Louisiana, and Texas. By the mid-thirteenth century, Spiroan traders had established outposts 170 miles west on the Canadian River and 150 miles south on the Red River to gather buffalo products and Osage orange wood to trade with the Mississippian chiefdoms to the east. Some people at Spiro practiced a form of cranial deformation that produced elongated, cone-shaped skulls as opposed to the flat-head style more common in the Mississippian world. It is possible that this distinctive head shape marked Spiroan traders, who would have been given safe passage throughout the region and beyond.

Brown and Copple Mounds reached their greatest size by 1250, but Craig

Mound continued to grow as ever-increasing amounts of wealth were added with each new burial. At about the same time, most of the people of Spiro left and took up residence in nearby villages, hamlets, and farmsteads — only the elite and their retainers remained in the ceremonial center. Over the next century, Spiro expanded its trade network and influence, but its most important exchange partner, Cahokia, fell into steep decline. By 1350, Brown and Copple Mounds were no longer in use, and Spiro's star had begun to fade. Around 1400, the elite at the site, perhaps in an attempt to return Spiro to its glory days, erected the final stage of Craig Mound, creating the so-called Great Mortuary, where they reinterred much of what had been buried in the mound over the previous several hundred years.

The grand gesture failed, and Spiro was abandoned by 1450, its decline likely due to a combination of the climatic stress of the Little Ice Age, which made cultivation a tricky proposition on the edge of the Great Plains; the encroachment of buffalo herds, which played havoc with agricultural fields; and a disruption to the exchange of Mississippian artifacts and raw materials. In fact, trade disruption affected the entire Mississippian world in the decades before and after 1400. Despite the prevalence of violence in Spiro artwork, its people do not appear to have met an abrupt or violent end. Spiro, unlike Cahokia, Etowah, and Moundville, was never enclosed by walls or ditches. Its people seem simply to have abandoned not only the ceremonial center but the entire area and the Mississippian way of life as well. When de Soto's army passed through the area in the 1540s, it encountered non-Mississippian seasonal buffalo hunters.

Etowah Indian Mounds Historic Site

The Etowah site has produced some extraordinary Mississippian artifacts and includes one of the largest platform mounds ever built in North America. The fifty-acre site once contained six mounds, the three largest of which still remain, and two plazas surrounded by a large moat and an impressive bastioned stockade. The site was home to at least three separate chiefdoms during the approximately 600-year span of the Mississippian period. The second chiefdom reached the apex of its complexity and influence between 1250 and 1375, when it appears to have exerted a kind of hegemonic influence throughout the region. Hernando de Soto and his army visited Etowah, known to the Spanish as Itaba, in 1541. At the time, it was no longer the seat of regional power, but merely the home of a subchief under the direct influence of the chief of Coosa, whose capital was located nearby. Today, visitors to Etowah Indian Mounds Historic Site can tour a small museum, cross a footbridge

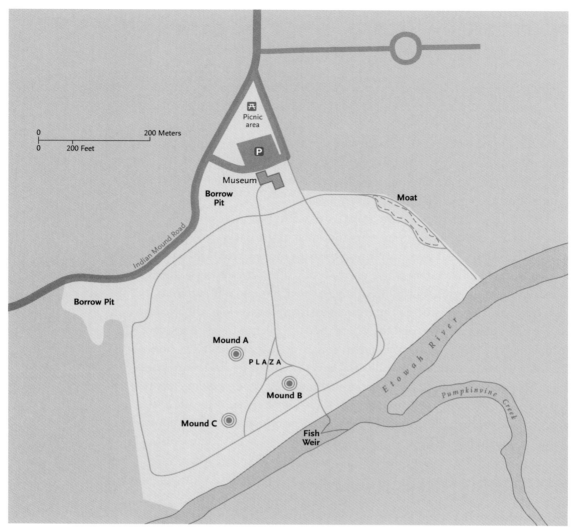

ETOWAH INDIAN MOUNDS HISTORIC SITE

over the remaining section of the moat, climb to the top of the mounds, and view a large stone fish weir in the Etowah River — all just a few miles northwest of the bustling metropolis of Atlanta.

Location

The Etowah site lies along the river of the same name in northwest Georgia, two and a half miles below the juncture of the Piedmont and the Ridge and Valley physiographic provinces. From the Ridge and Valley, the people of Etowah gathered and traded the high-quality grey-black chert used in the manufacture of stone tools. The Piedmont provided other mineral resources,

including hematite (red ochre), limonite (yellow ochre), galena, and quartz. In addition, the area had long been an important location for information and material exchange and was well positioned to take advantage of cross-regional Mississippian trade. Etowah sits near the southern terminus of the Appalachian Mountains, the source of such coveted material as copper and mica. At the same time, the people of Etowah had easy access to the Chattahoochee River, which served as a corridor to the equally coveted raw materials of the Gulf of Mexico, including marine shell.

The Ridge and Valley Province was home to exceptionally rich agricultural soils, particularly near its juncture with the Piedmont Province. From such a location the people of Etowah could easily exploit both the fertile soil of the Ridge and Valley and the considerable plant and animal resources of the oak-hickory forests of the Piedmont. There was a drawback, however. Since Etowah was located on the upstream side of the chiefdom, the majority

Village life at the capital of the Etowah chiefdom. Note the hunters returning with game, women processing foodstuffs, and corn being retrieved from a corncrib. (H. Tom Hall, National Geographic Stock)

of the society's population lived downstream. For the administration of the chiefdom, it would have made more sense for the capital to be centrally located, but subsistence factors seem to have outweighed logistics in the minds of the ruling elite. The same was true of other chiefdoms in the Ridge and Valley Province throughout the Mississippian Period, most of which located their capitals adjacent to the best agricultural soils within a particular river valley — no matter where in the valley that happened to be.

Features

MOUND A. Mound A, at sixty-seven feet, is second in height only to Monks Mound at Cahokia. The substantial terrace on its south side has slumped considerably since it was first erected. Most of the small amount of excavation conducted on the mound has been related to the construction of modern stairs ascending the ramp on the east side of the mound. It is not known in how many stages the mound was built, but construction was begun early in Etowah's occupational history and likely continued until the temporary abandonment of the site in 1375.

MOUND B. Mound B is a truncated pyramidal mound approximately thirty-five feet tall, located close to the Etowah River on the southwest side of Mound A. Like its larger counterpart, Mound B can be ascended via a ramp on its east side, which supports modern stairs. The area where Mound B was erected was originally used as a residential neighborhood — a number of houses had to be dismantled when the first stage of Mound B was constructed between 1100 and 1200. Mound B and several large, adjacent buildings constructed on prepared clay surfaces were surrounded by an interior stockade wall, presumably because activities within were reserved for elites.

MOUND C. Mound C was the third truncated pyramidal mound erected at Etowah. It has been completely excavated and reconstructed, so more is known about it than any other mound at the site. It was built and used exclusively between 1250 and 1375, the period of Etowah's greatest power and influence. Mound C was constructed in seven stages and grew to a height of 25 feet with a base of 150 square feet. It was surrounded by a light stockade probably designed to keep both children and dogs from climbing on the mound. Mound C was used to lay the elite of Etowah to rest — 350 burials have been recovered, along with some of the most magnificent artifacts of the Mississippian period.

There is some evidence of retainer burial as well, though not to the degree found at Cahokia. For example, burial 57 consisted of an adult male placed in an eight-foot-by-six-foot log tomb that was floored and roofed with two-inch-thick walnut planks. The seven other bodies surrounding the tomb seem to have been interred at the same time, the assumption being the people were killed specifically for this purpose. At least in part, these deaths represented another form of wealth to the elite man, who was buried also with eight conch-shell cups, a shell gorget representing a Falcon Warrior, two copper axes, two copper-covered earspools, five embossed copper plates, and an abundance of shell beads. It is possible to recognize clusters of burials within Mound C that may represent distinct elite lineages, though one artifact type crosscuts these lineage clusters — the Hightower-style shell gorgets, which were incised shell artifacts worn as pendants.

PLAZA. Etowah contained two plazas. The first, stretching out to the east from the foot of Mound A, was one of the most impressive built during the Mississippian Period. The word "built" is appropriate because the main plaza at Etowah was a 3-foot-tall, 330-square-foot raised clay platform. The second, more conventional plaza was located between Mounds B and C on the southern side of Mound A.

MOAT AND STOCKADE. The Etowah site was surrounded on three sides by a dry moat that, in tandem with the Etowah River, enclosed fifty acres. The moat, which was ten feet deep and thirty feet wide, was connected to two large borrow pits where some of the dirt used in the construction of

Shell gorget discovered in Mound C at Etowah and featuring a commonly depicted figure sometimes referred to as a Falcon Warrior. Note the wings, tail, and talons. (Photo courtesy of David H. Dye)

the mounds was obtained. Along the inside edge of the moat, the people of Etowah constructed a twelve-foot-tall stockade wall with bastions every eighty feet. Together, the moat and stockade provided a formidable defense, and the moat helped drain the site in heavy rains or floods.

FISH WEIR. The people of Etowah constructed a stone fish weir in the Etowah River adjacent to the site. It was used to funnel fish toward basketry traps where hundreds could be collected quickly at certain times of the year. The V-shaped weir remains in the river today and can be seen by visitors if the water is not running too high.

Research

The Reverend Elias Cornelius was credited with the "discovery" of Etowah in 1818 when he was led to the mounds by a Cherokee guide. Cornelius asked his guide about the site and its earthworks, but the Indian professed ignorance, a response that helped fuel the "Moundbuilder theory": most Americans believed the mounds of eastern North America had been built by a "superior" race of people who were eventually murdered by the "savage" Indians then inhabiting the area. In all likelihood, Cornelius misunderstood his guide. The Cherokee knew about mounds, of course, but the mounds at Etowah had been constructed by the ancestors of the Creek, not the Cherokee; that was the reason for the guide's answer. It took much of the rest of the century to put the Moundbuilder theory to rest.

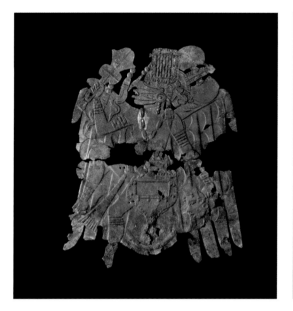

One of the first professional discussions of Etowah came in 1873 with the publication of *Antiquities of the Southern Indians* by Charles "C. C." Jones. Jones was a Savannah lawyer who eventually retired from law to pursue his fascination with southern Indians full-time. He was one of the first to attempt to prove that the ancestors of Native Americans built the mounds that dotted the southern landscape. In the early 1880s the Smithsonian Institution created the Division of Mound Exploration of the Bureau of Ethnology (later renamed the Bureau of American Ethnology) in an attempt to finally solve the question of who built the mounds. John Rogan, one of the bureau's archaeologists, was sent to investigate Etowah in 1884. Rogan conducted small test excavations in all the mounds but did his most significant work on Mound C, where he uncovered eleven burials from the summit. Among the many artifacts he recovered were the magnificent copper plates, each embossed with the image of a Falcon Warrior, which have come to be known as the Rogan plates.

During the 1920s, Warren King Moorehead undertook a series of excavations on Mounds B and C and in some nonmound areas of the site. Archaeological techniques at the time were not well developed according to today's standards, so the significance of Moorehead's work is somewhat limited. His published notes on the 1932 excavations have nonetheless been used to some effect by modern archaeologists. Moorehead unearthed more than one hundred burials from Mound C. Virtually all the Mississippian markers of status were discovered within these interments, including copper-covered

LEFT: Copper plates discovered in Mound C at the Etowah site in Georgia. They are known as the Rogan plates, after the archaeologist who unearthed them. (Donald E. Hurlbert, Smithsonian Institution)

RIGHT: A Rogan plate thought by some to be a female counterpart to the male depicted on the left. This warrior appears to have breasts and is carrying a masculine head, while the figure on the left lacks apparent breasts and carries the severed head of what appears to be a female. (Donald E. Hurlbert, Smithsonian Institution)

earspools and beads; columella pendants; shell beads worn at the neck, elbows, wrists, knees, and ankles; cooper-covered beads worn on the forelocks of men; flint swords and monolithic axes; stone and copper celts (instruments shaped like chisels or axe heads); stone palettes; and marine-shell cups.

Much of the archaeological work done at Etowah was undertaken during the 1950s. Arthur Randolph Kelly, who first came to Georgia to oversee the WPA excavations at Ocmulgee and stayed on to found the Department of Anthropology at the University of Georgia, excavated portions of Mound B and adjacent nonmound areas between 1954 and 1958. His work was preceded by the work of William Sears, who dug a series of test pits throughout the village area in 1952 and 1953. The most extensive investigation during the decade, however, was done by Lewis Larson, an archaeologist who worked for the state historical commission and later at the University of West Georgia. Larson completely excavated Mound C between 1954 and 1962, discovering the construction sequence in the process. He removed the remaining artifacts from the mound, including the marble statues that have become synonymous with the Etowah site.

Most of the archaeological work done at the site since the completion of Larson's excavations has been related to construction projects: the stairs that ascend Mounds A, B, and C; the bridge across the moat; and the visitor center. Instead of further excavations, scholars like Adam King have endeavored to synthesize the vast archival information related to the site, making great strides toward understanding Etowah's complex political history.

History

A series of large trash-filled pits dating from between 1000 and 1100 represent the earliest archaeological features at Etowah. A highly plausible scenario posits that the dirt from the pits was used to erect the original stage of Mound A, an event that culminated in a feast for the communal laborers, who threw the refuse into the borrow pits. In any case, the construction of Mound A signaled the establishment of a small chiefdom at the Etowah site. In the decades before Etowah's establishment, most of the villages in northwest Georgia were protected by walls, but the village at Etowah boasted no defensive measures, an indication that the elites of Etowah rose to power in part by reconciling formerly hostile groups. Although little is known about Etowah's relationship with neighboring groups, there were other societies in the region, including Ocmulgee, which was probably the most formidable chiefdom in the area.

Between 1100 and 1200 the size of the village at Etowah increased, construction of Mound A continued, the first two phases of Mound B were built, and the large borrow pits that would later form part of the moat were probably in their initial stages of excavation. The chiefdom of Etowah remained small during this period, but was no longer alone in the Etowah Valley — at least two other chiefdoms developed there during the twelfth century. Meanwhile, chiefdoms were emerging in many other parts of Georgia, Tennessee, and Alabama as the Mississippian way of life spread throughout the Mid-South. Around 1200, while societies in other areas continued to thrive, the chiefdoms of the Etowah Valley were abandoned rather rapidly. The reasons for the exodus are unknown, but the valley remained uninhabited for several decades.

Etowah was reoccupied in the mid-thirteenth century, and it was between 1250 and 1375 that Etowah reached the apogee of its political and artistic development. The elites who founded the new chiefdom appear to have brought foreign artifacts and perhaps a "foreign charter" to help legitimize their claim to leadership. The elaborate goods later buried in Mound C may have served as visual elements for a set of myths that explained the role of chiefs in the sacred order of the universe. The set of myths, and perhaps many of the artifacts, may have come directly from Cahokia. For instance, some have argued that the Rogan plates were manufactured in Cahokia, exchanged as part of a "missionary" package, and finally interred as antiques many generations later.

In any case, Etowah served as the capital of a quickly expanding chiefdom that included four other minor mound centers in the valley. And Etowah began to play a prominent role in the long-distance exchange network of the

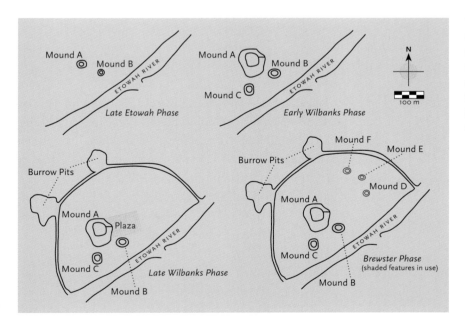

The development of the Etowah site over time, as seen through mound, plaza, and moat construction. (Redrawn from Adam King, *Etowah* [Tuscaloosa: University of Alabama Press, 2002], 61)

Mississippian world. By this and other means, it appears that the ruling elite of Etowah, who emerged as a result of the hegemonic influence of Cahokia, became a hegemonic force unto themselves, influencing chiefdoms as far away as the middle Chattahoochee River and northern Florida. For instance, the copper plates depicting Falcon Warriors discovered at the Lake Jackson site near Tallahassee, Florida (see the box feature Lake Jackson Mounds Archaeological State Park, page 112), may have been manufactured at Etowah and given to the elites of Lake Jackson in much the same way Etowah's elites had received the Rogan plates from Cahokia, and for much the same reason.

By 1325 a major portion of Mound A had been erected, including a ramp and an impressive set of stairs ascending to the summit, which was twenty-three feet wide and built of logs set in packed clay. The first three stages of Mound C were constructed as well, and the area between the three mounds became a small public plaza. In addition, despite the site's impressive size, the leaders decided to enclose it within an imposing moat and wall.

Between 1325 and 1375, the chiefdom of Etowah reached its largest size, both spatially and demographically, and the number of mound sites within the Etowah Valley grew to eight. Four more construction episodes occurred on Mound C, and Mounds A and B were added to as well. Stone-lined tombs were used instead of the earlier log-lined tombs, and several elite burials were placed in lobes on the mound slopes rather than on the summit itself. The most impressive architectural addition during this period was the more than 300-foot-long raised plaza built adjacent to Mound A.

Etowah appears to have been assaulted by a significant military force sometime around 1375, at which time the stockade was burnt, never to be rebuilt. Evidence suggests that the temple on the summit of Mound C was desecrated during the assault, the bones kept within were strewn on the ramp outside, and the sacred statues of the chiefdom's founding members were broken. Although it is impossible to know the details, it seems that one of the region's chiefdoms became strong enough and bold enough to attack and destroy the capital of Etowah, which had dominated the area for more than a century. In the wake of the attack, the entire Etowah Valley was abandoned and remained empty for about a hundred years, despite the fact that other chiefdoms continued to thrive in the surrounding region.

Etowah was reoccupied again around 1475, but it never regained the splendor that had once characterized the site. The new residents built three small mounds (D, E, and F) over the course of a seventy-five-year occupation. They may have used Mounds A and B, though they did not enlarge them, but it seems clear that Mound C was not used during this period. While Etowah lay dormant for a century, a new power rose in the region — the chiefdom of Coosa, located on the Coosawattee River, a few miles north of the Etowah

Valley — and Etowah became a minor mound center within the chiefdom. Coosa's territory was located within the Ridge and Valley Province along the west side of the Blue Ridge, and stretched from present-day Newport, Tennessee, near Knoxville, southwestward through Chattanooga, across northwest Georgia, and into northeast Alabama. As many as ten subchiefs within the area were allied to or at least paid deference to the chief of Coosa.

When Hernando de Soto met the chief, who appeared to be in his midtwenties, he was carried out to meet the Spaniard on a cushioned litter borne by his principal warriors while others played flutes and sang. The Coosa leader granted the invading conquistador food and burden bearers but balked at the Spaniard's request for women. Soto quickly clapped the chief and his sister, the mother of the chiefly heir, in irons. Using the hostage leader to ensure his people's cooperation, a common strategy of the invaders, Soto continued to march through Coosa territory, requisitioning food and supplies as he went. Although the Spaniards were quite impressed with both the regal nature of the chiefdom's leader and the quality of the land within its territory, they were once again disappointed at the lack of mineral wealth. Before he traveled on, Soto released the chief of Coosa but for unknown reasons refused to release the man's sister, an act that reduced the great Mississippian leader to tears of impotent rage. Adversely affected by the European invasion, the chiefdom of Coosa went into decline in the decades that followed. By 1600, Etowah had been abandoned for the final time.

Moundville Archaeological Park

Moundville Archaeological Park is one of the most spectacular remaining Mississippian sites. Moundville was intermittently occupied between 900 and 1650, and at its height the town encompassed more than 185 acres and included at least twenty-nine mounds and a large stockade wall, most of which was built between 1200 and 1450. During that period, Moundville was home to one of the most important and influential chiefdoms in the Ancient South, first as a bustling capital town and later as a necropolis, a "city of the dead." In fact, no other large Middle Mississippian site was used as a true necropolis in the manner of Moundville, and scholars have yet to explain this phenomenon. Today, twenty mounds, the majority of which surround a huge plaza, remain well preserved within the park's boundaries. Only Cahokia boasts more mounds, and Moundville, being more secluded and farther from urban sprawl, presents one of the most compelling extant visual images of the nearly lost and forgotten Mississippian world. Moundville Archaeological Park includes the Walter B. Jones Museum, five reconstructed houses, a nature trail with excellent views of the Black Warrior River, several picnic

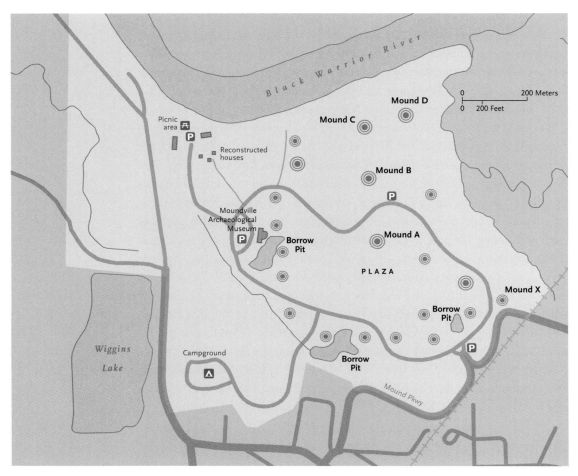

MOUNDVILLE ARCHAEOLOGICAL PARK

areas, and a well-shaded campground. The site is also home to the Nelson B. Jones Conference Center, which can be rented for larger events, and the De-Jarnette Research Center (not open to the public), where Moundville's artifacts are curated and studied.

Location

Moundville is located in west-central Alabama near the modern town of the same name, fifteen miles south of Tuscaloosa. The site was located at the convergence zone of two physiographic provinces, the Cumberland Plateau and the Gulf Coastal Plain, which allowed residents to exploit the resources of both areas efficiently. The people of Moundville fished and gathered freshwater mussels at the shoals of the Black Warrior River a few miles north of the site. Each fall they gathered the rich nut harvest from the oak-hickory forests on the Cumberland Plateau, which served as good hunting grounds for deer, bear, and turkey as well. In addition to a number of plant and animal resources, the Gulf Coastal Plain provided rich soils.

Moundville lies just north of the so-called Black Belt of central Alabama, a large swath of particularly fertile soils that have been coveted by farmers for more than a thousand years. The easily tilled soils were well suited for the growing of corn, beans, and squash. The Black Belt included extensive cane-brakes and prairies and provided a source of much-coveted cedar wood, used widely in the Ancient South in the construction of burial litters and other sacred artifacts. Of all the benefits of Moundville's location, perhaps the most important was its bluff-top setting. Residents could look down on the Black Warrior River fifty-five feet below, ensured that their houses, temples, and plaza were safe from virtually any flood. In addition, the many steep ravines that cut into the bluff were used as convenient garbage dumps by Mound-ville's citizens.

Features

MOUNDS. The twenty mounds at the site range in height up to fifty-five feet, but most are between twelve and fifteen feet tall. They are roughly oriented to the cardinal directions, though Mound A sits slightly askew of the others. The many mounds that surround the large plaza are grouped in pairs: a larger platform mound with no mortuary evidence linked with a smaller platform mound that contained elaborate burials. Each set of paired mounds may have represented a particular lineage within the chiefly family, or perhaps each set represented a different clan. In either case, it is apparent that the most impor-tant families occupied the mounds at the northern end of the plaza, since the burials were less elaborate toward the south end.

Mound B, the largest at the site at just over fifty-five feet tall, was likely the home of the ruling chief of Moundville. Today it is adorned with a re-constructed building often referred to as a temple, although it is more likely that the town's main temple was located atop Mound A. Mounds C and D were located away from the plaza to the north and east of Mound B, and both contained elite burials. The summits of most mounds included structures — houses, temples, or mortuary houses. Two mounds, however, one adjacent to the northern edge of the plaza and one adjacent to the south-ern edge, appear to have been used only for burials and did not include sum-mit architecture. Not all the mounds at Moundville were used at the same time. For instance, Mound X predated the construction of the stockade at Moundville and was destroyed during the wall's production.

PLAZA. The seventy-four-acre plaza at Moundville shows evidence of ar-tificial leveling. Unlike most Mississippian plazas, Moundville's includes a

large mound near its center, Mound A, though the reason behind its odd placement remains unknown. The remains of large buildings have been uncovered at the northeast and northwest corners of the plaza. The structures were built at ground level, indicating that they were public in nature. Within one of the buildings, archaeologists made a macabre discovery: a cache of human heads buried along the north wall. Several other Mississippian chiefdoms included public buildings such as these.

BORROW PITS. Moundville Archaeological Park includes four ponds that were created by the Mississippian residents of the site during mound production. In other words, earth for the mounds was taken from quarries with the deliberate intent of creating artificial ponds. The ponds, from which both copper and bone fishhooks have been collected, were stocked with fish and served as a ready source of protein — presumably, only for Moundville's elite residents. They still hold fish today, and visitors can occasionally see locals angling at these quaint ponds.

RECONSTRUCTED HOUSES. Residential structures at Moundville changed considerably throughout the centuries the site was occupied, but all were made with the materials at hand — wood, bark, and thatch — and were extremely small by modern standards. Visitors to the site can explore five replica houses built near the bluff overlooking the river. The people of Moundville lived in small, kin-based "neighborhoods" that consisted of at least a half-dozen houses, each of which was generally rebuilt several times in the same location over a period of decades.

Research

Moundville was mentioned by Ephraim Squier and Edwin Hamilton Davis in their classic work from 1848, *Ancient Monuments of the Mississippi Valley*, and later in the century Nathaniel Lupton produced a reasonably accurate map of the site. Very little work was conducted by the Bureau of Ethnology's Division of Mound Exploration at Moundville, in part because the local landowner demanded a fee, and the site was not even mentioned when the bureau published its seminal work on the mounds of eastern North America in 1894. The first significant archaeological investigations at Moundville were conducted by Clarence Bloomfield Moore, a lawyer from Philadelphia who spent part of each year cruising southern rivers in his steamboat, the aptly named *Gopher*, unearthing huge numbers of artifacts. Moore dug extensively at Moundville in 1906, and though his work was certainly not up to today's standards, his extensive records of the excavation have been of some use to modern archaeologists. Unfortunately, over the next two decades the site was looted extensively.

FACING PAGE: Mounds A and B at Moundville as seen from the plaza. Visitors can ascend to a reconstructed building atop the summit of Mound B. (Laura Shill, University Relations, The University of Alabama)

An excavation at Moundville Archaeological Park. Recovered artifacts are curated and studied at the DeJarnette Research Center, located on-site. (Department of Anthropology, University of Alabama)

By the mid-1920s, concerned local citizens such as Dr. Walter Jones (after whom the current museum is named) had begun a concerted effort to save Moundville. With the help of the Alabama Museum of Natural History, the land surrounding the mounds was slowly purchased. By 1933, the site had become officially known as Mound State Park, but it was not until 1938 that the park was developed. The Civilian Conservation Corps was brought in to stabilize the mounds against erosion, but it soon undertook other projects as well, including the construction of roads and buildings. The name of the park was changed to Mound State Monument, and the following year, 1939, the museum was opened to the public. Colloquially, the site has long been referred to as "Moundville," but this was made official only in 1991, when its name was changed to Moundville Archaeological Park.

Local efforts at preservation saved Moundville from certain destruction and led to years of serious archaeological inquiry at the site. Beginning in 1929 and continuing until America became involved in World War II, the Alabama Museum of Natural History undertook an extensive series of excavations under the direction of David DeJarnette and others. In all, those excavations uncovered an incredible 14 percent of the site — nearly five hundred thousand square feet. Among the voluminous materials recovered were more than three thousand human burials. Since it is much easier and quicker to remove artifacts than it is to analyze them, much of the material was left unstudied until the 1960s. It was then that Christopher Peebles began the onerous task of making sense of decades of accumulated artifacts, photos, and field notes. Over the years, many others have helped with the task, and excavations and analysis continue to the present day.

The burials unearthed from Moundville have revealed a great deal of information about how the people of the chiefdom lived. Human remains were recovered in virtually every part of the site with the exception of the plaza. About 95 percent of the burials were those of commoners interred with little in the way of material wealth. Virtually all the exotic artifacts recovered from the site were buried with the remaining 5 percent of Moundville's population. Among the elite burials recovered from mounds was an adult male who had been interred with a monolithic axe and an exquisite stone palette, which likely served as the symbols of chieftainship in Moundville. Although the elite were generally in better health than the commoners, the majority of the population suffered from iron-deficiency anemia as a result of a diet high in starch and low in protein. There was a high infant-mortality rate, and relatively few people lived into their fifth or sixth decade. Cranial deformation, the process of changing the shape of a person's skull in infancy, was a common practice at Moundville, too common to have been restricted to those of elite birth.

History

Moundville enjoyed a long history and was occupied at various times during all three Mississippian periods. It reached its height during the Middle Mississippian period between approximately 1200 and 1450, when it became one of the largest and most influential chiefdoms in the Ancient South. Corn cultivation was introduced to the area sometime after 900, but its introduction did little to alleviate the endemic violence in the Black Warrior River Valley, whose residents were forced to live in fortified villages for protection. Soon after construction was begun on two mounds at the Moundville site around 1100, the valley residents abandoned their nucleated settlements and spread out to occupy small homesteads. Apparently, the first chief of Moundville was able to forge peace between formerly hostile groups, and his newly formed chiefdom prospered as a result. At the same time, small chiefdoms were developing to the west and north of Moundville. The relationships that existed between those chiefdoms are currently unknown.

When beans were introduced to the area around 1200, the overall diet of the people improved, allowing both the capital and its surrounding hinterlands to support larger populations. It is probably no coincidence that the vast majority of mound construction at the site occurred during the thirteenth

century, when the population of Moundville rose from about a thousand people to as many as three thousand, and the rest of the chiefdom's population numbered several thousand more. The Moundville chiefdom grew during the thirteenth century to include at least three secondary mound centers and several additional villages within fifteen and a half square miles of the Black Warrior River Valley. By that time, Moundville had developed into a hege-monic force in the Deep South akin to that of Etowah's in the Mid-South.

Moundville's rise was not without its consequences, and early in the thir-teenth century the first of six stockades was erected around three sides of the capital, with the bluff protecting the fourth. The stockade enclosed an enor-mous area — nearly 185 acres — that included not only the mound and plaza complex, but extensive habitation areas as well. It is difficult to image the ex-pense and effort that went into the construction of a half-dozen walls within a hundred years. Moundville's secondary centers and subsidiary towns were fortified during this period, and must have periodically served as places of refuge for the thousands of Moundville citizens who lived in homesteads throughout the farming districts. It is difficult to determine exactly whom Moundville was protecting itself against. It may have been in conflict with one or more chiefdoms in the Mississippi Valley to the west, or perhaps even Etowah, located about 186 miles to the northeast, which was certainly large enough to challenge Moundville.

Moundville is particularly famous for its Hemphill-style pottery, which was smudged during the firing process to produce a black, glossy finish. Hemphill pottery, which was used by both the elite and the commoners, was traded throughout much of the Ancient South. In return, Moundville

An exquisitely crafted stone bowl representing a male wood duck. Discovered at Moundville in Alabama. (Courtesy, National Museum of the American Indian, Smithsonian Institution [165232.000]; photo, detail, by Ernest Amoroso.)

received pottery from as far away as the Caddo country of present-day East Texas. (See the box feature Caddo Mounds State Historic Site, page 166.) The artisans of Moundville produced as well a prodigious number of stone palettes, ranging from eight to twelve inches in diameter. Dozens of complete specimens and hundreds of fragments have been discovered, and most show evidence of pigments on their surfaces. Although palettes are found at Mississippian sites throughout the Ancient South, they are far more common at Moundville than anywhere else.

Moundville is also well known for its use of distinctive iconography, which scholars believe was associated with death and the Under World. Especially prevalent is the eye-in-hand motif, believed to be associated with the constellation Orion, which includes the only nebula visible to the naked eye. Some Native American groups associate this constellation with the path along which all souls must travel after death. Although the eye-in-hand motif has been discovered at Spiro and Etowah also, it is much more prevalent at Moundville. Some exquisitely crafted stone bowls have been unearthed at Moundville, as well as a series of copper pendants that appear to represent human scalps. On the other hand, engraved shell artifacts, quite common in most of the Mississippian world, are conspicuously absent from Moundville — only eight engraved shell gorgets and three shell cups were included in the three thousand burials recovered from the site. Human figural art is also rare at Moundville, despite having been found in some abundance at Cahokia, Spiro, and Etowah.

By the fourteenth century, the political realities in the region had changed. After a century in which people of the Moundville chiefdom constructed six

CADDO MOUNDS STATE HISTORIC SITE

Caddo Mounds State Historic Site, also known as the George C. Davis site, is located in the Neches River Valley southwest of Alto, Texas, in Cherokee County. Today, the 397-acre site includes three earthen mounds, a visitor center with exhibits, and a 0.7-mile interpretive trail. The first professional archaeology undertaken on the mounds was conducted in 1919 by the Bureau of American Ethnology. WPA workers conducted excavations at the site between 1939 and 1941, including a significant investigation of the largest mound. Excavations of the remaining mounds and the village area were conducted between 1968 and 1970, and the site was opened to the public in 1982.

The site was organized around two platform mounds and a conical burial mound, which began as a tomb for five individuals and grew in six construction stages until it reached about twenty feet in height and boasted a diameter approaching one hundred feet. After completion, it contained ninety people, who had been buried in thirty separate interments. The platform mounds appear to have been constructed in six stages as well, each of which served as the base for a building—one of which measured sixty feet across. Some of the earth used in the construction was taken from a quarry to the west of the smaller platform mound. The town was not protected by defensive fortifications of any kind.

The Caddo Mounds site was occupied from about 750 to 1300, a small chiefdom on the fringe of a regional Mississippian culture whose heartland was the Red River Valley. Though it was a frontier outpost—the site is farther from the Red River than any other associated mound site—the town's leaders still possessed the trappings of the elite. Some were buried with copper-covered earspools, stone effigy pipes, marine shell, and symbols of office such as spatulate celts (stone implements resembling shovels that have been beaten flat). The elite engaged in a regional trade for high-quality stone and were buried with hundreds of projectile points made from imported rock. The Caddo Mounds site reached its zenith about 1100, when it seems to have boasted its largest population and likely wielded its widest influence. The site was abandoned by 1300, but a final mantle placed on the mound hints of an orderly retreat from a frontier outpost that was no longer prosperous. Scholars have postulated that an expansion of the bison population into the region during the thirteenth century may have undermined the trade value of Caddo corn or made farming too difficult because of the presence of bison in the fields.

Life in a late prehistoric-period Indian village as depicted in a mural on display at Caddo Mounds State Historic Site in Texas. (Artwork created and provided by the Interpretive Services Branch, Texas Parks and Wildlife Department; permission to use provided by the Texas Historical Commission)

massive stockades, they no longer found it necessary to live behind walls, and between 1300 and 1450, the Moundville site was reduced to a small population of elite lineages and their retainers. The chiefdom itself, however, was growing. Five more secondary mound centers were built during this period, bringing the total to eight, and the valley was again filled with small homesteads. The population of the Moundville chiefdom was likely near 10,000.

Moundville itself served as a necropolis during this period, a place where certain people from throughout the chiefdom were brought for burial. So much of the site was used for that purpose that former neighborhoods became large cemeteries, perhaps used by the descendants of those who had once lived there. Several of the mounds at the site fell into disuse during the fifteenth century, and fewer and fewer burials occurred. During the sixteenth century, it appears that only two or three of the mounds at the site were still being used, and Moundville found itself in the shadow of other, more powerful chiefdoms. An increased level of competition within the region, perhaps related to the rise of the new political powers, led to the abandonment of homesteads within the Black Warrior River Valley and a return to walled villages. Although there was still a small chiefdom in existence when the Spanish explored the area in 1541, it fell soon after, and Moundville was permanently abandoned.

Town Creek Indian Mound

The Town Creek site is on the Little River, a tributary of the Pee Dee, in Montgomery County, North Carolina. Located near the town of Mount Gilead, and only a short drive from several metropolitan areas, the five-acre site has a complex history that belies its small size. Town Creek was occupied by Mississippians from approximately 1150 to 1450, when it consisted of a mound and plaza complex surrounded by a wooden stockade. Today, the site includes a museum and visitor center, as well as a number of impressive reconstructions. Town Creek is completely enclosed by a stockade with twin north and south fortified entrances. Half the stockade wall has been daubed, that is, covered with a mud plaster, and when the wall is approached from the visitor's center, the daubed section is all that can be seen. A platform mound with a wattle-and-daub, thatched-roof dwelling on its summit; a second dwelling on the ground level, enclosed by a light stockade of its own; and a third, circular building are located within the walls of Town Creek and can be explored by visitors. In addition, the center of the plaza is marked by a forty-foot-tall wooden post. Taken together, the Town Creek reconstructions offer a unique visual experience that helps one imagine what life was like within the walls of a small Mississippian capital.

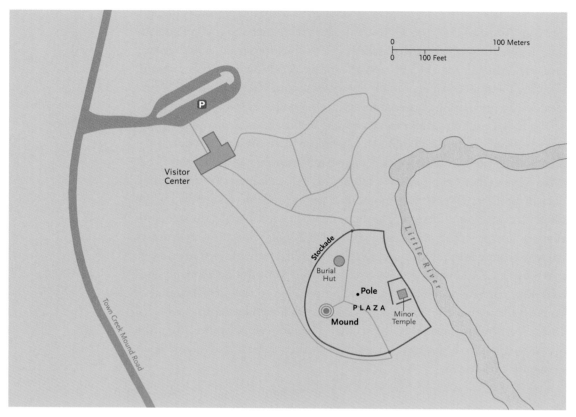

TOWN CREEK INDIAN MOUND

Location

The Town Creek site is located in the Piedmont of North Carolina and sits on a small bluff overlooking the Little River near its confluence with Town Creek, the stream from which the site gets its name. The roughly triangular bluff rises more than twenty feet above the river, high enough that ten-year floods do not inundate the site. The area around Town Creek is one of the most fertile places in the Little River Valley. It receives between 195 and 205 frost-free days a year, as well as more than forty-eight inches of rain — near perfect climatic conditions for a Mississippian farmer. Evidence of corn and squash, but not of beans, has been found at the site. Today the site is surrounded by woods, so it is hard to imagine what it would have looked like surrounded by fields, widely spaced houses, and scattered stands of nut or fruit trees.

The people of Town Creek had access to both bottomland and upland forests. In those wooded environments, they hunted deer, turkeys, and passenger pigeons and gathered hickory nuts, walnuts, and wild fruits. They ate

a number of fish and turtle species as well. Just east of the site, along the Little River, are the remains of a stone weir and several large boulders on which tools were ground and sharpened. Much of the rock used by the people of Town Creek is known locally as Carolina slate, and this material proved reliable enough that very little stone was imported into the area. The people of Town Creek had access to some exotic materials, however, since copper, mica, and marine shell have been recovered from the site.

Features

TOWN CREEK MOUND. Unlike many of the sites featured in this book, Town Creek has only one mound, a platform mound erected in four stages. The first construction episode resulted in a five-foot-tall mound, and the second added approximately three feet. The other additions brought it to its current size — 12 feet tall, with a base of 110 square feet and a ramp projecting 33 feet. Much of the current mound is a reconstruction, since much of the original mound was excavated. The mound was built over the location of two square buildings connected by an entrance trench. The smaller of the two was interpreted at the time of excavation (during the federal relief archaeological programs of the Depression) as an earth lodge like that found at Ocmulgee National Monument. Each of the mound summits held buildings of the same dimensions. It is likely that those structures served as a temple and chiefly residence. In addition, the edge of the mound facing the plaza may have included a ramada-like structure, but that section of the mound was destroyed by looters before any professional work was done.

PLAZA. The plaza associated with Town Creek Mound is approximately 150 by 200 feet, and appears to have been in use long before construction of the mound was begun. During the first century of Mississippian occupation of the site, the plaza included not only a large pole, but also a circle of smaller posts with a diameter of 112 feet, which has been compared with the so-called sun circles of Cahokia. By the time mound construction was begun, around 1250, however, the sun circle had been dismantled, though large posts were still being erected in the center of the plaza.

POLE. Today the most conspicuous feature of the plaza is the forty-foot-tall pole, and the same was true when the people of Town Creek used the plaza hundreds of years ago. In fact, six such large posts were erected in the plaza over the course of the three-hundred-year history of the site, as described by Joffre Coe, one of Town Creek's archaeologists:

> [The holes for the posts] had been dug in sequence, and each had a stepping ramp that entered from the southeast side of the hole. Although the holes were prepared at different points in time, the methods of construction seem to have been the same. The large butt end of the pole was slid down the ramp to the bottom of the posthole. The top end was then raised — pulled with ropes and propped up a little farther at a time with an X- or Y-shaped (frame) support, until the pole could be secured in a vertical position. Most were additionally secured by wedging large rocks into the ramp behind the pole as it was lifted.

Raising the post in the plaza at Town Creek, 1957. (Courtesy of the Research Laboratories of Archaeology, The University of North Carolina at Chapel Hill)

STOCKADE. A series of five stockades was built during the occupation of Town Creek, each one encompassing more area than the previous in order to accommodate a growing population. The nine-foot-high wall at the site today is a reconstruction of the smallest of the five stockades. In fact, its curvature had to be expanded to accommodate the mound — when the original stockade was erected, neither the mound nor the building that predated it had yet been built. In addition to the tower gates on the north and south sides of the wall, two tunnel-like gates ran under the stockade wall on the side facing the river. Those gates were located above a garbage dump on the terrace below the bluff. If the design of the gates is any indication, it seems that taking out the trash may have occasionally been dangerous. The trench under the wall was narrow and long (two feet wide by eight feet long), and the entrance small and easily defendable. It is not hard to imagine an enemy concealed in the trash waiting for an unsuspecting person.

A portion of the re-
constructed bastion
and stockade at Town
Creek in North Carolina.
(Courtesy of the Re-
search Laboratories of
Archaeology, The
University of North
Carolina at Chapel Hill)

RECONSTRUCTED BUILDINGS. Town Creek contained circular and square structures, and both are represented by reconstructions. It appears that the circular buildings were residential dwellings during the first century of Mississippian occupation and later, when the site was a mortuary center, became cemeteries. Thus, the reconstructed circular building is referred to as Mortuary D. The square buildings at the site have been interpreted as public structures, and the one atop the mound is referred to as a "townhouse," after the public buildings of historical southern Indians. It is possible that the square structures built at ground level were public in nature, but it is doubtful that the buildings atop the mound were equally accessible.

Research

The Town Creek Mound was first mentioned in print in 1881, and the site was known to Cyrus Thomas of the Smithsonian Institution, but no professional work was undertaken there in the nineteenth century. It was donated to the State of North Carolina in 1937 by the property owner, Floyd Frutchey, who first contemplated plowing it down because the pothunters who regularly visited the site were becoming a nuisance. Other investigators, with slightly nobler intentions, visited the site before 1937. For instance, in 1926 a local school principal excavated a small portion of the mound with the help of a few students. Unfortunately, he returned the following year with mules and used a drag pan to "investigate" the eastern half of the mound, destroying valuable evidence in the process. Douglas Rights, who would go on to publish a book about North Carolina Indians in 1947, visited the site in 1929 and was instrumental in convincing Mr. Frutchey to donate the mound and a small parcel of land surrounding it to the state.

The first professional excavations at Town Creek began in 1937 under the direction of Joffre Coe, a student from the University of North Carolina at Chapel Hill. The investigations were part of the federal relief archaeology program, and Coe received workers from both the WPA and the National Youth Administration. Between 1937 and 1940, Coe concentrated his efforts on the mound and its immediate surroundings, excavating all but a small portion of it and salvaging what he could for posterity. The two burials used to develop the facial reconstructions on display at the museum today were discovered and excavated by relief workers in 1942, not long before the program was discontinued because of World War II.

Following the war, the administration of Town Creek fell to the North Carolina Division of State Parks, and despite the lack of federal relief workers, excavations continued under Joffre Coe, who implemented an innovative research approach. Inspired by his experience interpreting aerial photographs during the war, Coe developed a plan to photograph all the features of the site in situ, that is, without removing them from the ground. Although the plan seemed grandiose at first, it was realistic for two reasons — the site was relatively small, only five acres, and it was owned by the state, so the project could be carried out over many years. Coe and his crew would remove a layer of soil from a small area of the site, use the photographic tower he designed to take pictures of the exposed features in that area, and then refill the excavated area without disturbing the features further. By 1984, the vast majority of the site had been photographed, and archaeologists now have a map of virtually all the buried features at Town Creek. In other words, Coe and his crews found and photographed all site features but left their excavation to future archaeologists — an incredible bit of foresight considering the state of archaeology in the mid-twentieth century.

In 1950 and 1952, additional land was purchased, and the development of Town Creek as a tourist site became a focus of activity. In 1955 the North Carolina Department of Archives and History took over administration of the newly designated Town Creek Indian Mound State Historic Site. The land around the mound had long been cleared for farming, so a reforestation project was undertaken in which approximately 10,000 pine and cedar

Stan South using a camera and photo tower to record subsurface archaeological features in an excavation unit at Town Creek. (Courtesy of the Research Laboratories of Archaeology, The University of North Carolina at Chapel Hill)

seedlings were planted. One of the most imposing and impressive of the reconstruction projects was the stockade wall, the only fully reconstructed Mississippian stockade, which was built using 1,060 juniper posts, each one twelve to fourteen feet in length. Within the wall, the mound was stabilized, and a building was constructed on the summit in 1957. The structure still stands today, though it needs occasional roof repairs. A second building was erected near the wall along the river's edge and was surrounded by a palisade much less substantial than the outer wall. In 1961 a final building was added, a round structure that includes an exhibit of a burial at Town Creek.

During much of the excavation and restoration activity, Town Creek was less than fully functional — for instance, the site facilities did not include electricity and running water until 1960. Yet people still came to see the mound and other reconstructions — 11,162 people in 1958, to be exact. Attendance increased after the facilities were upgraded, especially when a paved road was added in 1962. That same year, construction finally began on a proper museum, which was opened to the public in 1963. In 1965, Town Creek was designated a National Historic Landmark, and the following year more than 65,000 people visited the site. Archie Smith, who was first appointed site manager in 1974, updated the museum and opened new exhibits in 1983. Investigations at Town Creek continue to the present.

History

The Town Creek site is located within the territory of what archaeologists refer to as Pee Dee culture, a variant of Mississippian found in eastern South Carolina and south-central North Carolina. Pee Dee marks the eastern extent of the Mississippian culture area, and Town Creek is located on the boundary's northeastern edge, adjacent to the Mississippian frontier. The site served as the capital of a small chiefdom that probably did not exceed fifteen or twenty miles in diameter, though not enough work has yet been done to adequately define the spatial limits of Town Creek society. The many scattered farmsteads in the area would have looked to Town Creek not only as a ceremonial center, but also as a place of refuge in times of war. It is possible that the chiefdom at Town Creek developed around the brokerage of goods from the north and east, goods that were eventually distributed throughout the Ancient South.

Archaeologists at the site have uncovered a copper axe, copper pendants, copper-covered wooden earspools, copper-covered wooden rattles, columella beads, and shell gorgets. The source of the copper was the Great Lakes region, and the shell came from the Atlantic coast. In addition, mica from North Carolina, like the mica discs that have been found at the site, was widely exchanged throughout the Mississippian world. In return, Town Creek was the recipient of goods and ideas from other parts of the Mississippian world — of the ten stone and pottery effigies uncovered there, five are representations of the long-nosed god found so conspicuously at Cahokia. One stone palette was uncovered as well but has since disappeared. Taken in conjunction with the large number of chunkey stones discovered at the foot of the mound — eighty-one made of stone and more than eleven hundred made of pottery — it seems clear that Town Creek was influenced, at least indirectly, by societies in the American Bottom.

TOP: A copper axe discovered at Town Creek. Such axes are thought to have been ceremonial in nature, since the metal was too soft to be of practical value. (Courtesy of the Research Laboratories of Archaeology, The University of North Carolina at Chapel Hill)

ABOVE, LEFT: A carved stone face found at Town Creek that likely depicts the so-called long-nosed god, representations of which have been found throuhout the Ancient South. (Courtesy of the Research Laboratories of Archaeology, The University of North Carolina at Chapel Hill)

ABOVE, RIGHT: Mica discs bearing a cross-in-circle motif thought to represent the four cardinal directions of the universe. (Tommy Charles, retired SCIAA archaeologist)

That is not to say, however, that Town Creek was not a locally developing phenomenon, just that the Pee Dee peoples were more receptive to Mississippian ideas and technology than their neighbors to the north and east. The village at Town Creek was established at what had been a nonresidential mortuary site between the ninth and eleventh centuries. There may even have been a low mound erected over the primary burial area. It is possible that the founders of the town had some knowledge of the site's former function. Whatever the case, by no later than 1150, newcomers had established the first Mississippian village at Town Creek.

The focal point of the community was the plaza, around which approximately ten circular dwellings were arranged, along with a pair of square buildings on the western side. Within the plaza was a sun circle of standing posts, within which a larger post, approximately forty feet tall, was erected. Although the population of the site at that time is unknown, it is clear that the majority of structures built between 1150 and 1250 were residential in nature, indicating a significant number of inhabitants. The village was surrounded by a stockade that was rebuilt as many as four times during that hundred-year period, a clear indicator of some level of endemic violence between the people of Town Creek and their non–Pee Dee neighbors.

By 1250, the nature of the site had changed significantly. A platform mound was erected on the western edge of the plaza over the spot formerly occupied by public buildings. Most of the mound was constructed between 1250 and 1350 — perhaps three of the four construction episodes — and the summit was capped with paired buildings on the western side of the mound and a ramada on the eastern side. A large post remained in the plaza as before, but the circular monument was no longer standing, replaced by a rectangular enclosure on the eastern side of the plaza. It housed a mortuary structure where most of the exotic artifacts recovered from the site were found. During this phase in Town Creek's history, only a small resident population of elite personages and their servants lived there. Many areas that once contained dwellings had become cemeteries, and the function of the site became increasingly ceremonial. Town Creek was still surrounded by a stockade in 1250, but it was rebuilt only once during the ensuing century, perhaps an indication that local violence had lessened with the political changes.

Town Creek's fortunes waned considerably after 1350, perhaps in part because of the drastic decline in long-distance regional trade that affected the entire Mississippian world by the turn of the fifteenth century. In any case, Town Creek was abandoned by 1450 at the latest.

CHAPTER FIVE
THE LATE MISSISSIPPIAN
PERIOD, AD 1400–1600

THE CLIMATIC UPHEAVAL of the Little Ice Age and the social and political upheaval of the late fourteenth century continued into the fifteenth century. In some cases, these factors combined to have devastating effects — for example, almost the entire Savannah River Valley in Georgia was abandoned between 1400 and 1450. Other areas experienced similar occurrences; the chiefdoms west of the Mississippi River were hit particularly hard. The Mississippian world was not disappearing, but changing. New, far-flung, powerful chiefdoms developed throughout the Ancient South during the late fifteenth and early sixteenth centuries. Some of those societies emerged in areas previously home to large chiefdoms; for instance, Coosa, Tascaluza, and Apafalaya rose in the territories of Etowah and Moundville. Other places that had once been powerful, such as Cahokia and Spiro, were not reoccupied during the Late Mississippian period.

Although the Late Mississippian chiefdoms did not boast the same level of finery as their Middle Mississippian predecessors, they still manufactured ceremonial weapons, marine-shell jewelry (particularly beads and gorgets), copper-covered earspools, and chunkey stones. The craftsmanship, however, was decidedly inferior to that of the previous period. Many places in the Ancient South were still characterized by fortified towns, but large swaths of the Mississippian world were free of walls during the sixteenth century, including northern Florida and much of Georgia and South Carolina. However, the peoples of the Late Mississippian period were forced to deal with an intrusion undreamed of by their ancestors, one that no walls could defend against — European invasion.

Because the Europeans who were present in the Ancient South during the sixteenth century recorded their observations, we know more about the

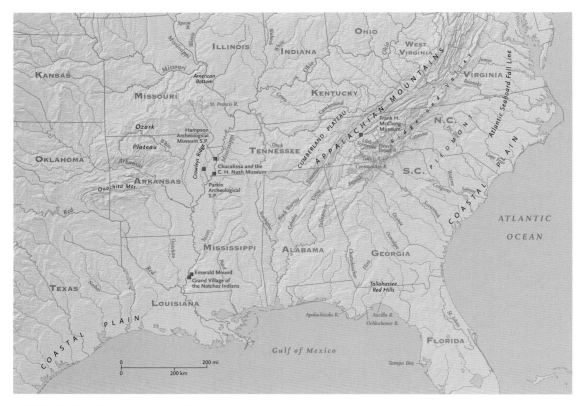

LATE MISSISSIPPIAN SITES

social geography of the Late Mississippian than that of the previous two periods. Through the careful combination of archaeological and historical data, the names by which many of these chiefdoms referred to themselves, along with the names of their friends and enemies, are known. In fact, by analyzing the Indian words recorded by early Europeans, scholars have been able to determine which languages were spoken in many sixteenth-century chiefdoms. The conquistadors Hernando de Soto, Tristán de Luna, Juan Pardo, and others were not interested in Mississippian peoples beyond discovering a way to subjugate and exploit them, and much of what they recorded was thus related to politics and warfare.

Several Spanish military expeditions made contact with the Apalachee chiefdom in northern Florida, a fierce warrior society on the edge of the Mississippian world. Among the chiefdoms in the lower South during the Late Mississippian period were a number of particularly powerful societies, including Cofitachequi in South Carolina, Ocute in Georgia, Tascaluza in Alabama, and Coosa, which occupied parts of Tennessee, Georgia, and Alabama. (See the box features Frank H. McClung Museum, pages 182–83, and

PHOTO, PAGES 178–79: The mound at Parkin Archeological State Park in Arkansas, a site likely visited by Hernando de Soto and his army in 1541. (Arkansas Department of Parks and Tourism)

Duck River Cache, page 184.) The Mississippi Valley was home to a number of particularly bellicose chiefdoms, including Chicaza and Quiqualtam in Mississippi, and Casqui and Pacaha in Tennessee and Arkansas.

Despite the chiefdoms' courage, valor, and conviction, the stresses they were subject to as a result of European contact — military losses, disease, and political destabilization — were too great a shock to absorb in conjunction with the climatic downturn of the Little Ice Age. Consequently, the Mississippian world was in serious decline by 1600, though chiefdoms held on in some places into the seventeenth century.

Chucalissa and the C. H. Nash Museum

Chucalissa, a Choctaw word meaning "abandoned house," was occupied intermittently between 1000 and 1550, reaching nearly twelve acres in size, with a population numbering between eight hundred and a thousand people. Chucalissa served as the home village of one of the subchiefs of the Quizquiz chiefdom, a name recorded by the Hernando de Soto expedition. Today the site is located adjacent to T. O. Fuller State Park, about six miles south of Memphis, Tennessee. The park is adjacent to the Mississippi River in a wooded area that seems far removed from the bustle and noise of the nearby city. Chucalissa includes multiple mounds, a sunken plaza, an arboretum, and a half-mile interpretive trail. The site is also home to a hands-on archaeology lab and the C. H. Nash Museum, which features exhibits on contemporary and prehistoric Native American cultures, including a large diorama to help visitors imagine Chucalissa as it might have looked more than five hundred years ago. The museum store offers an excellent collection of books for sale, the most comprehensive selection available at any of the sites featured in this book, with titles of interest to both amateurs and scholars.

Location

Chucalissa is located on the edge of the Chickasaw Bluffs, overlooking the floodplain of the Mississippi River about a hundred feet below. When the site was occupied, the river was significantly closer to the bluff than it is today, having been diverted when track was laid for the Yazoo and Mississippi Valley Railroad — which can be seen from the site today. Much of the floodplain was covered by a huge expanse of now-extinct forest dominated by cypress and tupelo interspersed with a variety of species of water-tolerant trees. The residents of Chucalissa exploited the bottomland forests as well as the numerous oxbow lakes scattered throughout the floodplain for turtles, slow-water fish species, waterfowl, and river cane. More important, however, was the huge swath of fertile soil that stretched over four miles north to De Soto

FRANK H. McCLUNG MUSEUM

The Frank H. McClung Museum, located on the campus of the University of Tennessee in Knoxville, features several exhibits on the prehistory, natural history, and geology of the region. The award-winning permanent exhibition *Archaeology and the Native Peoples of Tennessee* features five huge murals, hundreds of beautifully displayed artifacts, and interactive exhibits for both old and young—there is even a dog burial in the floor, visible through glass. The stunning variety of the artifacts includes the Duck River cache (see the box feature Duck River Cache, page 184); a number of carved-shell gorgets, masks, and cups; sandstone statues; and an impressive collection of pottery. The artifacts were recovered by University of Tennessee archaeologists between 1934 and 1982, with most coming from sites in valleys now inundated by Tennessee Valley Authority reservoirs. The Mississippian section of the exhibit is based in large part on the excavations of the Toqua site and includes scale models of the both the village and the chief's house.

Toqua, a walled village with two mounds and a borrow pit maintained as a pond, was located on the west bank of the Little Tennessee River a few miles from the river's mouth. At the time of the Hernando de Soto expedition, the place was known as Tali. The town was built in the thirteenth century, and the bastioned stockade surrounding it enclosed almost ten acres. At some point in the following decades, the wall burned and had to be rebuilt. The new wall enclosed only about five acres, yet the population, estimated at three hundred people, had not decreased. Despite the overcrowding, the town maintained a plaza in front of Mound A, the larger of the two mounds at the site. The oval platform mound was built in at least sixteen stages, eventually reaching a height of 25 feet, with a diameter of more than 150 feet. Each successive summit held a group of structures that included a large temple connected by a covered walkway to an adjacent smaller residential structure. In front of those buildings, on the leading edge of the mound, was a large ramada, under which the chief could play host to his guests. As the mound grew in size, the structures in back were built on a raised terrace in order to maintain their visibility from the plaza. People were buried on the summit and in the sides of Mound A and were often interred with weapons—one man was buried with a pot where his head should have been.

Mound B, another oval platform mound, was located about two hundred feet southeast of Mound A, near the corner of the second stockade wall. At its largest, the mound measured about six feet tall and one hundred feet in diameter. It was built in at least three stages, each of which held a single building, probably a mortuary house. The burials discovered in Mound B contained a great deal of pottery and many shell artifacts but no weapons, an interesting contrast with the burials discovered in Mound A. It is apparent from the hundreds of skeletons recovered from the site that the people of Toqua suffered from iron-deficiency anemia, which was associated with a diet overreliant on corn and deficient in

protein. Men averaged five feet six inches tall, and women just five feet one inch. Life expectancy was low, in part because of the high infant-mortality rate, and evidence of violence among the skeletal remains was common.

During the sixteenth century, the Little Tennessee Valley was heavily populated and included many walled towns. Spanish chroniclers mention Tali only in passing, noting that the residents had to be bullied before they would ferry the army across the river in dugouts. In the years following the Soto expedition, the Mississippian way of life faded, and the Koasati-speaking peoples abandoned the area. They were soon replaced by Cherokee speakers who came down from the higher country to claim the abandoned land of one of their traditional enemies.

A mural on display at the Frank H. McClung Museum on the campus of the University of Tennessee in Knoxville. It depicts a number of leading men atop a mound in a late prehistoric town. (Greg Harlin, Frank H. McClung Museum)

DUCK RIVER CACHE

The Duck River cache consists of more than forty exquisitely crafted flint artifacts that were buried together a foot above a pair of human statues, one male and one female. The cache was found along the Duck River in Humphreys County, Tennessee, near Nashville in the west-central part of the state. The area is part of the Highland Rim region, and its well-watered and -drained alluvial bottomland was perfect for Mississippian farmers. Although the artifacts were located within the boundaries of the Link site, named after the first Euro-American owners of the property, they were not found within a mound, but had been buried in the habitation area, perhaps in the floor of a house. It is likely the artifacts were made and interred during the Middle Mississippian period, since many of them resemble items depicted in the hands of Falcon Warriors carved on shell gorgets found throughout the Ancient South in the thirteenth and fourteenth centuries.

With the exception of the statues, nearly the entire cache was made of Dover flint, found exclusively near Dover, Tennessee. All the artifacts were ceremonial, that is, none of them had been used or were intended for utilitarian purposes. The flint had been chipped into a variety of forms, including monolithic axes, maces, hooks that represented claws or talons, swords, sun discs, turtle effigies, and several knives and daggers. The two statues were made of sandstone or perhaps decayed limestone, and they have come to be known as "Adam and Eve." Adam is about thirty inches in height, weighs about eighty pounds, and is in a half-kneeling, half-squatting position, with very prominent eyes. Eve is twenty-four inches tall, weighs about fifty pounds, and is in a kneeling position, with her hands placed on her knees. Her eyes are not very prominent, but unlike Adam's, her mouth is open.

The flints were discovered in late December 1894 or perhaps early January 1895 on the Link farm, though there is some disagreement about who uncovered the cache. The statues were found in March 1895. The Duck River cache was quickly sold, and it was resold and moved several times before finally being returned to Tennessee more than fifty years later. The forty-six chipped-flint artifacts are now on display at the Frank H. McClung Museum in Knoxville, Tennessee—a potent and permanent reminder of the artistic genius of the Mississippian peoples. The story of Adam and Eve, however, is less than inspiring. The statues were originally sold separately from the other items of the cache, and the whereabouts of Eve is currently unknown. The two were photographed together only one time, the year they were discovered. They seem to have stayed together until 1935, when the collection of Edward Payne was sold and the statues were purchased separately. Adam, who is also known as Tennessee Man, eventually ended up in the Metropolitan Museum of Art after having once been the property of Nelson Rockefeller.

The Duck River Cache, a spectacular array of more than forty stone artifacts buried together in Humphreys County, Tennessee, near Nashville. (Frank H. McClung Museum)

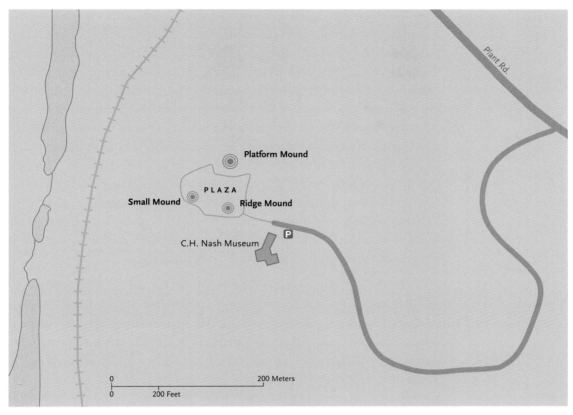

CHUCALISSA AND THE C. H. NASH MUSEUM

Park on the Memphis riverfront, where the capital of the chiefdom to which Chucalissa belonged is believed to have been located.

The people of Chucalissa had easy access by trail to their fields at the foot of the bluff, where they grew corn, beans, and squash, yet their houses remained safe from the frequent floods of the Mississippi. When Soto's army passed through the area in 1541, the population of the region was quite large, and virtually the entire stretch of bottomland soil between Chucalissa and Memphis was under cultivation. In addition, the people planted gardens in the loess soils of Chickasaw Bluffs for crops such as tobacco, sunflowers, and gourds. The upland forests, dominated by species of oak, hickory, and pine, were within easy reach and provided a number of plant and animal resources, including hickory nuts, persimmons, pawpaws, blackberries, elderberries, deer, black bears, and turkeys. In short, the bluff-top village at Chucalissa was an excellent location for a Mississippian settlement, with only one major disadvantage: the lack of direct dugout access from the village to the river — something other sites in the region usually had.

Features

PLATFORM MOUND. Platform Mound has a base 150 by 100 feet and rises to a height of 25 feet. The mound was built in several stages, each averaging about a foot and a half in thickness. Some of the fill for mound construction came from the floodplains at the foot of the bluff, and some of the surviving borrow pits can be seen along the interpretive trail. Each successive summit supported a pair of structures, which were rebuilt two to four times before a new mantle of earth was laid over the mound and the process begun again. On the western half of the summit was a square, semisubterranean structure that measured fifty feet per side. On the eastern half of the summit was a second, smaller semisubterranean structure. That pattern, a temple paired with a chiefly residence, was seen in many places throughout the Mississippian world. The summit may have included a ramada, for feasting and audiences with the chief, on the leading edge of the mound.

SMALL MOUND. Southwest of the main mound was a second platform mound; however, erosion and plowing have reduced its size and changed its shape. Even at its maximum size, it was smaller than the main platform mound, despite being about a hundred years older. Little is known about its summit architecture, but burials from this mound show evidence of differential treatment at death — not only material evidence such as marine-shell jewelry and earspools, but biological evidence as well. The people, both male and female, interred in the Small Mound are taller on average than the rest of the population, a probable indicator of better diet and nutrition over several generations. It is likely the nutritional stress faced by commoners was due to the high level of military action in the region; areas for hunting and gathering were small and contested, and the elite received the lion's share of the most desirable food.

RIDGE MOUND. Ridge Mound is actually a series of small, overlapping mounds that served as the foundation for a number of residential buildings erected along the summit. Those structures were rebuilt as many as four times before a new mantle of earth was added to the mound. Each of the square houses measured eighteen to twenty-two feet per side and was home to one of the elite lineages that resided at Chucalissa. Ridge Mound is no longer readily identifiable as a mound, but instead resembles a long, low rise along the southern edge of the plaza.

PLAZA. The plaza at Chucalissa is rare in that it is sunken, that is, it is about two feet lower than the rest of the site. It is bordered on three sides by mounds and measures approximately 175 feet square. The sunken plaza may have been the source of some of the fill for mound construction, or its appear-

ance may be related to excavations and therefore not an original feature of the site. Today the plaza contains ball poles for use in stickball, the southern Native American version of lacrosse.

STOCKADE. A wooden stockade surrounded Chucalissa on at least three sides — the bluff side may have been left open. Further archaeological work is needed to determine its exact size and the number of times it was rebuilt. It is possible that the site did not include a wall during the earliest stages of its occupation, but stockades were ubiquitous on both sides of the Mississippi River in this stretch of the valley during the fifteenth and sixteenth centuries.

HOUSE RECONSTRUCTIONS. The village at Chucalissa formerly included two reconstructed wattle-and-daub, thatched-roof Mississippian houses for the education and enjoyment of visitors, but they deteriorated to the point that they had to be dismantled. Plans are in place to rebuild these structures in 2012. During the height of its occupation, Chucalissa was crowded with dozens of buildings.

Research

After it was abandoned, Chucalissa went unnoticed for approximately four hundred years. Unlike many of the sites in this book, it was neither the object

Platform Mound and plaza at the Chucalissa site, near Memphis, Tennessee. (C. H. Nash Museum at Chucalissa)

of nineteenth-century speculation nor the victim of early collectors. For the most part, it remained hidden away on the forested bluff south of Memphis, though a few hunters, loggers, and moonshiners knew of the mounds. The site first came to the attention of archaeologists just before World War II, when T. O. Fuller Park was being developed by the state. The University of Tennessee was responsible for some of the early excavation at the site, including that done in 1940 under the direction of one of the most highly respected early archaeologists of the Southeast, T. M. N. Lewis. Unfortunately, work at Chucalissa, which at the time was referred to as either the Ensley Plantation site or the T. O. Fuller mound site, was halted when the nation went to war.

After World War II, interest in the T. O. Fuller mounds was maintained by the Memphis Archaeological and Geological Society, which oversaw a number of minor excavations at the site and, perhaps more importantly, brought the value of the site to the attention of the public. In late 1954, the Tennessee State Department of Conservation decided to invest in the site, funding both the construction of a museum and the development of the mounds and village for tourism. Incidentally, much of the labor for museum construction was provided by prisoners. The person most responsible for bringing the whole project to fruition was the archaeologist Charles H. Nash, for whom the museum was eventually named. Nash had worked as an archaeologist in the South for more than twenty years, much of it with the Tennessee Valley Authority, when he was appointed Tennessee State Parks archaeologist in 1957. He was to oversee excavations as well as the reconstruction of several houses at the newly named Chucalissa site.

Between 1957 and 1967, a number of investigations were undertaken at Chucalissa, including the analysis of stone and bone artifacts and human and animal remains. In 1962 administration of the site passed into the hands of the Interdisciplinary Program in the College of Arts and Sciences at Memphis State University, now the University of Memphis. In the ensuing years, Nash helped develop the school's archaeology program, and since that time, Chucalissa has served as the focus for a number of university field schools and graduate projects. The site has provided countless educational opportunities for local children, particularly during the annual Summer Education Program.

History

Little is known concerning the earliest occupation of Chucalissa, but for much of its history, it served as a minor mound center for a chiefdom whose capital was located in Memphis. The elite at Chucalissa lived adjacent to the plaza in houses that contained the highest percentage of decorated pottery and tradeware; those of the highest rank occupied residences on the sum-

A stickball game being played in the plaza at Chucalissa. Stickball does not seem to have occupied as prominent a role in the Mississippian world as the game of chunkey. (C. H. Nash Museum at Chucalissa)

mits of mounds. The houses of commoners, smaller than those of the elites, were clustered in the southernmost portion of the site and north of Platform Mound. Some of the town's residents lived along the ridges formed by ravines that cut through part of the bluff. They and others at the site used the ravines as a garbage dump.

Burials seem to be located just about everywhere within the site, with the exception of the plaza and Platform Mound, though one burial found in the flank of the mound appears to have occurred after the site was abandoned. Most of the interments associated with the late fifteenth and early sixteenth centuries were extended primary burials, 64 percent of which included one or two pots placed by the head and shoulders. When two vessels were present, one was a bowl and the other a bottle, one of which was an effigy vessel. Although rare, there were some grave goods besides pottery, including shell gorgets and beads, a shell spoon, earspools, and trophy skulls. Burials outside the mounds are found in clusters, but do not seem to be associated with particular house floors — often, commoners were buried in the open. Like many Mississippian populations, the people of Chucalissa suffered from a high infant-mortality rate, and a relatively small percentage of people lived to be elderly. Cranial deformation was present at the site and grew in popularity over time, but never included more than a small percentage of the total population, perhaps having been reserved for the elite.

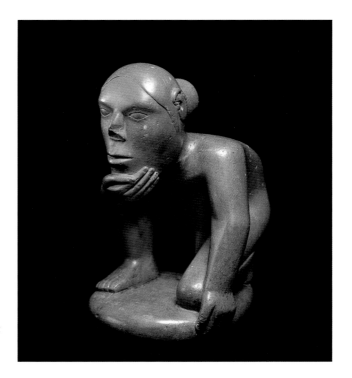

A pipe of Missouri flint clay carved into the likeness of a crouching man holding his chin in his hand. Effigy pipes made of this material have been found throughout the Ancient South. (Courtesy of Shiloh National Military Park)

During the late fifteenth and early sixteenth centuries, Chucalissa was a subsidiary mound site within the chiefdom of Quizquiz, which was itself a tributary of the chiefdom of Pacaha, whose ruler controlled at least three other chiefdoms on both sides of the Mississippi. The territory of the chiefdom of Quizquiz included parts of present De Soto County, Mississippi, and Shelby County, Tennessee, and the capital was probably located on the site of Fort Pickering—a Civil War–era facility located four and a half miles north of Chucalissa at De Soto Park in Memphis. Two mounds still survive in diminished form at the park, but the site originally included at least seven mounds, a number of which delineated a plaza. Like Chucalissa and unlike most of the other major sites in the region, the capital of Quizquiz was located along a bluff that overlooked the floodplain of the Mississippi.

Chucalissa was the largest of the chiefdom's subsidiary mound sites. The others were six to ten acres in size and were generally located about two to four miles apart throughout the chiefdom. Six smaller, nonmound sites have been discovered in the area, but there were probably more; it is difficult to determine how many were occupied at any given time. Five of the six known nonmound sites were located on natural levees near oxbow lakes in the floodplain of the Mississippi River. The sixth, located four miles up the Loosahatchie Valley, was likely used as a base to exploit upland forest resources.

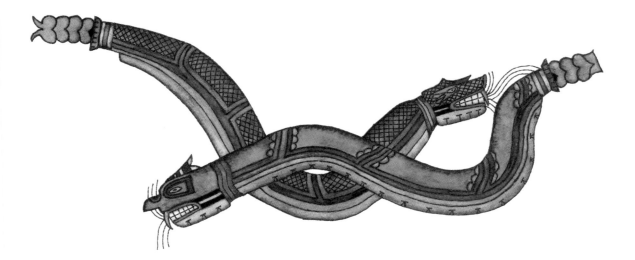

The nonmound villages were one to three acres in extent, and it is unclear whether they were fortified. Within the southernmost area of the Quizquiz chiefdom were quite a number of homesteads that almost certainly lacked stockades, and hunting camps have been found up to twenty miles away from the mound centers.

Members of the chiefdom of Quizquiz were encountered by the Soto expedition, but the Spaniards did not visit the town of Chucalissa, and European artifacts have yet to be recovered there. Chucalissa may have been abandoned by that time. The Europeans, after having traveled for eight and a half days northwest across an uninhabited area of the hill country of northern Mississippi, surprised the first town of Quizquiz and captured three hundred women and children; most of the men of the town were away. The subchief of the town was a feeble old man, but he remained defiant toward the Spaniards. Communicating only through messengers, he refused to help Soto until the captives — among whom was his mother — were released. Because of the poor condition of his men, Soto agreed, but once the prisoners were returned, the people of Quizquiz fled their towns without providing him with the dugout canoes he desired. Soto was able to obtain corn and pecans from the abandoned towns and encamped near the river, where his men spent twenty-seven days building four large boats to ferry themselves across the Mississippi.

A mural of paired, multicolored snakes at Chucalissa. The image represents mythological serpents common in Mississippian cosmology and art. (C. H. Nash Museum at Chucalissa)

Parkin Archeological State Park

Parkin, a seventeen-acre mound site located north of I-40 in the town of the same name in Cross County, Arkansas, was occupied between 1350 and 1600. The site was oriented around one large mound and a number of smaller

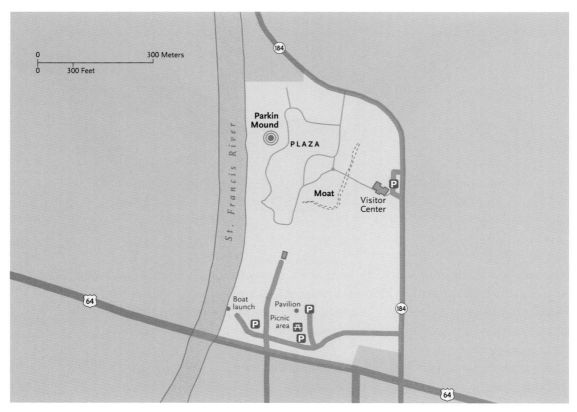

PARKIN ARCHEOLOGICAL STATE PARK

mounds, all of which were adjacent to a small plaza. Parkin, which was surrounded by a moat and stockade wall, served as the capital town of a sixteenth-century chiefdom whose twenty thousand people were spread throughout the valleys of the St. Francis and Tyronza Rivers. According to the most widely accepted route taken by Hernando de Soto, the conquistador and his army stopped at Parkin in 1541. Today, Parkin Archeological State Park includes the large mound, remnants of the town's defensive ditch, and an excellent museum exhibit, which includes Spanish artifacts recovered from the site as well as replicas of Spanish and Indian weapons and gear from the period. Parkin is a National Historic Landmark and is on the National Register of Historic Places.

Location

The Parkin site is located on the east bank of the St. Francis River just below its confluence with the Tyronza. The majority of the towns in the Parkin chiefdom, including the capital, were built atop natural levees that represent the third and fourth meander belts of the Mississippi River, into which the St. Francis flows. The people of the chiefdom took full advantage of the rich levee soils, cultivating corn, beans, squash, pumpkins, and other vegetables in their fields and gardens. Interestingly, the soil around the Parkin site was not the best available within the territory of the chiefdom, yet Parkin was far and away the largest town. It was so large, in fact, that some of the town's food had to be brought in from other parts of the chiefdom. It thus appears that the location of the capital was chosen for its strategic location at the confluence of rivers, presumably for the ease of collecting goods and information from the rest of the chiefdom.

The Mississippi Delta consisted of a tangle of oxbow lakes, bayous, and sloughs weaving through bottomland forests of sweet gum, cypress, tupelo, and submergible oaks, from which a host of edible plants, animals, and fish were extracted. The Mississippi flyway was regularly filled with enormous flocks of waterfowl. In fact, it appears the people of the Parkin chiefdom relied more heavily on fish and waterfowl than the common Mississippian fare of deer and turkey, though those too were available just to the west along Crowleys Ridge, a narrow, north-south-running ridge with a mixed southern hardwood forest of oak, hickory, and pine. The resources of that forest complemented the resources available in the floodplain forests closer at hand. In addition to game birds and animals, the upland forests provided a variety of fruits and nuts, including persimmons, grapes, and hickory nuts. Crowleys Ridge was also the source of stone for the knives, arrowheads, and other tools used by the people of Parkin.

Features

PARKIN MOUND. Parkin Mound, overlooking the St. Francis River on the western edge of the site, is about twenty feet tall with an extension on its southern flank that rises more than five feet above the level of the village. Some of the fill used in the construction of the mound came from a borrow pit on the north side of the site beyond the moat and wall. Little archaeological work has been done on the mound itself, but evidence of pothunters — two looter's pits on the summit — is still visible. The southern extension of the mound, which has been more thoroughly investigated, appears to have been erected in fifteen construction stages. Both the mound summit and the extension served as platforms for a series of buildings. The building on the summit, which, the Spaniards noted, was adorned with buffalo skulls, served as the home of the chief, the main temple, or both. The structures on the mound's extension were almost certainly houses of the chief's many wives and other important members of his family. No other mounds exist today at Parkin, but six small mounds were reported in 1940. Those mounds, none of which reached a height greater than three feet, are referred to as house mounds because they were used as foundations for the houses of some of

Parkin's elite citizens. The mounds were located adjacent to the plaza, defining the town's sacred, ceremonial space.

PLAZA. There was a small plaza in front of Parkin Mound. The plaza was sunk below the level of the surrounding village, and though the area has since been filled in by farmers, it would have appeared much like the plaza that can be seen at Chucalissa. The plaza was not dug out; rather, the rest of the village was built up. The Parkin site is raised almost ten feet above the surrounding ground by a combination of fill from the digging of the moat and the occupational debris accumulated from many generations of people living within the walls of the town.

MOAT. The Parkin site was enclosed on three sides by a very wide but fairly shallow moat, with the St. Francis River framing the fourth side. In addition to its defensive use, the moat drained the site during heavy rains or floods, in effect "flushing" the site of accumulated waste. In fact, considering its shallowness, that may have been the primary purpose of the moat. The town was protected also by a wooden stockade, a familiar pattern throughout the chiefdom. The presence of so many walled towns in the region, along with the accounts of Spanish explorers, makes it clear that violence was endemic in the Central Mississippi Valley during the fifteenth and sixteenth centuries.

Research

The first written accounts that mention the Parkin site are those of the Soto expedition, which came to the area in 1541 and referred to the chiefdom here as Casqui. Those eyewitness accounts of the capital have helped shape modern researchers' understanding of the site, and the Spaniards' discussion of regional politics has shed light on the nature of military competition between Mississippian chiefdoms. Scientific research cannot be said to have begun at Parkin until 1879, when Edwin Curtis of Harvard's Peabody Museum visited the site, which was known at the time as the Stanley Mounds. Although he did not write a report on his excavations, Curtis unearthed a number of important artifacts, including a shell-and-copper necklace, and noted a large number of house mounds that have since been destroyed. During the next decade, a man named C. W. Riggs put together a large collection of artifacts from Parkin and surrounding sites, which he displayed during the World's Columbian Exposition in 1893 in Chicago. Much of the collection was later sold to the Field Museum of Natural History in Chicago and the Buffalo Museum of Science.

Edward Palmer of the Smithsonian Institution tested a number of sites in the vicinity of Parkin in 1894 as part of Cyrus Thomas's mound project for the Bureau of Ethnology. As mentioned in the last chapter, during the first decade of the twentieth century, Clarence Bloomfield Moore, a lawyer turned amateur archaeologist, traveled up many southern rivers in his steamboat, the *Gopher*, digging at prominent mound sites in hope of finding museum-quality artifacts. In one day at Parkin, Moore excavated nineteen burials, from which he removed twenty-five unbroken pots, but finding significant evidence of looters, he abandoned the site. In 1906 land that included the Parkin site became part of the Northern Ohio Cooperage and Lumber Company, which soon built a loading dock on the St. Francis River near the mound and a boardinghouse for workers that intruded on the southern edge of the site. Workers often dug for pots in their spare time, selling those they unearthed.

Shortly before the United States entered World War II, the archaeologists James Griffin, James Ford, and Philip Phillips recorded several sites in the Parkin vicinity as part of their Lower Mississippi Valley Survey, a project undertaken by the Peabody Museum. The map they produced of the Parkin site included the main mound and six house mounds, considerably fewer than the number noted in 1879 by Curtis. Their most important contribution was the identification of a pattern among the sites in the area—

ABOVE: A warehouse belonging to the Lansing Wheelbarrow Company, located on the St. Francis River near Parkin, late nineteenth or early twentieth century. (Parkin Archeological State Park)

RIGHT: Employees of the Northern Ohio Cooperage and Lumber Company, c. 1906. (Parkin Archeological State Park)

compact, densely settled, walled towns with mounds on the western edge of the site — which are recognized today as constituting the chiefdom of Casqui. Work did not resume at Parkin until 1965, when the University of Arkansas Museum, in conjunction with the Arkansas Archeological Society, conducted a nine-day excavation that tested four areas of the site. The following summer the university held an archaeological field school at Parkin that focused on the extension on the southern edge of the mound. The most interesting discovery of the summer came not from the extension but from the summit of the mound itself — the remains of a very large post of charred cypress wood that may have been part of the crucifix Soto erected on the chief's mound at Parkin.

The most extensive modern archaeological work in the region was undertaken in 1978–79 to determine whether Parkin should become a state park. The Parkin Archeological Project not only investigated the site, but also visited all twenty-one known Mississippian sites in the St. Francis and Tyronza basin. The results of the study greatly increased our understanding of the settlement system of the chiefdom of Casqui. It was determined that Parkin was the largest site in the vicinity, that the people of the chiefdom lived within walled villages instead of on scattered farmsteads, and that they brought agricultural products to the capital, which was not located on the richest soils in the chiefdom. The project also investigated the possibility that the army of Hernando de Soto visited the site, an idea that has since been accepted by most scholars. Today work continues at Parkin, which is home to an Arkansas Archeological Survey research station. The site also contains a Native American repatriation cemetery, where the remains of ancestors long held in museum collections can be reinterred.

History

Parkin was originally settled in the second half of the fourteenth century, during the Middle Mississippian period after Cahokia had faded and much of the Central Mississippi Valley had been abandoned. At first the new inhabitants of the area lived in scattered homesteads. The Parkin site was a small, fortified village where homesteaders went to participate in ceremonies and offer part of their harvest to the chief. Homesteaders could retreat to Parkin if the chiefdom was attacked, though their living arrangements imply the possibility was rare. Things soon changed, however, and for most of the occupational history of the area, people were forced to live behind walls, their mortal enemies a pressing, daily concern.

The chiefdom of Casqui was bounded on the west by Crowleys Ridge and on the north and east by a series of swamps and wetlands. Its capital was perfectly situated to receive goods from the rest of the chiefdom and to act as a staging area for trade along the Mississippi River. Villages within the chiefdom were spaced about every two and a half miles up both the St. Francis and Tyronza Rivers. The sites varied in size, but three of the four largest were located five miles away from Parkin, each home to an important subchief. All the towns of the chiefdom shared a number of characteristics. They were rectangular in shape and up to seventeen acres in size. Villages were elevated by being built upon the occupational debris of many lifetimes, and plazas were generally the lowest areas within communities. Fourteen towns had mounds built on the western edge of the site, including Parkin. Spanish accounts describe the chiefdom as consisting of many fortified towns of various sizes. Most of the towns contained fifteen to forty houses, though larger towns had up to four hundred. Between the towns were miles of fields that also contained scattered groves of fruit- and nut-bearing trees. The Spanish chroniclers commented that at least one town was visible from any other.

The region that included Casqui and its neighboring chiefdoms was known for its distinctive human-head effigy pottery. At the Parkin site, five such pots have been discovered. It is clear that each pot represented a different person, but archaeologists differ about whether the likenesses were of the individuals with whom the pots were buried, or of enemies vanquished in combat. Other distinctive pottery discovered in the area includes a dog-effigy "teapot," fish effigies, and a cat-serpent effigy vessel. Two sixteenth-century European artifacts have been recovered from the Parkin site: a brass Clarksdale bell (a common Spanish artifact of the period, first found in Clarksdale, Mississippi) in a child's grave and a glass chevron bead found on the surface. Both items were a regular part of the diplomatic gift package given by Spaniards to Indians they encountered.

A human-head effigy pot discovered at the Parkin site in Arkansas. Pots depicting human heads in this manner have been found only in northeastern Arkansas and adjacent parts of the Mississippi Valley. (Arkansas Department of Parks & Tourism)

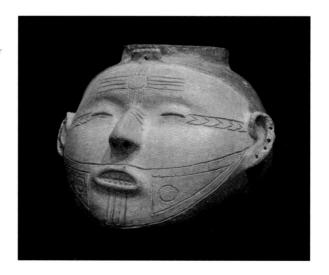

Casqui was in conflict with all the surrounding chiefdoms, including the one known as Pacaha, whose villages lay as close as a single day's travel away. Artifacts from the Pacaha chiefdom are on display at nearby Hampson Archeological Museum State Park. (See the box feature Hampson Archeological Museum State Park, page 200.) Once Soto discovered the feud between Casqui and Pacaha, he endeavored to play one off against the other for his own benefit — a strategy he regularly employed on his expedition through the Ancient South. When he first entered the territory of the chief of Casqui, he caught the occupants off guard and took several prisoners. Soon, the Casqui chief sent the conquistador presents of fish and mulberry-fiber shawls. When Soto approached the capital town at the Parkin site, Casqui, a man of about fifty years, marched out to greet him, accompanied by a chorus and a large retinue of followers. (It was common in the Mississippian world for a chief to take the name of his chiefdom.)

Soto presented himself as an important person, something akin to the greatest chief in the realm. Unconvinced, Casqui asked the Spaniard to produce a potent sign of his alleged power, perhaps war medicine, or rain to ease the drought his people had been experiencing. The following day, Soto ordered his men to construct a large crucifix, which was then erected on the summit of the mound. The Spaniards formed a procession, with each kneeling in front of the cross, while between fifteen thousand and twenty thousand Indians watched from the far side of the St. Francis River. One can only guess what they must have thought when the drought was broken by a soaking rain later that night.

Apparently convinced of Soto's power, or at least sensing an opportunity to best his enemies, Casqui agreed to supply the conquistador with five thousand warriors for a joint raid against the chiefdom of Pacaha. When the combined force of Spaniards and Indians arrived at Pacaha's capital town, the chief and his people fled. The warriors of Casqui quickly ransacked the temple, stealing the valuables and strewing the bones of Pacaha's ancestors on the ground, while Soto's forces gathered all the stored food available in the town. Pacaha and five thousand of his people were a few miles from the abandoned capital, hiding on a small island in the Mississippi River. When Soto discovered them, Pacaha and his people fled to the east side of the Mississippi, and the Spanish again collected what they had left behind in haste. A handful of warriors from Casqui took some of what the Europeans had claimed as their own — an act that so enraged Soto that he engineered a peace with Pacaha so that the two could attack Casqui in concert.

Before an expedition could be organized, Chief Casqui sent what can only be described as a clown to "entertain" Soto and Pacaha, and the Indians at least were quite amused. A very bold Casqui, accompanied by only forty

HAMPSON ARCHEOLOGICAL MUSEUM STATE PARK

The Hampson Archeological Museum State Park, near Wilson, Arkansas, houses a small but spectacular collection of artifacts associated with the Upper Nodena archaeological site. The museum boasts dozens of whole and reconstructed pots, including a virtual menagerie of animal effigies and a startlingly realistic headpot (a pot in the shape of a human head). The museum sits on a lot shaded by a group of stately cypress trees, among which are several picnic tables for the enjoyment of visitors. The Upper Nodena site was located a few miles away on a 5,000-acre farm that has been owned by the Hampson family since 1879. After having done some minor digging as a child, Dr. James K. Hampson began extensive excavations at the site in the 1920s. Although Hampson was only an amateur archaeologist, he was conscientious about his work and shared his results with scholars. In 1932 he invited Walter Jones, a professional archaeologist, to lead an investigation at Upper Nodena, and they unearthed about thirteen hundred burials; unfortunately, many of the records have since disappeared. In the 1940s, Hampson opened a museum at the site, which he operated until his death.

Upper Nodena was constructed on the levee ridge of a former channel of the Mississippi River; the channel was an active bayou when the site was occupied, from about 1400 to 1600. The village of just over fifteen acres was home to 1,000–1,500 people. Upper Nodena was the second largest of a group of twenty-one sites clustered around present Wilson and Joiner, Arkansas, dating to the Late Mississippian period. Though not all of them may have been occupied at once, the sites represent a chiefdom allied to Pacaha, whom Hernando de Soto encountered in 1542, though the Spaniard did not visit Upper Nodena or its neighboring sites.

At least three mounds were present at Upper Nodena, all of which were adjacent to the plaza. Mound A was a two-tiered mound with a single structure on the top tier and two structures on the lower tier. Mound B had a single circular structure on its summit. Mound C contained the contemporaneous burial of a large number of people perhaps killed in battle or by disease—one skull at the site identified as Caucasian had an unhealed wound caused by an arrow. Most burials appear to have been grouped in kin-based cemeteries within the village. The deceased were generally interred in an extended position, often with a bowl and a bottle near their heads. Very little seems to have distinguished mound burials from those in cemeteries.

BELOW, LEFT:
A human-head effigy pot on display at Hampson Archeological Museum State Park near Wilson, Arkansas. The head may represent the person it was buried with or an enemy slain in battle. (Hampson Archeological Museum State Park)

BELOW, RIGHT:
One of the mounds of the Upper Nodena site, 1930s. Many of the artifacts unearthed there are on display at Hampson Archeological Museum State Park. (Hampson Archeological Museum State Park)

warriors, followed the clown and delivered a speech that, even in translation, moved the Spaniards. Although apologetic, Casqui reminded Soto about the devotion his people had shown the Spaniards' cross and asked him whether he now intended to use his power against the people of Casqui. In the end, Soto forgave him, and instead of a battle, he held a banquet. At dinner, an argument erupted between the two chiefs over which should sit at Soto's right hand. As they vied for the honored seat, the Spaniards were impressed with the seemingly regal nature of their argument. The younger Pacaha claimed to rule a much larger area and to have come from a more distinguished lineage than Casqui, who did not refute Pacaha's claims but instead pleaded his own case, noting that he was much older than Pacaha and that his people were greater warriors because they kept the larger forces of Pacaha from invading. Pacaha was ultimately awarded the seat, and Casqui brooded.

Soto, his scouts having informed him that no corn-producing societies existed to the north, soon gathered his army and headed west, leaving Casqui and Pacaha to sort out their differences. Soto not only enflamed an already hot war between the two chiefdoms, but also severely depleted the food supplies of both societies. Though the region was suffering a summertime drought before the new corn was ripe, Soto demanded from Casqui enough corn to feed several hundred Spaniards and their slaves for sixteen days and ransacked all the food stored in Pacaha's capital. Although the details are lost, both chiefdoms were ruined — perhaps as the result of a lasting increase in the level of violence following the Soto expedition. In any case, the region was devoid of Mississippian settlements by 1600 at the latest.

Grand Village of the Natchez Indians

Grand Village of the Natchez Indians, formerly known as the Fatherland site, is a National Historic Landmark located about three miles from the Mississippi River in Adams County, Mississippi, within the Natchez city limits. This wooded 128-acre site contains three platform mounds, a reconstructed winter house, a ramada, a corncrib, two short nature trails, and a small museum. Grand Village, founded as early as 1350, was intermittently occupied by the Natchez people until 1730. It is likely that the original inhabitants of the site were related to the people who lived at Emerald Mound, located a few miles to the northeast and abandoned for unknown reasons sometime after the founding of Grand Village. (See the box feature Emerald Mound, page 204.) The army of Hernando de Soto was attacked on the Mississippi River near Grand Village by a fleet of Natchez in dugout canoes, the second such fleet the Europeans had encountered. In the early eighteenth century, the Natchez had extensive interactions with French colonists from

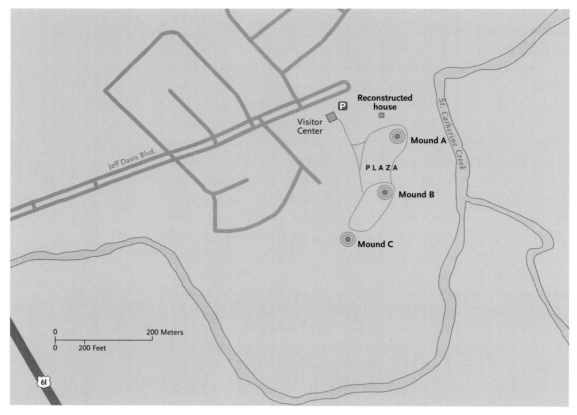

GRAND VILLAGE OF THE NATCHEZ INDIANS

Louisiana. Thanks to the efforts of a number of local businesses and the donation of a substantial portion of private land, Grand Village was set aside in 1972 for both posterity and the continued enjoyment of visitors. The site is administered by the Mississippi Department of Archives and History.

Location

Grand Village of the Natchez Indians sits along St. Catherine Creek, a small tributary of the Mississippi River. Just to the northwest of the site at the Natchez River landing is a gap in the Natchez Bluffs that leads from the floodplains to the rim, and from which the hills slope gradually down to the valley of St. Catherine Creek. The stream was diverted, perhaps in 1871, and the mouth is now thirteen river miles upstream of its location when the site was occupied. The creek, which originally separated the village from the mound and plaza area, was not as deeply entrenched as it has become since it was diverted, and it presented a weaker barrier to movement across the site than it does today. Tucked away in their small valley, the people of Grand Village

were safe from the floodwaters of the Mississippi and had access to the resources of oxbow lakes, swamps, bluff forests, and prairies.

The bluff hills, which rise in places up to 150 feet, are sometimes referred to as loess hills because of the nature of their soil, which was deposited by wind during the Ice Age. Loess soil is particularly susceptible to erosion; deeply entrenched pathways like those still visible along sections of the Natchez Trace were one result. Loess soil is also well suited for horticulture, which the Natchez people took advantage of by cultivating corn, beans, and squash on small farmsteads throughout the bluff hills. The forests there provided habitat for a number of bird and animal species, including deer, black bear, rabbit, turkey, and wood duck. A number of other waterfowl were regularly hunted, and fish were taken in abundance, including alligator gar, largemouth bass, sturgeon, and both flathead and channel catfish. Wild plant foods gathered from the forests, prairies, and swamps — pecans, grapes, persimmons, and walnuts most importantly — constituted a small but important part of the Natchez diet.

Mounds B and C at Grand Village of the Natchez Indians. The visitors in the left corner of the photo provide scale. (Mississippi Department of Archives and History)

EMERALD MOUND

Emerald Mound is located along the Natchez Trace about ten miles north of Natchez, Mississippi. The site was donated to the National Park Service in 1950 and became a National Historic Landmark in 1989. Its name derives from a pre–Civil War era plantation in the area, but the site was known to Euro-Americans as Selzertown in 1838, when the first recorded excavation of the mound took place. The most extensive investigations took place in the late 1940s, and the most recent work was done in 1972. Emerald Mound was stabilized in 1955 by the National Park Service, and today the mound is open and free to the public. Emerald Mound was constructed over a small natural ridge, and by any measure the mound is huge. Its base covers eight acres (770 by 435 feet), from which it rises to its main platform, which is 35 feet tall. On this platform are two mounds, one on the east and one on the west. The western mound has a base 190 by 160 feet and rises another 30 feet from the main platform. The eastern mound is about 8 feet tall. At one time, the platform supported a row of three small mounds on the north and another three on the south. Those six mounds were destroyed in the nineteenth century by a combination of plowing and erosion. Burials containing exotic artifacts were found in the east mound during the 1838 dig, but the whereabouts of those materials is unknown.

Very little is known concerning the occupational history of Emerald Mound. It was built and used by the ancestors of the Natchez Indians between 1200 and 1600. The site served as the principal ceremonial center in the area, but the majority of the population who used it lived in scattered farmsteads. The territory of the Emerald chiefdom stretched from about Vicksburg on the north to the Homochitto River on the south.

Enormous Emerald Mound, located along the Natchez Trace in Mississippi. Note the cars for scale. (NPS / © Eagleview Industries)

Features

MOUND A. Although at one time it was likely the tallest mound at the site, Mound A was not in use during the historical-period occupation of Grand Village. The mound appears to have been abandoned when it began eroding into St. Catherine Creek, probably during the late fifteenth or early sixteenth century. Mound A was tested in 1924, 1930, and again in 1962, but very little is known concerning either the construction stages or summit architecture. Today the creek flows to the east of the remnant of Mound A.

MOUND B. Mound B, which may have included a ramp facing Mound C, was built in four stages. Each stage supported a building, only the last of which contained European artifacts. Evidence suggests each structure was rebuilt at least once before a new mantle of earth was applied to the mound, and there appears to have been a structure built at ground level before the initial stage of the mound was constructed. The first mound stage was about two and a half feet tall with a base of eighty by ninety feet; the second enlarged it to a height of about five feet. At that point, the summit measured about seventy by eighty feet and supported a building with dimensions of approximately forty-five by forty feet. The third mound-construction stage added another four feet to the mound's height, and the final stage increased it by two feet or more, bringing it to a height of at least eleven feet. The buildings atop Mound B were used as the chiefly residence for the ruler of the Natchez people. Historical sources describe a windowless building about fifty feet square and twenty feet tall. The walls were plastered with daub and then covered with split-cane mats, and the roof was thatched with grass. There was no chimney. Instead, the fire pit was placed close to a corner of the building where the walls were purposefully not adjoined, and that small opening served also as a door. A length of river-cane fence near the open corner served as a windbreak. The "door" drew air inside, and smoke dissipated through the thatch, which helped keep insects out of the house. But fire was a constant danger. Within the house, a French colonist from the early eighteenth century noted "a number of beds on the left hand entering; but on the right is only the bed of the great chief, ornamented with different painted figures."

MOUND C. Mound C was located about 450 feet south of Mound B and was also built in four stages. Evidence suggests, however, that the first two mound stages did not serve as foundations for buildings. The first stage was three feet tall, and the second added only a foot. The third construction stage added another two feet to the mound's height, along with a ramp leading down to the plaza between Mounds C and B. Two successive buildings were erected on the summit, each resembling the Natchez temple later described

This effigy pipe depicting a mythological creature known as an underwater panther was recovered from Emerald Mound near Natchez, Mississippi. (Courtesy of Milwaukee Public Museum)

by French colonists. Both structures consisted of a large rear room about forty feet square and a front room that was probably a less substantially built ramada, with some sort of door connecting the two rooms. The height of the mound was not increased from six feet during the fourth construction stage, but the mound itself was extended about ten feet to the northeast, and the temple on top was increased in size. The extension covered part of the ramp, which was also enlarged. According to early French accounts, the temple roof was surmounted by at least two carved wooden statues of birds. The room beyond the ramada contained the sacred fire, baskets full of the bones of former Natchez leaders, wood and stone statues of humans, and live temple guardians, who were responsible for keeping the sacred fire burning. The Natchez temple was not a public place; only certain members of elite lineages were generally allowed in the rear room. Among the many items recorded by the French as being kept within the temple were freshwater pearls, rattlesnake effigies, carved wooden heads, stuffed owls, crystals, and an altar.

PLAZA. A plaza located between Mounds B and C was surrounded by the houses of the elite members of Natchez society. When Mound A was in use there was likely a plaza between it and Mound B as well, though whether both plazas were ever in use at the same time is unknown. The French witnessed several public ceremonies in the plaza at Grand Village, including the funeral of Tattooed Serpent, the brother of the chief, at which a number of people were ritually strangled in order to accompany him as servants and companions in the afterlife. Just before the site was permanently abandoned, the French dug a siege trench, later discovered by archaeologists, through part of the plaza.

HOUSE RECONSTRUCTION. Grand Village includes reconstructions of a Natchez winter house, corncrib, and ramada. The house, built by museum staff members in 1988, is an accurate replica, with the following exceptions: Johnson grass, a nonnative grass introduced from the Mediterranean area, was used for the roof thatching because the grass species used by the Natchez is no longer found in the area; cement was mixed with the mud daub to form the plaster for the walls; and because of the difficulty of maintaining them, no split-cane mats were used to cover the exterior walls. Those minor exceptions take nothing away from the reconstructions.

Research

Most chiefdoms in the Ancient South collapsed before coming into contact with Euro-Americans, a fact that has made Mississippian chiefdoms difficult to study. The Natchez, for reasons not yet fully explained, were able to maintain some vestiges of their chiefdom until the 1730s, when their society was destroyed by the French and the refugees were forced to join other Indian groups. Numerous historical sources, primarily French, refer to the Natchez, and descriptions by them can be read throughout the museum at Grand Village. The Natchez were first recorded by that name in 1682, when the Sieur de LaSalle encountered the group. The most extensive writings concerning them were penned by a Dutch-born French planter, Antoine Simon Le Page du Pratz, who lived near the Natchez between 1720 and 1728. These French accounts have been invaluable in reconstructing the social and political organization of the Mississippian world, in part because they discuss in some detail cultural practices only alluded to in the documents of the Spanish explorers.

Professional archaeology commenced at the site when Warren K. Morehead tested one of the mounds in 1924 as part of an extensive survey of Adams County. Investigations continued in 1930 when Moreau Chambers, who worked for the Mississippi Department of Archives and History, excavated portions of all three mounds, though the majority of his work was conducted on Mound C. Much of what Chambers unearthed is now held by the Mississippi State Historical Museum. Twenty-five of the thirty-eight burials recovered from Grand Village were unearthed by Chambers, and all were removed from Mound C. Primary and secondary burials were discovered, along with individual skulls. Some of the skeletons showed evidence of cranial deformation.

More than thirty years passed before another archaeologist investigated Grand Village. In 1962, Robert S. Neitzal, also an employee of the Mississippi Department of Archives and History, began work at the site. He quickly discovered why locals hadn't found arrowheads or broken pottery on the surface — the site was buried under a thick layer of soil that had washed into it after abandonment. Since Grand Village is surrounded by bluff hills, periodic episodes of erosion had laid down a tremendous amount of soil on top of the habitation surface of the original village — about twenty-six thousand tons. Neitzal was unprepared to deal with such conditions and was forced to further investigate the mounds. In 1972, Neitzal returned to remove the overburden in order to excavate the village portion of the site. In 1973 a cypress canoe dating to the middle of the fifteenth century was discovered not far from Natchez, as were the remains of a large wooden weir. The focus at Grand Village today is public outreach, and no further excavations are planned for the site.

History

Much of our understanding of the occupational history of Grand Village comes from information gleaned in 1971 by Harvard University's Lower Mississippi Valley Survey. Although there is some evidence for activity in the vicinity between 1200 and 1350, it appears that Grand Village was not founded until approximately 1350, with the majority of mound-building episodes occurring during the fifteenth and sixteenth centuries. Mounds A and B seem to have been completed by 1500, and Mound C was begun about the same time. It is not known whether Mounds A, B, and C were used contemporaneously. In any case, Mound A began to erode into the creek during the early sixteenth century, and the focus of the site shifted to Mounds B and C and the plaza between them.

During the entire occupation of Grand Village, a span of almost four centuries, the settlement pattern in the area was dispersed. Although population figures do not exist for the late prehistoric era, in 1700 the Natchez numbered about thirty-five hundred people living in four hundred homesteads scattered throughout the hills within twenty miles of Grand Village. The region was divided into seven residential districts, each of which owed a percentage of its harvest to the Natchez chief, known as the Great Sun. Grand Village was home to the Great Sun and his family, who lived atop Mound B. The priests, temple guards, and other elite families also lived at Grand Village, dwelling in houses adjacent to the plaza. There were several houses across

St. Catherine Creek and in the area north of Mound B that had once been a plaza.

Archaeologically speaking, the prehistoric occupation of the site resembles the historical one, so it can be assumed the earlier residents were organized in much the same way as those encountered by the French — though the Natchez population was larger during the sixteenth century than in 1700. The warriors of Grand Village almost certainly took part in an attack on what was left of Soto's forces as they fled down the Mississippi River after four years in the Ancient South. A Natchez fleet of fifty dugout canoes harassed the Spanish expedition throughout the day of July 5, 1543, keeping up a steady fire of arrows and even boarding one of the Spanish vessels long enough to liberate one of the few Indians remaining with the conquistadors, a woman. After following the army throughout the night, the fleet stopped pursuing the exhausted Europeans about ten o'clock on the morning of July 6.

The Natchez had not seen another of the bearded intruders along the great river for almost a hundred and fifty years when they briefly encountered LaSalle in 1682. The first meeting with the French was hardly noteworthy, but after the founding of the Louisiana colony around 1700, French traders began to visit Grand Village regularly. The colony sought an alliance with the Natchez against their English competitors in the region. Some of the Natchez sided with the English, however, who were willing to trade exotic European goods to even the common people of the Natchez chiefdom. Those new economic opportunities undermined the social stratification on which Natchez society was based, and whatever hold the Great Sun still had on his people was gone completely by the time of his death in 1728. The following year, the Natchez attacked the French fort that had been erected in their territory; though temporarily successful, they were soon driven from their homes by the Europeans. A number of them escaped to other Indian societies, where they forged new identities, but more than two hundred Natchez were captured by the French and sold into slavery in Hispaniola.

CHAPTER SIX

THE DECLINE OF THE
MISSISSIPPIAN WORLD

WHAT HAPPENED TO the Mississippian chiefdoms of the Ancient South? There is no simple answer. But it is possible to identify some factors that led to the abandonment of the Mississippian way of life. The first was the invasion of the Ancient South by Europeans ultimately bent on conquering and colonizing. Their exploratory military forays, or *entradas*, as the Spanish referred to them, inflicted not only physical casualties but mental ones as well. That is to say, European expeditions undermined the authority of Mississippian chiefs and forced commoners to question the efficacy of their leaders. The second factor, more disruptive by far than the first, was the introduction of European diseases against which the Native peoples had no natural immunity. As large numbers of people fell victim to epidemics, chiefdoms became destabilized, and many collapsed. The chiefdoms that survived into the second half of the seventeenth century met an opponent against which they could not persevere, however — the emerging world market system, the third and most devastating of the factors that destroyed the Mississippian world. The last vestiges of chiefly authority in the Ancient South disappeared as commoners gained access to the exotic goods of European markets and became enmeshed in the violent conflicts of the trade in deerskins and Indian slaves.

European Invasion

In the sixteenth century, the Mississippian world was invaded by foreign nations, Spain foremost among them. The Spaniards considered all of eastern North America "La Florida," so named in 1513 by Juan Ponce de León, who later attempted, but failed, to found a colony in the newly discovered lands. In

211

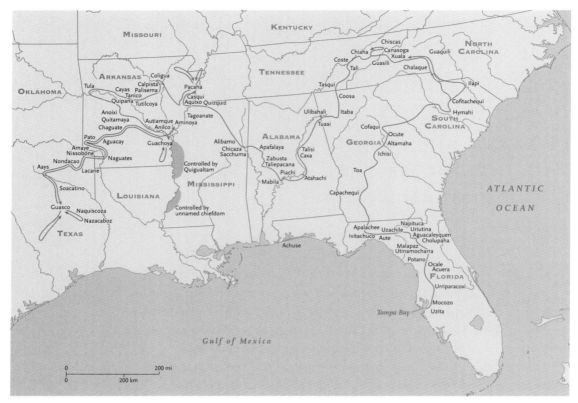

THE HERNANDO DE SOTO EXPEDITION, 1539–1543

(Based on Hudson and Tesser, *Forgotten Centuries*, 76–77)

1526, Lucas Vásquez de Ayllón tried to establish a settlement along the coast of present-day South Carolina, but he too was unsuccessful. Despite these early, short-lived attempts, Spaniards believed that Florida held riches like those of the Aztec and Incan Empires, which they had already conquered, and they continued to try to establish a beachhead. Two years later, Pánfilo de Narváez made a third attempt to colonize the region; he and nearly every member of his party died in the effort. In 1539, Hernando de Soto and his army of six hundred men and more than two hundred horses landed near Tampa Bay and began a four-year odyssey through the Ancient South, during which they inflicted significant military losses on a number of Mississippian chiefdoms. (See the box feature De Soto National Memorial, page 213.)

Soto's was not a modern army — men supplied their own equipment and received a percentage of the spoils of war in lieu of a salary. The army was forced to procure food as it traveled, and the men and horses devoured the stored produce of chiefdom after chiefdom. They were a formidable group. Foot soldiers generally wore steel helmets and some type of body armor, often long shirts of brigandine (made by attaching steel plates to padded

The De Soto National Memorial is a twenty-seven-acre site in Bradenton, Florida, near the entrance to Tampa Bay. The nine ships in Soto's fleet spotted the coast on Sunday, May 25, 1539, on the feast of Espiritu Santo. The following day, they discovered a channel into the bay, probably the southwest channel just below Egmont Key. It took five days to pilot all the ships into Tampa Bay because they had to be very cautious of shallow water, and it took them several days to unload as well. They had to winch more than two hundred horses over the side of the ships and swim them to shore. In addition, more than six hundred men had to be ferried ashore along with all their equipment, including war dogs and Soto's herd of pigs. On June 3, the Spaniard formally claimed the country for Emperor Charles V.

Although not the actual landing site of the Soto expedition, which was probably at a stretch of open, sandy beach on Piney Point, the memorial's nature trail through an otherwise impenetrable mangrove swamp allows visitors to imagine the environment the Spaniards encountered. In the sixteenth century, much of the coast of Tampa Bay was lined with similar kinds of swamps, most of which have been removed. The memorial contains a small museum focused on period armor, weapons, and other Spanish artifacts, including replicas that can be handled and worn. From mid-December to mid-April, daily living-history programs are featured at the memorial. Some of the performers belong to a group called Calderon's Company, named after Captain Pedro Calderón of Soto's army. Founded in 1993, the group takes part in several interpretive events throughout Florida and other parts of the South, including the winter camp event at De Soto State Historic Site in Tallahassee in January.

Reenactors dressed and equipped like sixteenth-century Spanish conquistadors. They can be seen seasonally at the De Soto National Memorial in Bradenton, Florida. (Courtesy of the De Soto National Memorial)

DE SOTO STATE HISTORIC SITE

The De Soto State Historic Site is located about three-fourths of a mile from the capitol in Tallahassee, Florida, on Lafayette Street, which is an extension of Old St. Augustine Road, the seventeenth-century mission road that connected Tallahassee with St. Augustine. The site was discovered by B. Calvin Jones when he conducted archaeological investigations before the start of a construction project. Coincidentally, the site was found in 1987, just in time for the 450th anniversary of the Soto expedition. A ten-month excavation confirmed the site to be the location of Soto's first winter encampment, which was within the capital town of the Apalachee chiefdom. The town was called Anhaica and contained about 250 houses when the Spaniards arrived.

Soto and his entire army stayed there for five months over the winter of 1539–40. The Spaniards burnt the section of the site they weren't using and erected a stockade around the rest for protection. A relatively large number of Spanish artifacts have been recovered from the site, including a number of trade beads, the steel tip of a crossbow quarrel, more than two thousand links of iron chain mail and twenty of brass, several wrought-iron nails, and five copper coins dating from the late fifteenth and early sixteenth centuries. Pig bones were found within a burned structure that dates from the sixteenth century.

Also known as the Governor Martin site, because it was owned by former governor John Martin, the De Soto State Historic Site is still being developed. Although open to the public, it currently contains no interpretive elements. The mansion, guesthouse, and garage on the property are being used as offices for state employees. Each January, however, the site hosts an interpretive event commemorating Soto's first winter encampment, where the first Christmas Mass within the present boundaries of the United States was performed.

A crossbow bolt and several links of chain-mail armor discovered among the remains of Hernando de Soto's winter encampment of 1539 in present-day Tallahassee, Florida. (Photograph courtesy of Roy Lett, Florida Division of Historical Resources)

leather armor), which ended up proving most effective in stopping arrows. They generally carried either a halberd or a sword and shield, but a few wielded battle-axes or crossbows. Soto even brought a handful of primitive guns known as harquebuses — heavy single-shot weapons that took a good deal of time to load and were useless in wet, damp conditions. Although they created quite a noise and spectacle, matchlocks were not relied on as important weapons, and by the end of the expedition the army had long been out of powder and shot.

The real power of Soto's army was the horses and the lancers who rode them. The cavalrymen wore chain-mail shirts that weighed as much as thirty pounds, plate armor on their legs and arms, and gauntlets on their hands. This was not the full plate armor of medieval knights, but it still made it difficult for the Indians to inflict fatal wounds. Their mounts were trained warhorses that wore armor of their own and trampled men to death, continuing to carry their riders even after receiving an injury or with the death sounds of other horses in their ears. The Mississippians had never even seen a horse, let alone attempted to stand their ground against a charging lancer. Horsemen were considered so important in the New World that they were given twice the share of foot soldiers when the spoils of war were divided. Except when mired in swamps or inhibited by darkness, the cavalry had a terrible advantage over the unmounted Indians. Spanish horses may have worn small copper bells known to archaeologists as Clarksdale bells, and if so, the sound of them must have been terrifying to the Mississippians.

In addition to the horses, Soto brought dogs and a small herd of pigs. Although the number and breeds were not recorded, the Spanish typically used greyhounds, wolfhounds, and mastiffs as dogs of war. The large animals wore spiked collars and sometimes padded armor on their flanks. They were trained to attack vulnerable areas such as the genitals and to disembowel their victims. Dogs were used to drive Indians from places of cover out into the open, where they were extremely vulnerable to cavalry. Dogs were used also to terrorize Indians during interrogations.

It was hard to get meat for the entire army, and they went without it for long stretches because Soto allowed their pigs to be eaten only when the army could find no other food and was on the verge of starvation. The remains of pigs have been found at the site of Soto's first winter encampment in modern Tallahassee, Florida. (See the box feature De Soto State Historic Site, page 214.)

To the Mississippians, the Spanish forces were something akin to a supernatural invasion. Although the Spaniards appeared human, their complexions were unlike any the Mississippians had seen. They had weapons and armor made of unknown material and capable of inflicting grievous wounds.

They rode on the backs of huge, fearsome animals the likes of which had never been seen, and they drove a herd of strange animals before them. Although Indians were familiar with dogs, they were not prepared for the ferocity of the invaders' canines, which surpassed that of even wild animals. And this army of hundreds traveled through the countryside demanding food, slaves to carry their goods, and women to be used for the pleasure of the strange men, all the while proclaiming to have been sent by an unknown god and punishing with violence those who disobeyed.

Mississippians were far from helpless against the invading horde. The weapons and tactics of the warriors of the Ancient South have been discussed in detail, but a word or two about their effectiveness against Spanish conquistadors is in order. Although Mississippian warriors were no match for mounted lancers, whenever the advantage of horses could be reduced or nullified, they were generally the equal of their European foes. Cane arrows could be used successfully against chain-mail armor because they splintered on contact and drove shards between the chain links and into the flesh. Mississippian archers were accurate enough to send arrows into elbows, knees, and eyes — the parts of the body most difficult to protect with armor. They were equally deft with clubs, wielding them effectively against Spanish foot soldiers armed with swords and maces. In fact, the Spaniards never ceased to be impressed by their opponents' courage and valor, their intense loyalty to their families and leaders, and their ability to endure hardship and pain.

Although Soto and his army failed to find a society rich in gold and silver, they did not fail to occasionally conquer those they encountered. Soto used existing Native political conflicts to his own advantage, inflaming chronic violence between rival chiefdoms. It may not have taken military action on the part of the Spaniards to destabilize some of the chiefdoms through which they traveled, especially because so many chiefs must have looked ineffectual to their people when facing Soto and his army of strange men and even stranger animals and technology. By the time of the expeditions of Tristán de Luna in 1559–61 and Juan Pardo in 1566–68, some chiefdoms were already in decline. Yet those military expeditions were just harbingers of the truly catastrophic changes to come.

Old World Diseases

Old World diseases delivered a much more terrible blow to the Mississippian way of life than the early *entradas*. The peoples of the New World had no way to combat the many diseases brought across the ocean with the foreign invaders. Native Americans had been biologically separate from the peoples of the rest of the world for at least fourteen thousand years, during which time the majority of the most important plant and animal species of the Old World were originally domesticated — animals such as the cow, horse, pig, sheep, chicken, and goat, and plants such as wheat, barley, and rice. The process of domestication also resulted in the development of many deadly communicable diseases such as smallpox, measles, typhus, and influenza among human populations, likely as a result of the new, close contact between humans and herd animals. Over hundreds and even thousands of years, Old World people slowly developed some ability to resist the disease-causing microbes. When those diseases arrived in the New World, they attacked populations that had never encountered them.

It is difficult to imagine the impact of those diseases. An epidemic striking a series of towns could infect nearly all the people and eventually kill a significant number of them. That would have been dreadful enough, but the survivors were just as likely to succumb to another outbreak in the future. It took many generations to build up immunity, so Native Americans continued to be deleteriously affected by disease throughout the colonial and early American experience. The successive waves of epidemics that washed over the Mississippian world eventually reduced the overall population of the Ancient South by 75 to 90 percent, and because the Mississippians were preliterate — they did not have written forms for their diverse languages — many of their cultural traditions were lost, anything that the survivors did not know or remember. Many songs, dances, stories, and religious ceremonies, along with practical knowledge and experience, disappeared forever when disease devastated the chiefdoms.

Mississippian societies were fairly unstable to begin with, and the authority of the chief, though sacred in nature, was far from inviolable. A drastic reduction in population affected all aspects of a chief's power. The planting and harvesting of crops were disrupted by disease epidemics, and a reduced yield endangered the supply of excess corn needed to finance the chiefly elite. A decline in population reduced a chief's fighting force and made the chiefdom more vulnerable to attacks from its enemies. Finally, the diseases themselves were difficult to explain in any other way than as the result of having offended the gods, with the blame resting at the feet of the chief — the link to and representative of those gods. These simple examples reduce the complexity of the experience, but they make plain the devastating and insidious nature of the epidemics.

It is difficult to be specific about the effects of these epidemics during the sixteenth and seventeenth centuries because much of the devastation occurred in the interior, far from early Euro-American colonies. It is not even known when diseases first appeared in the Mississippian world, but they may have arrived early in the sixteenth century with the colonization attempts of

Ponce de León and Lucas Vásquez de Ayllón. They may be linked also with the expedition of Hernando de Soto, who brought not only men but pigs as well, a likely vector for disease. Once the Spaniards established a small colony in northern Florida in 1565, it was only a matter of time until diseases spread throughout the region. Through that port of entry to the Mississippian world came not only soldiers but women and children, the latter of whom were more likely than adults to carry the diseases so devastating to the Indians. The colony was linked by small-scale trade to interior Indian towns that the Spanish did not visit, but to which disease was sometimes inadvertently carried along with trade goods.

As devastating as the diseases were, they did not completely destroy the Mississippian world. Some chiefdoms continued to operate, and one of these was the Apalachee chiefdom, where the Spaniards founded a mission in the 1630s. In fact, it was the elite lineages of the Apalachee who invited the Franciscan friars from St. Augustine. It seems the Apalachee leaders were losing their authority over their subjects, and they invited the missionaries not because they brought soldiers to enforce their rules, but because they gave special privileges to the Indian elite, including access to European-manufactured goods. (See the box feature Museum of the Mississippi Delta, page 219.) The Spaniards liked to administer their colonies and missions through existing Native political channels, as they had in Mexico and South America, and so they bolstered the faltering power of the Apalachee elite. Unfortunately, the remnant chiefdoms that survived the initial disruptions of invasion and disease were soon faced with an even more insidious enemy: the emerging world market economy.

World Market Economy

Despite having a colonial presence in the region for more than a hundred years, the Spaniards had yet to develop a robust economy by the mid-seventeenth century. The exchange the friars carried out with both mission and interior Natives was used mainly as a means of diplomacy, and profit margins were not a top priority. Trade items included hatchets, scissors, knives, jewelry, and blankets, but the Spaniards outlawed the sale of firearms to Native peoples. Thus, in Spanish Florida the adoption of European manufactured goods was a gradual process occurring over many decades. At first the process even mimicked old methods of distribution, with the chief and other elites serving as the primary consumers of European goods but passing a few items along to their commoner constituents.

Other European powers besides Spain had their sights set on the New World, often with profit as the primary aim. During the middle decades of

The Museum of the Mississippi Delta is located in Greenwood, Mississippi, and should be of particular interest to those fascinated by the expedition of Hernando de Soto. The museum contains the largest collection of Indian trade beads in the country, including an unparalleled assortment of sixteenth-century Spanish beads. Although the conquistadors might conjure up images of golden treasure and knightly armor and weapons, with a few notable exceptions, most sixteenth-century Spanish artifacts found in the region were much more prosaic—horseshoes, nails, chisels, and wedges. Occasionally, the metal tip of a crossbow bolt may be uncovered, but those small, rusted metal pieces hardly call to mind the fierce weapons of which they were once part. Rounding out the small variety of artifacts were the bells used on trappings for the horses.

The collection in the L. B. Jones archaeology exhibit at the Museum of the Mississippi Delta includes a huge assortment of Indian artifacts, such as projectile points, stone axes, hoes, and a small variety of both ceremonial stone blades and pipes crafted from stone and ceramics. In addition, there are several displays of whole and reconstructed pots. Many of the pots are painted and come in a wide variety of shapes, including an assortment of effigy vessels. Most of the pottery came from the Humber-McWilliams site, located in northern Mississippi. The site was occupied during the Middle Mississippian period between approximately 1200 and 1450.

Glass chevron beads. Vividly colored beads were part of a "diplomatic package" of European-manufactured goods brought by Spaniards to the Ancient South. (Museum of the Mississippi Delta)

the seventeenth century, the French, Dutch, and English developed a sub-stantial exchange system with Native peoples of the northeastern part of the continent. In return for beaver pelts, which were used to manufacture coats and hats that protected people from the cold and rain of northern Europe, Indians received all the goods mentioned above as well as firearms and liquor. Guns could be used to great advantage against Native groups that possessed only bow-and-arrow technology, so any Indian group that could obtain firearms did its best to keep them out of the hands of their neighbors. As competition for European trade increased and firearms began to flood the market, the region became enmeshed in a series of violent conflicts known collectively to historians as the Beaver Wars.

One of the results of these small fierce wars was that the losers often had to relocate their communities, sometimes hundreds of miles from their original homes. A number of such groups were forced south, where they sought new European trading partners. In the mid-seventeenth century, Virginia began to expand its commercial interests beyond the Tidewater region, and in addition to animal pelts, the Virginians desired cheap labor for their tobacco fields. Since the nascent Atlantic slave trade was then centered in the Caribbean far to the south, the cheapest available labor was that of Indian slaves. By the late 1650s, Indians armed with European firearms were traveling to Florida in the employ of Virginia traders to conduct slave raids along the borders of the Spanish mission system. When the Carolina colony was founded in 1670, the demand for Indian slaves increased tremendously.

Within a few decades, slave catchers had exacted a terrible toll on populations already reeling from drastic demographic decline. Some groups were so reduced they had little choice but to turn to Europeans for help. Known to Carolinians as "settlement Indians," the groups performed difficult or menial jobs for the colonists in return for being allowed to live in or near the colonial settlements. Meanwhile, the elite lineages of successful groups were losing their authoritative grip on their societies as commoners gained access to the market and thus to the kinds of goods that had formerly been reserved for chiefs. The unpredictable disease epidemics combined with the added pressure of slave raids forced refugees to form essentially new societies. These groups, described by historians as confederacies, were established primarily through nonaggression pacts for the purpose of mutual defense.

Within the new societies there was no room for chiefs — the uncertainties of the day prevented many practices that were vital to the maintenance of chiefdoms. It had become quite difficult to produce a large enough surplus of food to finance the elite, who also had a problem maintaining the chiefly line because, with so much death, it was hard to determine the rightful successor. In addition, chiefs were no longer able to control the flow of exotic goods, because Europeans distributed them to anyone who brought in skins and slaves to trade. So although they had strong roots in the Mississippian world, the social, political, and cultural lives of southern Indian societies of the colonial period, such as the Creek, Cherokee, Chickasaw, Catawba, and Choctaw, were created during the meeting of the Old World and the New. Yet despite long odds, bits and pieces of the Mississippian world, which had produced the most complex societies to develop north of Mexico, still exist in the form of earthworks and imperishable artifacts, some of which can be viewed by the public. It is hoped this guide will lure you into that mysterious time when the South was first born.

GLOSSARY

American Bottom. The floodplain created by the confluence of the Missouri, Illinois, and Mississippi Rivers. A large wetland area up to twelve miles wide, containing a maze of waterways connecting oxbow lakes and tributary streams to the main channel of the Mississippi.

Ancient South. Term developed by Charles Hudson as a complementary concept to that of the "Old South." The Ancient South, which covered roughly the same territory as the Old South, was inhabited by Mississippian farming societies, which dominated the area from about 900 to the European invasion in the sixteenth and seventeenth centuries.

bastion. Watchtowers on stockades. They served the dual purpose of buttressing the large walls and providing elevated platforms from which archers could defend a town.

black drink. A caffeinated drink similar to tea or coffee made from the leaves and twigs of the yaupon holly. (See the box feature Black Drink, page 18.)

borrow pits. A by-product of mound construction resulting from the excavation of earth to use for mound fill. Some borrow pits were converted into ponds that were stocked with fish.

buffer zone. Uninhabited wilderness areas separating chiefdoms. Of varying size, buffer zones served as political boundaries and as areas where members of a chiefdom could hunt, fish, gather wild foods, and collect firewood and other nonfood resources.

causeway. A narrow, elevated man-made ridge that sometimes connected the bases of mounds to each other or led from mounds to borrow pits. They may also have been used as pathways to facilitate movement across low-lying areas of a site.

celt. Another name for an axe. Most celts were made of ground and polished stone, but copper celts intended for ceremonial use have been discovered throughout the Ancient South as well.

chert. A common name for a type of stone particularly suited for the production of tools. Chert found throughout the southern Coastal Plain is typically tan in color, while that found in the Ridge and Valley Province is grey-black.

chiefdom. A society characterized by the hereditary transfer of leadership positions and a social system that included both elites and commoners, but smaller and less complex than a state.

chunkey. A variation of the hoop-and-pole game common throughout North America. Chunkey stones, used to play the game, are found at Mississippian Period sites, and chunkey players are regularly depicted in Mississippian art. (See the box feature Chunkey, page 65.)

Civilian Conservation Corps (CCC). A Depression-era, government-funded work-relief program designed specifically for young men. CCC crews built trails, visitor centers, lodges, and archaeological and historical reconstructions throughout the nation's parks and monuments.

Coles Creek culture. Society predominating in the Lower Mississippi Valley between 700 and 1100. Coles Creek societies shared some characteristics with the emerging Mississippian culture but were not integrated into hierarchical regional polities like Mississippian chiefdoms.

columella pendant. Ornaments made from the center (or columella) of lightning whelk, emperor helmet, or horse conch. It was removed in the production of shell drinking cups.

corncrib. Small storage shed built on legs several feet high. All manner of food-stuffs were kept in corncribs, and the space below them were often used as outdoor kitchens. (See the box feature Mississippian Homes, pages 30–31.)

cradleboard. A wooden backpack-like devise used to transport and protect infants.

cranial deformation. The practice of binding an infant's head to a cradleboard in order to slowly alter the shape of the head. Cranial deformation, generally seen as a mark of beauty, was a widespread but not necessarily common characteristic of the Mississippian world.

double-cropping. The practice of planting successive crops in a field during the same year, which could be done only where the climate provided enough frost-free days. The practice allowed Mississippian chiefs to store relatively large amounts of food.

dugout canoe. Varying greatly in size, dugouts were canoes carved from the trunk of a single tree, often pine or cypress. Though long, narrow, and shallow of draft, dugouts could carry a large amount of cargo. Most Mississippian towns included a canoe landing. (See the box feature Dugout Canoes, pages 22–23.)

earspool. An earring-like stone or wooden disc inserted into a slit made in the earlobes.

effigy pottery. Pottery made in the shape of a human or other animal. Vessels of this type are often featured prominently in museum displays.

exogamous. Marrying outside a specified group. During the historical period, southeastern Indian clans were exogamous, that is, marriage was forbidden within the same clan.

Fort Ancient culture. A society that developed on the northeastern edge of the Mississippian culture area. Fort Ancient societies grew corn, squash, and, eventually, beans and built plazas and walled towns, but did not erect platform mounds or enshrine sacred leaders.

gorget. A relatively large pendant. Mississippian gorgets were generally made of shell or copper and were sometimes engraved or embossed with a variety of geometric designs and fantastic creatures.

hickory milk. Hickory nut oil. It was obtained by boiling nutmeats while periodically skimming off the substance that rose to the surface. Hickory milk was used much like olive oil.

intercropping. The practice of planting corn, beans, and squash in the same field. The beans used the corn stalk for support and helped fix nitrogen in the soil, while the squash spread out between the corn and beans and helped keep weeds out while retaining moisture in the soil.

litter. Refers to the palanquin-like platform that Mississippian leaders were sometimes carried about on by retainers. Litters were often made of red cedar and have been found among the burial goods of chiefs.

Little Ice Age. Period from 1300 to 1850. It consisted of a series of unpredictable stretches of cold years interspersed with more moderate weather. During the early part of the period, many of the largest Mississippian centers were abandoned.

mace. A club. Maces were often depicted in Mississippian art, and stone maces intended solely for ceremonial use were sometimes included with the burial goods of leaders.

mantle. A cloak. In the Ancient South, mantles were made of a variety of animal skins, with deer predominating, but were also woven of mulberry fiber. They could be made also by attaching feathers, often from turkeys or Carolina parakeets, to a sort of netting.

matrilineage. Descent through a female family member. Mississippian matrilineages resulted in extended families composed of related women and their children. The females of each matrilineage owned the houses they lived in (despite the fact that their husbands built them), the produce of the gardens and fields they worked, and the children they bore.

matrilineal kinship. A system in which a person's blood relatives are restricted to the males and females on the mother's side, traced only through females. Thus, not only was no one on a person's father's side of the family considered a blood relative, but neither were any of the children of males on a person's mother's side.

matrilocal residence. The practice in which a newlywed couple constructs their home among the bride's people. A typical extended family was composed of mothers and their children, maternal aunts and their children, and maternal grandmothers. The only males related by blood that resided among a matrilineage were the unmarried sons of the women; all adult males were husbands.

Medieval Warm Period. A period of particularly good weather that lasted from 900 to 1300, which coincided with the development and maximum growth of Mississippian societies.

Mississippian culture. Type of society predominating in the Ancient South between 900 and 1600. Mississippian societies were ruled by powerful, hereditary leaders who often lived on top of earthen mounds in fortified towns and were often buried with riches acquired through pillage and long-distance trade.

Mississippi Flyway. A north-south corridor for migratory birds through the Mississippi Valley. During certain seasons, the oxbow lakes in the valley teem with several species of geese and ducks.

monolithic axe. An axe and handle made from a single piece of stone. Monolithic axes were symbolically charged works of art not intended for practical use.

mortuary house. A building used to house the dead while they were prepared for secondary burial. Mortuary houses were often constructed on the tops of mounds.

NAGPRA. The Native American Graves Protection and Repatriation Act, a federal mandate to protect Native American burial sites and provide a means for Native peoples to seek the return of tribal artifacts and human remains taken in the American conquest of the continent.

old fields. Horticultural fields in a fallow state. Old fields were useful because they soon grew into a tangle of underbrush that included several edible species attractive to humans and game animals.

Oneota culture. A society that developed along the northern edge of the Mississippian world. Oneota societies adopted both corn and shell-tempered pottery around 1050, but never built platform mounds and were not ruled by hereditary chiefs.

Osage orange. A tree species whose wood is particularly well suited for making bows. The species occurred along the western margins of the Ancient South, and staves of Osage orange were traded throughout the Mississippian world.

oxbow lake. Formed from cutoffs of meandering rivers such as the Mississippi, oxbow lakes were among the best places to live for Mississippian farmers. The levee soils between oxbows and the main river channel were the richest soils for corn horticulture in the Ancient South.

parry fracture. A fracture, usually of one of the lower-arm bones, that results from warding off the blow of a club or other handheld weapon.

Pee Dee culture. A variant of Mississippian culture found in eastern South Carolina and south-central North Carolina. Pee Dee marked the eastern extent of the Mississippian way of life.

Plum Bayou culture. A society lasting from 650 to 1050 and found within the Arkansas and White River basins. It was contemporaneous with the emerging Mississippian culture of the American Bottom. Plum Bayou shared some but not all Mississippian cultural traits.

primary burial. The burial of a body shortly after death, in either an extended or a fetal position. (See the box feature Burial Methods, pages 36–37.)

ramada. A kind of freestanding porch designed to protect against rain and sun during the summer months. Ramadas had no walls but sometimes had a raised floor to protect against flooding and to facilitate breezes moving under the ramada as well as through it. (See the box feature Mississippian Homes, pages 30–31.)

retainer sacrifice. The ritual killing of retainers, slaves, or relatives, often by strangulation, on the occasion of a chief's death. Those killed were to serve the chief in the afterlife. (See the box feature Burial Methods, pages 36–37.)

ridge and swale. Topography consisting of parallel curving ridges and swales (depressions). Some are barely noticeable, while others are prominent features on the landscape.

river cane. A species of bamboo native to the southeastern United States. River cane was so widely used as a raw material for such a huge variety of items that it is analogous to modern-day plastic. (See the box feature River Cane, page 9.)

scalplock. The ponytail worn by most southeastern Indian males, the rest of whose heads were shaved clean. Scalplocks were often taken as war trophies.

secondary burial. The burial of bodies that had first been processed in some way. The most common type of processing was the defleshing of bones, which were then bundled together and kept in baskets or buried. (See the box feature Burial Methods, pages 36–37.)

shell-tempered pottery. Pottery made with a tempering agent of shell, which was burnt and then crushed into fine particles before being added to the clay. Shell-tempered pottery was very widespread, but not universal, in the Mississippian world. (See the box feature Pottery, page 25.)

sofkee. A kind of gruel or porridge made of cracked hominy treated with wood-ash lye. Sofkee was a staple of southeastern Indian cuisine, and there was usually a pot of it ready to eat in any household.

stockade. A defensive wall built of logs set vertically into the ground at closely spaced intervals, with smaller laths woven between them. The entire wall was usually plastered with daub. Stockades were typically nine to twelve feet tall and often included bastions.

wattle and daub. A construction technique in which walls were built of small round posts set vertically into the ground, evenly spaced, with a few inches between each. Long split-cane withes were then woven between the posts, and both sides were plastered over with mud that had been mixed with plant fibers. (See the box feature Mississippian Homes, pages 30–31.)

weir. A basketry fish trap placed in a moving body of water with the opening facing upstream. Weirs, which allowed fish to swim in but not back out, could be used to capture large numbers of fish with little work.

winter house. The typical residential structure used by Mississippians. Referred to as winter houses because of their insulating properties, they were single-room, wattle-and-daub buildings with steep thatched roofs (See the box feature Mississippian Homes, pages 30–31.)

woodhenge. A sequence of five concentric circles constructed at Cahokia of evenly spaced, upright logs. These so-called sun circles could be used to determine the solstices, equinoxes, and other important dates on the agricultural calendar. They may have been used in conjunction with other posts at the site as an engineering tool to help lay out the community.

Works Progress Administration (WPA). A Depression-era, government-funded work-relief program. There were a large number of WPA archaeological excavations in the South, in part because it was possible to work outside year-round.

yaupon holly. See Black Drink.

SELECTED BIBLIOGRAPHY

Adair, James. *The History of the American Indians*. Edited by Kathryn E. Holland Braund. Tuscaloosa: University of Alabama Press, 2005.

Ahler, Steve A., and P. J. DePuydt. *A Report on the 1931 Powell Mound Excavations, Madison County, Illinois*. Reports of Investigations no. 43. Springfield: Illinois State Museum, 1987.

Alt, Susan. "Cahokian Change and the Authority of Tradition." In *The Archaeology of Traditions: Agency and History before and after Columbus*, edited by Timothy R. Pauketat, 141–56. Gainesville: University Press of Florida, 2001.

———. "Identities, Traditions, and Diversity in Cahokia's Uplands." *Midcontinental Journal of Archaeology* 27 (2002): 217–36.

———. "Spindle Whorls and Fiber Production at Early Cahokian Settlements." *Southeastern Archaeology* 18 (1999): 124–33.

Ambrose, Stanley H., Jane Buikstra, and Harold W. Krueger. "Status and Gender Differences in Diet at Mound 72, Cahokia, Revealed by Isotopic Analysis of Bone." *Journal of Anthropological Archaeology* 22 (2003): 217–26.

Anderson, David G. *The Savannah River Chiefdoms: Political Change in the Late Prehistoric Southeast*. Tuscaloosa: University of Alabama Press, 1994.

Anderson, David G., and Robert C. Mainfort, eds. *The Woodland Southeast*. Tuscaloosa: University of Alabama Press, 2001.

Bareis, Charles J., and James W. Porter, eds. *American Bottom Archaeology: A Summary of the FAI-270 Project Contribution to the Culture History of the Mississippi River Valley*. Urbana: University of Illinois Press, 1984.

Barker, Alex W., and Timothy R. Pauketat, eds. *Lords of the Southeast: Social Inequality and the Native Elites of Southeastern North America*. AP3A No. 3. Washington, D.C.: Smithsonian Institution Press, 1992.

Barrett, S. A. *Ancient Aztalan*. Westport, Conn.: Greenwood, 1970.

Bartram, William. *The Travels of William Bartram*. Edited by Francis Harper. Naturalist Edition. Athens: University of Georgia Press, 1998.

Beck, Robin A. "Consolidation and Hierarchy: Chiefdom Variability in the Mississippian Southeast." *American Antiquity* 68 (2003): 641–61.

Bell, Robert E., ed. *Prehistory of Oklahoma*. Orlando, Fla.: Academic Press, 1984.

Bense, Judith A. *Archaeology of the Southeastern United States: Paleoindian to World War I*. New York: Academic Press, 1994.

Birmingham, Robert A., and Leslie E. Eisenberg. *Indian Mounds of Wisconsin*. Madison: University of Wisconsin Press, 2000.

Birmingham, Robert A., and Lynne G. Goldstein. *Aztalan: Mysteries of an Ancient Indian Town*. Madison: Wisconsin Historical Society Press, 2005.

Black, Glenn A. *Angel Site: An Archaeological, Historical, and Ethnological Study*. 2 vols. Indianapolis: Indiana Historical Society, 1967.

Blakely, Robert L., ed. *The King Site: Continuity and Contact in Sixteenth-Century Georgia*. Athens: University of Georgia Press, 1988.

Blitz, John H. *Ancient Chiefdoms of the Tombigbee*. Tuscaloosa: University of Alabama Press, 1993.

———. "Mississippian Chiefdoms and the Fission-Fusion Process." *American Antiquity* 64 (1999): 577–92.

———. *Moundville*. Tuscaloosa: University of Alabama Press, 2008.

Blitz, John H., and Karl G. Lorenz. *The Chattahoochee Chiefdoms*. Tuscaloosa: University of Alabama Press, 2006.

———. "The Early Mississippian Frontier in the Lower Chattahoochee-Apalachicola River Valley." *Southeastern Archaeology* 21 (2002): 117–35.

Boudreaux, Edmond A. *The Archaeology of Town Creek*. Tuscaloosa: University of Alabama Press, 2007.

Bowne, Eric E. *The Westo Indians: Slave Traders of the Early Colonial South*. Tuscaloosa: University of Alabama Press, 2005.

Brain, Jeffrey P. *Winterville: Late Prehistoric Culture Contact in the Lower Mississippi Valley*. Archaeological Report, No. 23. Jackson: Mississippi Department of Archives and History, 1989.

Brose, David S., ed. *The Northwest Florida Expeditions of Clarence Bloomfield Moore*. Tuscaloosa: University of Alabama Press, 1999.

Brown, James A. *The Spiro Ceremonial Center: The Archaeology of Arkansas Valley Caddoan Culture in Eastern Oklahoma*. Museum of Anthropology, Memoir 29. Ann Arbor: University of Michigan, 1996.

Butler, Brian M., and Paul D. Welch, eds. *Leadership and Polity in Mississippian Society*. Center for Archaeological Investigations, Occasional Papers, no. 33. Carbondale: Southern Illinois University, 2006.

Carneiro, Robert L. "The Chiefdom: Precursor of the State." In *Transitions to Statehood in the New World*, edited by G. Jones and R. Kantz, 37–79. Cambridge: Cambridge University Press, 1981.

Chapman, Jefferson. *Tellico Archaeology: Twelve Thousand Years of Native American History*. Knoxville: University of Tennessee Press, 1994.

Cherry, James F. *The Headpots of Northeast Arkansas and Southern Pemiscot County, Missouri*. Fayetteville: University of Arkansas Press, 2009.

Clayton, Lawrence A., Vernon James Knight Jr., and Edward C. Moore, eds. *The de Soto Chronicles: The Expedition of Hernando de Soto to North America in 1539–1543*. 2 vols. Tuscaloosa: University of Alabama Press, 1993.

Cobb, Charles R. *From Quarry to Cornfield: The Political Economy of Mississippian Hoe Production*. Tuscaloosa: University of Alabama Press, 2010.

———. "Mississippian Chiefdoms: How Complex?" *Annual Review of Anthropology* 32 (2003): 63–84.

Cobb, Charles R., and Brian M. Butler. "The Vacant Quarter Revisited: Late Mississippian Abandonment of the Lower Ohio Valley." *American Antiquity* 67 (2002): 625–41.

Cobb, Charles R., and Patrick H. Garrow. "Woodstock Culture and the Question of Mississippian Emergence." *American Antiquity* 61 (1996): 21–37.

Cobb, Charles R., and Adam King. "Re-inventing Mississippian Tradition at Etowah, Georgia." *Journal of Archaeological Method and Theory* 12 (2005): 167–92.

Coe, Joffre Lanning. *Town Creek Indian Mound: A Native American Legacy*. Chapel Hill: University of North Carolina Press, 1995.

Cole, Fay-Cooper, Robert Bell, John Bennett, Joseph Caldwell, Norman Emerson, Richard MacNeish, Kenneth Orr, and Roger Willis. *Kincaid: A Prehistoric Illinois Metropolis*. Chicago: University of Chicago Press, 1951.

Collins, James M., and Michael L. Chalfant. "A Second-Terrace Perspective on Monks Mound." *American Antiquity* 58 (1993): 319–32.

Cook, Robert A. *Sun Watch: Fort Ancient Development in the Mississippian World*. Tuscaloosa: University of Alabama Press, 2007.

Crane, Verner W. *The Southern Frontier, 1670–1732*. Tuscaloosa: University of Alabama Press, 2004.

Crosby, Alfred W. *Ecological Imperialism: The Biological Expansion of Europe, 900–1900*. Cambridge: Cambridge University Press, 1986.

Dalan, Rinita A., George R. Holley, William I. Woods, Harold W. Watters Jr., and John A. Koepke. *Envisioning Cahokia: A Landscape Perspective*. DeKalb: Northern Illinois University Press, 2003.

DeJarnette, David L., and Steve B. Wimberly. *The Bessemer Site: Excavations of Three Mounds and Surrounding Village Areas Near Bessemer, Alabama*. Museum Paper 17. Tuscaloosa: Geological Survey of Alabama, 1941.

d'Iberville, Pierre LeMoyne. *Iberville's Gulf Journals*. Translated by Richebourg Gaillard McWilliams. Tuscaloosa: University of Alabama Press, 1981.

Dickens, Roy, Jr., and H. Trawick Ward, eds. *Structure and Process in Southeastern Archaeology*. Tuscaloosa, University of Alabama Press, 2002.

Dickinson, Jonathan. *Jonathan Dickinson's Journal: A True Story of Shipwreck and Torture on the Florida Coast in 1696*. Port Salerno, Fla.: Classics Library, 1985.

Drooker, Penelope Ballard. *Mississippian Village Textiles at Wickliffe*. Tuscaloosa: University of Alabama Press, 1992.

Dye, David H., and Cheryl Anne Cox, eds. *Towns and Temples along the Mississippi*. Tuscaloosa: University of Alabama Press, 1990.

Earle, Timothy. "Chiefdoms in Archaeological and Ethnohistorical Perspective." *Annual Review of Anthropology* 16 (1987): 279–308.

———. *How Chiefs Come to Power: The Political Economy in Prehistory*. Stanford: Stanford University Press, 1997.

Eastman, Jane M., and Christopher B. Rodning, eds. *Archaeological Studies of*

Gender in the Southeastern United States. Gainesville: University Press of Florida, 2001.

Emerson, Thomas E. *Cahokia and the Archaeology of Power*. Tuscaloosa: University of Alabama Press, 1997.

Emerson, Thomas E., and Douglas K. Jackson. *The BBB Motor Site (11-Ms-595)*. American Bottom Archaeology, FAI-270 Site Reports no. 6. Urbana: University of Illinois Press, 1984.

Emerson, Thomas E., and R. Berry Lewis, eds. *Cahokia and the Hinterlands: Middle Mississippian Cultures of the Midwest*. Urbana: University of Illinois Press, 1991.

Ethridge, Robbie. *From Chicaza to Chickasaw: The European Invasion and the Transformation of the Mississippian World*. Chapel Hill: University of North Carolina Press, 2010.

Ethridge, Robbie, and Charles Hudson, eds. *The Transformation of the Southeastern Indians, 1540–1760*. Jackson: University Press of Mississippi, 2002.

Ethridge, Robbie, and Sheri Shuck-Hall, eds. *Mapping the Mississippian Shatter Zone: The Colonial Indian Slave Trade and Regional Instability in the American South*. Lincoln: University of Nebraska Press, 2009.

Ewen, Charles R., and John H. Hann. *Hernando de Soto among the Apalachee: The Archaeology of the First Winter Encampment*. Gainesville: University Press of Florida, 1998.

Fagan, Brian. *The Little Ice Age: How Climate Made History, 1300–1850*. New York: Basic Books, 2002.

Fairbanks, Charles H. *Archaeology of the Funeral Mound: Ocmulgee National Monument, Georgia*. Tuscaloosa: University of Alabama Press, 2003.

Feinman, Gary M., and Jill E. Neitzel. "Too Many Types: An Overview of Sedentary Prestate Societies in the Americas." In *Advances in Archaeological Method and Theory 7*, edited by Michael B. Schiffer, 39–102. New York: Academic Press, 1984.

Fortier, Andrew C., and Dale L. McElrath. "Deconstructing the Emergent Mississippian Concept: The Case for the Terminal Late Woodland in the American Bottom." *Midcontinental Journal of Archaeology* 27 (2002): 171–215.

Fowler, Melvin L. *The Cahokia Atlas: A Historical Atlas of Cahokia Archaeology*. Revised Edition. Urbana: University of Illinois Press, 1997.

Fowler, Melvin L., Jerome Rose, Barbara Vander Leest, and Steven A. Ahler. *The Mound 72 Area: Dedicated and Sacred Space in Early Cahokia*. Reports of Investigations no. 54. Springfield: Illinois State Museum, 1999.

Fritz, Gayle J. "Multiple Pathways to Farming in Precontact Eastern North America." *Journal of World Prehistory* 4 (1990): 387–435.

Fundaburk, Emma Lila, ed. *Southeastern Indians Life Portraits: A Catalogue of Pictures, 1564–1860*. Tallahassee: Rose Printing, 1996.

Fundaburk, Emma Lila, and Mary Douglass Foreman, eds. *Sun Circles and Human Hands: The Southeastern Indians; Art and Industry*. Tuscaloosa: University of Alabama Press, 2001.

Gallay, Alan. *The Indian Slave Trade: The Rise of the English Empire in the American South, 1670–1717.* New Haven, Conn.: Yale University Press, 2002.

Galloway, Patricia. *Choctaw Genesis, 1500–1700.* Lincoln: University of Nebraska Press, 1995.

———, ed. *The Southeastern Ceremonial Complex: Artifacts and Analysis.* Lincoln: University of Nebraska Press, 1989.

Garland, Elizabeth B. *The Obion Site: An Early Mississippian Center in Western Tennessee.* Report of Investigation 7. Starkville: Cobb Institute of Archaeology, Mississippi State University, 1992.

Green, William, and Roland L. Rodell. "The Mississippian Presence and Cahokia Interaction at Trempealeau, Wisconsin." *American Antiquity* 59 (1994): 334–59.

Griffin, James B., ed. *Archaeology of Eastern United States.* Chicago: University of Chicago Press, 1952.

Hall, Robert L. *An Archaeology of the Soul: North American Indian Belief and Ritual.* Urbana: University of Illinois Press, 1997.

Hally, David J. *King: The Social Archaeology of a Late Mississippian Town in Northwest Georgia.* Tuscaloosa: University of Alabama Press, 2008.

———, ed. *Ocmulgee Archaeology, 1936–1986.* Athens: University of Georgia Press, 1994.

———. "The Territorial Size of Mississippian Chiefdoms." In *Archaeology of Eastern North America: Papers in Honor of Stephen Williams,* edited by J. B. Stoltman, 143–68. Archaeological Report no. 25. Jackson: Mississippi Department of Archives and History, 1993.

Hammerstedt, Scott. "Mississippian Status in Western Kentucky: Evidence from the Annis Mound." *Southeastern Archaeology* 24 (2005): 11–27.

Hann, John H. *Apalachee: The Land between the Rivers.* Gainesville: University Press of Florida, 1988.

Harn, Alan D. *The Prehistory of Dickson Mounds: The Dickson Excavation.* Illinois State Museum Reports of Investigations, no. 35. Springfield: Illinois State Museum, 1980.

———. *Variation in Mississippian Settlement Patterns: The Larson Settlement System in the Central Illinois River Valley.* Illinois State Museum Reports of Investigations, no. 50. Springfield: Illinois State Museum, 1994.

Helms, Mary W. *Craft and the Kingly Ideal: Art, Trade, and Power.* Austin: University of Texas Press, 1993.

Hilgeman, Sherri L. *Pottery and Chronology at Angel.* Tuscaloosa: University of Alabama Press, 2000.

Holley, George R., Rinita A. Dalan, and Phillip A. Smith. "Investigations in the Cahokia Site Grand Plaza." *American Antiquity* 58 (1993): 306–19.

Hudson, Charles M. *Black Drink: A Native American Tea.* Athens: University of Georgia Press, 1979.

———. *Conversations with the High Priest of Coosa.* Chapel Hill: University of North Carolina Press, 2003.

————. *Knights of Spain, Warriors of the Sun: Hernando de Soto and the South's Ancient Chiefdoms*. Athens: University of Georgia Press, 1997.

————. *The Southeastern Indians*. Knoxville: University of Tennessee Press, 1976.

Hudson, Charles, and Carmen Chaves Tesser. *The Forgotten Centuries: Indians and Europeans in the American South, 1521–1704*. Athens: University of Georgia Press, 1994.

Iseminger, William, ed. *Cahokia: City of the Sun*. Collinsville, Ill.: Cahokia Mounds Museum Society, 1992.

Jeter, Marvin D. *Edward Palmer's Arkansas Mounds*. Tuscaloosa: University of Alabama Press, 2010.

Johnson, Gregory A. "Organizational Structure and Scalar Stress." In *Theory and Explanation in Archaeology: The Southampton Conference*, edited by C. Renfrew, M. Rowlands, and B. Segraves, 389–421. New York, Academic Press, 1989.

Johnson, Jay K. *The Development of Southeastern Archaeology*. Tuscaloosa: University of Alabama Press, 1993.

Jones, B. Calvin. "Southern Cult Manifestations at the Lake Jackson Site, Leon County, Florida: Salvage Excavation of Mound 3." *Midcontinental Journal of Archaeology* 7 (1982): 3–44.

Jones, Charles C. *Antiquities of the Southern Indians*. Tuscaloosa: University of Alabama Press, 1999.

Kehoe, Alice B. "Wind Jewels and Paddling Gods: The Mississippian Southeast in the Postclassic Mesoamerican World." In *Gulf Coast Archaeology: The Southeastern United States and Mexico*, edited by N. M. White, 260–80. Gainesville: University Press of Florida, 2005.

Kelly, John E. "The Archaeology of the East St. Louis Mound Center: Past and Present." *Illinois Archaeology* 6 (1994): 1–57.

————. "The Pulcher Tradition and the Ritualization of Cahokia: Perspective from Cahokia's Southern Neighbor." *Southeastern Archaeology* 21 (2002): 136–48.

Kelton, Paul. *Epidemics and Enslavement: Biological Catastrophe in the Native Southeast, 1492–1715*. Lincoln: University of Nebraska Press, 2007.

King, Adam. *Etowah: The Political History of a Chiefdom Capital*. Tuscaloosa: University of Alabama Press, 2003.

————, ed. *Southeastern Ceremonial Complex: Chronology, Content, Contest*. Tuscaloosa: University of Alabama Press, 2007.

Knight, Vernon James, Jr. "The Institutional Organization of Mississippian Religion." *American Antiquity* 51 (1986): 675–87.

————, ed. *The Moundville Expeditions of Clarence Bloomfield Moore*. Tuscaloosa: University of Alabama Press, 1996.

Knight, Vernon James, Jr., James A. Brown, and George E. Lankford. "On the Subject Matter of Southeastern Ceremonial Complex Art." *Southeastern Archaeology* 20 (2001): 129–53.

Knight, Vernon James, Jr., and Vincas P. Steponaitis, eds. *Archaeology of the Moundville Chiefdom*. Washington, D.C.: Smithsonian Institution Press, 1998.

Krech, Shepard. *Spirits of the Air: Birds and American Indians in the South*. Athens: University of Georgia Press, 2009.

Kwachka, Patricia B, ed. *Perspectives on the Southeast: Linguistics, Archaeology, and Ethnohistory*. SAS Proceedings, no. 27. Athens: University of Georgia Press, 1994.

Larson, Lewis H. "Archaeological Implications of Social Stratification at the Etowah Site, Georgia." In *Approaches to the Social Dimensions of Mortuary Practices*, edited by James A. Brown, 58–67. Memoir 25. Washington, D.C.: Society for American Archaeology, 1971.

———, ed. *The Georgia and South Carolina Coastal Expeditions of Clarence Bloomfield Moore*. Tuscaloosa: University of Alabama Press, 1998.

Laudonniere, Rene. *Three Voyages*. Translated by Charles E. Bennett. Tuscaloosa: University of Alabama Press, 2001.

LaVere, David. *The Caddo Chiefdoms: Caddo Economics and Politics, 700–1835*. Lincoln: University of Nebraska Press, 1998.

Lawson, John. *A New Voyage to Carolina*. Edited by Hugh Talmage Lefler. Chapel Hill: University of North Carolina Press, 1967.

Le Page du Pratz, Antoine-Simon. *The History of Louisiana*. Baton Rouge: Louisiana State University Press, 1975.

Lewis, R. Barry, ed. *Kentucky Archaeology*. Lexington: University of Kentucky Press, 1996.

Lewis, R. Barry, and Charles Stout, eds. *Mississippian Towns and Sacred Spaces: Searching for an Architectural Grammar*. Tuscaloosa: University of Alabama Press, 1998.

Loughridge, R. H. *Report on the Geological and Economic Features of the Jackson Purchase Region*. Frankfort: Kentucky Geological Survey, 1888.

Lumb, Lisa Cutts, and Charles H. McNutt. *Chucalissa: Excavations in Units 2 and 6, 1959–67*. Memphis State University Anthropology Research Center Occasional Papers, no. 15. Memphis: Memphis State University, 1988.

Lyon, Edwin A. *A New Deal for Southeastern Archaeology*. Tuscaloosa: University of Alabama Press, 1996.

Mainfort, Robert C., and Marvin Jeter, eds. *Arkansas Archaeology: Essays in Honor of Dan and Phyllis Morse*. Fayetteville: University of Arkansas Press, 1999.

Mason, Carol I. *The Archaeology of Ocmulgee Old Fields, Macon, Georgia*. Tuscaloosa: University of Alabama Press, 2005.

McNutt, Charles H., ed. *Prehistory of the Central Mississippi Valley*. Tuscaloosa: University of Alabama Press, 1996.

Mehrer, Mark W. *Cahokia's Countryside: Household Archaeology, Settlement Patterns, and Social Power*. DeKalb: Northern Illinois University Press, 1995.

Milanich, Jerald T. *Archaeology of Precolumbian Florida*. Gainesville: University Press of Florida, 1994.

———. *Florida Indians and the Invasion from Europe*. Gainesville: University Press of Florida, 1995.

Milanich, Jerald T., and Susan Milbrath, eds. *First Encounters: Spanish Explorations in the Caribbean and the United States, 1492–1570*. Gainesville: University Press of Florida, 1991.

Milanich, Jerald T., and William C. Sturtevant. *Francisco Pareja's 1613 'Confession-ario': A Documentary Source for Timucuan Ethnography.* Tallahassee: Division of Archives, History, and Records Management, Florida Department of State, 1972.

Milner, George. *The Cahokia Chiefdom: The Archaeology of a Mississippian Society.* Washington, D.C.: Smithsonian Institution Press, 1998.

———. "Mississippian Period Population Density in a Segment of the Central Mississippi Valley." *American Antiquity* 51 (1986): 227–38.

———. *The Moundbuilders: Ancient Peoples of Eastern North America.* New York: Thames and Hudson, 2004.

———. "Warfare in Prehistoric and Early Historic Eastern North America." *Journal of Archaeological Research* 7 (1999): 105–51.

Mitchem, Jeffrey M., ed. *The East Florida Expeditions of Clarence Bloomfield Moore.* Tuscaloosa: University of Alabama Press, 1999.

———, ed. *The West and Central Florida Expeditions of Clarence Bloomfield Moore.* Tuscaloosa: University of Alabama Press, 1999.

Mooney, James. *History, Myths, and Sacred Formulas.* Asheville, N.C.: Bright Mountain Books, 1992.

Moore, Alexander, ed. *Nairne's Muskhogean Journals: The 1708 Expedition to the Mississippi River.* Jackson: University Press of Mississippi, 1988.

Moore, David G. *Catawba Valley Mississippian: Ceramics, Chronology, and Catawba Indians.* Tuscaloosa: University of Alabama Press, 2002.

Moorehead, Warren King. *The Cahokia Mounds.* Tuscaloosa: University of Alabama Press, 2000.

———. *Exploration of the Etowah Site in Georgia.* Gainesville: University Press of Florida, 2000.

Morgan, William N. *Precolumbian Architecture in Eastern North America.* Gainesville: University Press of Florida, 1999.

Morse, Dan F., ed., *Nodena: An Account of Ninety Years of Archeological Investigation in Southeast Mississippi County, Arkansas.* Arkansas Archeological Survey Research Series, no. 30. Fayetteville: Arkansas Archeological Survey, 1989.

Morse, Dan F., and Phyllis A. Morse. *Archaeology of the Central Mississippi Valley.* New York: Academic Press, 1983.

———, eds. *The Lower Mississippi Valley Expeditions of Clarence Bloomfield Moore.* Tuscaloosa: University of Alabama Press, 1998.

Morse, Phyllis A. *Parkin: The 1978–1979 Archaeological Investigations of Cross County, Arkansas Site.* Arkansas Archeological Survey Research Series, no. 13. Fayetteville: Arkansas Archaeological Survey, 1981.

Muller, Jon. *Mississippian Political Economy.* New York: Plenum, 1997.

———. "Mississippian Specialization and Salt." *American Antiquity* 49 (1984): 489–507.

Nassaney, Michael S. "The Historical and Archaeological Context of Plum Bayou Culture in Central Arkansas." *Southeastern Archaeology* 13 (1994): 36–55.

Nassaney, Michael S., and Kenneth E. Sassaman, eds. *Native American Inter-*

actions: Multiscalar Analyses and Interpretations in the Eastern Woodlands. Knoxville: University of Tennessee Press, 1995.

Neitzel, Jill E. *Great Towns and Regional Polities in the Prehistoric American Southwest and Southeast.* Albuquerque: Amerind Foundation / University of New Mexico Press, 1999.

Neitzel, Robert S. *Archeology of the Fatherland Site: The Grand Village of the Natchez.* Archaeological Report no. 28. Jackson: Mississippi Department of Archives and History, 1997.

———. *The Grand Village of the Natchez Revisited: Excavations at the Fatherland Site, Adams County, Mississippi, 1972.* Archaeological Report no. 12. Jackson: Mississippi Department of Archives and History, 1983.

Nuttall, Thomas. *A Journal of Travels into the Arkansas Territory during the Year 1819.* Edited by Savoie Lottinville. Fayetteville: University of Arkansas Press, 1999.

O'Brien, Michael J. *Mississippian Community Organization: The Powers Phase in Southeastern Missouri.* New York: Kluwer Academic / Plenum, 2001.

O'Brien, Michael J., and Robert C. Dunnell, eds. *Changing Perspectives on the Archaeology of the Central Mississippi Valley.* Tuscaloosa: University of Alabama Press, 1998.

O'Brien, Michael J., and W. Raymond Wood. *The Prehistory of Missouri.* Columbia: University of Missouri Press, 1998.

O'Brien, Patricia J. "Cahokia: The Political Capital of the 'Ramey' State?" *North American Archaeologist* 10 (1989): 275–92.

O'Connor, Mallory McCane. *Lost Cities of the Ancient Southeast.* Gainesville: University Press of Florida, 1995.

Pauketat, Timothy R. *Ancient Cahokia and the Mississippians.* Cambridge: Cambridge University Press, 2004.

———. *The Ascent of Chiefs: Cahokia and Mississippian Politics in Native North America.* Tuscaloosa: University of Alabama Press, 1994.

———. *Chiefdoms and Other Archaeological Delusions.* Lanham, Md.: AltaMira Press, 2007.

———. "A Fourth-Generation Synthesis of Cahokia and Mississippianization." *Midcontinental Journal of Archaeology* 27 (2002): 149–70.

———. "Refiguring the Archaeology of Greater Cahokia." *Journal of Archaeological Research* 6 (1998): 45–89.

———. "Resettled Farmers and the Making of a Mississippian Polity." *American Antiquity* 68 (2003): 39–66.

Pauketat, Timothy R., and Thomas E. Emerson, eds. *Cahokia: Domination and Ideology in the Mississippian World.* Lincoln: University of Nebraska Press, 1997.

———. "The Representation of Hegemony as Community at Cahokia." In *Material Symbols: Culture and Economy in Prehistory,* edited by J. Robb, 302–17. Occasional Paper no. 26. Carbondale: Center for Archaeological Investigations, Southern Illinois University, 1999.

Peebles, Christopher S., and Susan M. Kus. "Some Archaeological Correlates of Ranked Societies." *American Antiquity* 42 (1977): 421–48.

Peregrine, Peter N. *Mississippian Evolution: A World-System Perspective.* Madison, Wisc.: Prehistory Press, 1992.

Phillips, Philip. *Archaeological Survey in the Lower Yazoo Basin, Mississippi, 1949–1955.* Papers of the Peabody Museum of Archaeology and Ethnology no. 60. Cambridge, Mass.: Harvard University Press, 1970.

Phillips, Philip, and James A. Brown. *Pre-Columbian Shell Engravings: From the Craig Mound at Spiro, Oklahoma.* Paperback ed. Part 1. Cambridge, Mass.: Peabody Museum Press, 1978.

Phillips, Philip, James A. Ford, and James B. Griffin. *Archaeological Survey in the Lower Mississippi Alluvial Valley, 1940–1947.* Papers of the Peabody Museum of Archaeology and Ethnology no. 25. Cambridge, Mass.: Harvard University Press, 1951.

Polhemus, Richard, ed. *The Tennessee, Green, and Lower Ohio Valley Expeditions of Clarence Bloomfield Moore.* Tuscaloosa: University of Alabama Press, 2002.

Pollack, David. *Caborn-Welborn: Constructing a New Society after the Angel Chiefdom Collapse.* Tuscaloosa: University of Alabama Press, 2004.

Power, Susan C. *Early Art of the Southeastern Indians: Feathered Serpents and Winged Beings.* Athens: University of Georgia Press, 2004.

Redmond, Elsa M., ed. *Chiefdoms and Chieftaincy in the Americas.* Gainesville: University Press of Florida, 1998.

Rees, Mark A., and Patrick Livingood, eds. *Plaquemine Archaeology.* Tuscaloosa: University of Alabama Press, 2006.

Rogers, J. Daniel, and Bruce D. Smith. *Mississippian Communities and Households.* Tuscaloosa: University of Alabama Press, 1995.

Rolingson, Martha Ann. "The Toltec (Knapp) Mounds Group in the Nineteenth Century." In Mainfort and Jeter, *Arkansas Archaeology,* 119–42.

———. *Toltec Mounds and Plum Bayou Culture: Mound D Excavations.* Arkansas Archeological Survey Research Series, no. 54. Fayetteville: Arkansas Archeological Survey, 1998.

Romans, Bernard. *A Concise Natural History of East and West Florida.* Edited by Kathryn E. Holland Braund. Tuscaloosa: University of Alabama Press, 1999.

Scarry, John F., ed. *Political Structure and Social Change in the Prehistoric Southeastern United States.* Gainesville: University Press of Florida, 1996.

Schnell, Frank T., Vernon J. Knight, Jr., and Gail S. Schnell. *Cemochechobee: Archaeology of a Mississippian Ceremonial Center on the Chattahoochee River.* Gainesville: University Press of Florida, 1981.

Sheldon, Craig T., ed. *The Southern and Central Alabama Expeditions of Clarence Bloomfield Moore.* Tuscaloosa: University of Alabama Press, 2001.

Silverberg, Robert. *Mound Builders of Ancient America: The Archaeology of a Myth.* Greenwich, Conn.: New York Graphic Society, 1968.

Simon, Mary L. "Red Cedar, White Oak, and Bluestem Grass: The Colors of Mississippian Construction." *Midcontinental Journal of Archaeology* 27 (2002): 273–308.

Sloan, Kim. *A New World: England's First View of America*. Chapel Hill: University of North Carolina Press, 2007.

Smith, Bruce D., ed. "The Archaeology of the Southeastern United States: From Dalton to de Soto, 10,500–500 B.P." *Advances in World Archaeology* 5 (1986): 1–92.

———. *The Mississippian Emergence*. Washington, D.C.: Smithsonian Institution Press, 1990.

———. *Mississippian Settlement Patterns*. New York: Academic Press, 1978.

Smith, Marvin T. *Archaeology of Aboriginal Culture Change in the Interior Southeast: Depopulation during the Early Historic Period*. Gainesville: University Press of Florida, 1987.

———. *Coosa: The Rise and Fall of a Southeastern Mississippian Chiefdom*. Gainesville: University Press of Florida, 2000.

Squier, Ephraim G., and Edwin H. Davis. *Ancient Monuments of the Mississippi Valley*. Edited by David J. Meltzer. Washington, D.C.: Smithsonian Institution Press, 1998.

Steponaitis, Vincas P. *Ceramics, Chronology, and Community Patterns: An Archaeological Study at Moundville*. Tuscaloosa: University of Alabama Press, 2009.

———. "Prehistoric Archaeology in the Southeastern United States, 1970–1985." *Annual Review of Anthropology* 15 (1986): 363–404.

Stoltman, James B., ed. *New Perspectives on Cahokia: Views from the Periphery*. Madison, Wisc.: Prehistory Press, 1991.

Sullivan, Lynne P., ed. *The Prehistory of the Chickamauga Basin in Tennessee*. 2 vols. Knoxville: University of Tennessee Press, 1995.

Sullivan, Lynne P., and Robert C. Mainfort, eds. *Mississippian Mortuary Practices*. Gainesville: University Press of Florida, 2010.

Sullivan, Lynne P., and Susan C. Prezzano, eds. *Archaeology of the Appalachian Highlands*. Knoxville: University of Tennessee Press, 2001.

Swanton, John R. *Chickasaw Society and Religion*. Lincoln: University of Nebraska Press, 2006.

———. *Creek Religion and Medicine*. Lincoln: University of Nebraska Press, 2000.

———. *Early History of the Creek Indians and Their Neighbors*. Gainesville: University Press of Florida, 1998.

———. *Indians of the Southeastern United States*. Washington, D.C.: Smithsonian Institution Press, 1979.

———. *Indian Tribes of the Lower Mississippi Valley and Adjacent Coast of the Gulf of Mexico*. Mineola, N.Y.: Dover, 1998.

———. *Myths and Tales of the Southeastern Indians*. Norman: University of Oklahoma Press, 1995.

———. *Source Material for the Social and Ceremonial Life of the Choctaw Indians*. Tuscaloosa: University of Alabama Press, 2001.

Taylor, Alan. *American Colonies: The Settling of North America*. New York: Penguin, 2001.

Thomas, Cyrus. *Report on the Mound Explorations of the Bureau of Ethnology*. Washington, D.C.: Smithsonian Institution Press, 1985.

Townsend, Richard F., ed. *Hero, Hawk, and Open Hand: American Indian Art of the Ancient Midwest and South*. New Haven, Conn.: Yale University Press, 2004.

Trubitt, Mary Beth. "Mound Building and Prestige Goods Exchange: Changing Strategies in the Cahokia Chiefdom." *American Antiquity* 65 (2000): 669–90.

Upham, Steadman. "A Theoretical Consideration of Middle Range Societies." In *Chiefdoms in the Americas*, edited by R. D. Drennan and C.A. Uribe, 345–68. Lanham, Md.: University Press of America, 1987.

Walthall, John A. *Prehistoric Indians of the Southeast: Archaeology of Alabama and the Middle South*. Tuscaloosa: University of Alabama Press, 1980.

Ward, H. Trawick, and R. P. Stephen Davis Jr. *Time before History: The Archaeology of North Carolina*. Chapel Hill: University of North Carolina Press, 1999.

Waring, Antonio J. "The Southern Cult and Muskogean Ceremonial." In *The Waring Papers: The Collected Works of Antonio Waring, Jr.*, edited by Stephen Williams, 30–69. Papers of the Peabody Museum of Archaeology and Ethnology no. 58. Cambridge, Mass.: Harvard University Press, 1968.

Waselkov, Gregory A., and Kathryn E. Holland Braund. *William Bartram on the Southeastern Indians*. Lincoln: University of Nebraska Press, 2002.

Weinstein, Richard A., David H. Kelley, and Joe W. Saunders, eds. *The Louisiana and Arkansas Expeditions of Clarence Bloomfield Moore*. Tuscaloosa: University of Alabama Press, 2004.

Welch, Paul D. *Archaeology at Shiloh Mounds, 1899–1999*. Tuscaloosa: University of Alabama Press, 2006.

———. *Moundville's Economy*. Tuscaloosa: University of Alabama Press, 1991.

———. "The Occupational History of the Bessemer Site." *Southeastern Archaeology* 13 (1990): 1–26.

Wesler, Kit W. *Excavations at Wickliffe Mounds*. Tuscaloosa: University of Alabama Press, 2001.

Williams, Mark, and Gary Shapiro, ed. *Lamar Archaeology: Mississippian Chiefdoms in the Deep South*. Tuscaloosa: University of Alabama Press, 1990.

Williams, Stephen, and Jeffrey B. Brain. *Excavations at the Lake George Site, Yazoo County, Mississippi, 1958–1960*. Papers of the Peabody Museum of Archaeology and Ethnology no. 74. Cambridge, Mass.: Harvard University Press, 1983.

Wilson, Gregory D. *The Archaeology of Everyday Life at Early Moundville*. Tuscaloosa: University of Alabama Press, 2007.

Worth, John E. *The Timucuan Chiefdoms of Spanish Florida*. 2 vols. Gainesville: University Press of Florida, 1998.

Yerkes, Richard W. "Microware, Microdrills, and Mississippian Craft Specialization." *American Antiquity* 48 (1983): 499–518.

Yoffee, Norman. "Too Many Chiefs? (or Safe Texts for the '90s)." In *Archaeological Theory: Who Sets the Agenda?*, edited by N. Yoffee and A. Sherratt, 60–78. Cambridge: Cambridge University Press, 1993.

Young, Biloine Whiting, and Melvin L. Fowler. *Cahokia: The Great Native American Metropolis*. Chicago: University of Illinois Press, 2000.

Young, Gloria A., and Michael P. Hoffman, eds. *The Expedition of Hernando de Soto West of the Mississippi, 1541–1543*. Fayetteville: University of Arkansas Press, 1993.

INDEX

208; plaza of, 202, 206–7, 208–9; population of, 208, 209; research concerning, 207–8; settlement pattern of, 208

Natchez Trace, 203, 204

National Youth Administration, 173

Neitzal, Robert S., 208

Nelson B. Jones Conference Center, 158

North Carolina Department of Archives and History, 173

North Carolina Division of State Parks, 173

ochre, red, 11, 74, 84, 149

ochre, yellow, 11, 84, 149

Ocmulgee chiefdom, 98–99, 106, 154; decline of, 107; duration of, 99, 106, 107; earth lodge, 99, 102, 103, 105, 107; elites of, 107; environmental setting of, 100; history of, 105–7; moat of, 106, 107; mounds of, 99, 106, 107; origins of, 105–6; plazas of, 106; research concerning, 103–5; stockade of, 106, 107

Ocmulgee National Monument, 98, 102, 103, 154, 170

Ocute, 180

Oklahoma Archaeological Survey, 144

Oklahoma Historical Society, 144

Oklahoma Tourism and Recreation Department, 144

old fields, 17, 60

Oneota culture, 89, 120

Osage orange, 48, 145, 146

oxbow lake, 7–8, 67, 91, 123, 181, 190; mentioned, 69, 193, 203

Pacaha, 181, 190, 199, 200, 201

palette, 112, 154, 163, 165, 175

Palmer, Edward, 95, 96, 195

Pardo, Juan, 180, 216

Parkin Archeological Project, 197

Parkin Archeological State Park, 191, 192

Parkin chiefdom, 191–92, 193; decline of, 201; duration of, 191; elites of, 193–94, 201; environmental setting of, 192–93; history of, 197–99, 200; long-distance trade of, 198; moat of, 192, 193, 194; mounds of, 191–92, 193–94, 198, 199; plaza of, 192, 194; population of, 192, 199; research concerning, 195, 197; settlement pattern of, 192–93, 197, 198; stockade of, 192, 193, 194

Patrick, John, 76, 77, 81

Pauketat, Timothy, 87

Payne, Edward, 184

Peabody Museum, 76, 95, 195

Pee Dee culture, 175, 177

Peebles, Christopher, 163

Phillips, Philip, 136, 195

Piedmont, 10–11, 13, 100, 148–49, 168

pine barrens, 11

plaza, 32, 33–34, 35, 46, 57

Plum Bayou culture, 66, 91, 92–93, 97–98, 145

Pocola Mining Company, 143, 144

Pottery, manufacture of, 24, 25, 64

Purdue, A. H., 118

Putnam, Frederick Ward, 76

Quiqualtam, 181

Quizquiz, 181, 190, 191

ramada, 30

ridge and swale, 68, 74

Ridge and Valley, 12, 148, 149, 150, 157

Riggs, C. W., 195

Rights, Douglas, 173

river cane, 8, 9, 100, 133, 181, 205

Rogan, John, 153

Rogan plates, 110, 153, 155, 156

Rolingson, Martha Ann, 96, 97

sacred fire, 34, 57, 206

salt, 27, 64, 115, 121, 145

scalping, 47

Sears, William, 154

University of Tulsa, 144
University of West Georgia, 154
University of Wisconsin-Milwaukee, 77
Upper Nodena site (Hampson Archeological Museum State Park), 199–200
Upper World, 53, 57

Vinson, Carl, 103

Walter B. Jones Museum, 157
warfare, 4, 46–51; depicted in artwork, 47–48; fortifications for, 46–47; naval, 51; skeletal evidence of, 47; tactics of, 49–50; weapons of, 48
wattle and daub, 124, 167, 187
weir, fish, 19, 88, 148, 152, 169, 208
Wickliffe chiefdom, 121, 130; decline of, 131; duration of, 121, 130; elites of, 124, 125, 130, 131; environmental setting of, 123–24; history of, 130–31; mounds of, 121, 124–25, 130–131; plaza of, 124, 130; population of, 121, 131; research concerning, 125–27, 130; settlement pattern of, 130

Wickliffe Mound Research Center, 127, 130
Wickliffe Mounds State Historic Site, 121
Wied, Maximilian von, 75
winter house, 30
Winterville chiefdom, 109, 110, 131–32; causeways of, 134, 135; decline of, 138; duration of, 137, 138; elites of, 131–32; environmental settings of, 132–33; history of, 137–38; long-distance trade of, 138; mounds of, 131, 134–35, 138; plazas of, 134, 135, 138; research concerning, 135–37; settlement pattern of, 132
Winterville Mounds State Park, 131, 132
woodhenge, 67, 72, 87, 90. *See also* sun circles
Woolaroc Museum, 144
Works Progress Administration (WPA), 76, 103, 116, 118–19, 144, 173; mentioned, 96, 136, 154

yaupon holly, 11, 17, 18, 28